Ad Hoc and Sensor Wireless Networks: Architectures, Algorithms and Protocols

Editors:
Hai Liu, Xiaowen Chu, Yiu-Wing Leung
Dept of Computer Science
Hong Kong Baptist University

eBooks End User License Agreement

CONTENTS

FOREWORD

It is a pleasure to introduce you to this book which focuses on fundamental challenges and issues in the field of ad hoc networks and sensor wireless networks, one of the most active research areas in recent years. The book covers representative problems in MANETs and WSNs, including QoS topology control, connected dominating set backbone, broadcasting, energy-efficient routing, geographic routing, distributed localization, data gathering and data aggregation and sensor area coverage. Compared with existing books, this book gives comprehensive investigation without sacrificing theoretical depth of the selected topics. In particular, I believe the book will be a valuable companion and comprehensive reference for students who are taking a course in wireless networking.

The authors of chapters of the book are distributed in a large number of countries and many of them are prominent researchers in ad hoc and sensor wireless networks. Readers of the book can get absorbed by perspectives, suggestions, knowledge and experiences by these authors who have been working with this area for several years.

Peng-Jun Wan
Department of Computer Science
Illinois Institute of Technology
2009

PREFACE

Mobile ad hoc networks (MANETs) and wireless sensor networks (WSNs) have received significant attention in recent years due to their potential applications in environment monitoring, traffic monitoring and controlling, mining and shipping security, animal tracking, battlefield, disaster relief operations and so on. Nodes in these networks are usually powered by batteries and self-organized into a network via wireless communications. However, unexpected failure of nodes, rapid changes of topologies, high error rates, collision interference, and bandwidth and power constraints together pose new challenges for this type of networks.

This book presents some latest and representative developments in MANETs and WSNs. It focuses on some major and important problems in MANETs and WSNs and provides comprehensive survey of various architectures, algorithms and protocols for these problems.

The book consists of eight chapters. Chapter 1 discusses topology control which is one of fundamental problems in wireless ad hoc and sensor networks. The authors survey the existing work and describe their own work in both homogeneous and heterogeneous networks. Chapter 2 introduces an important concept called connected dominating set (CDS), which normally serves as a virtual backbone to reduce routing overhead in wireless networks. The concept can be extended to k-connected m-dominating sets (kmCDS) to provide fault tolerance. Energy efficient routing and broadcasting are fundamental topics and they are discussed in chapter 3 and chapter 4, respectively. Chapter 5 discusses geographic routing from both theoretical and practical perspectives. Chapter 6 discusses distributed localization which is a challenging problem in sensor networks since sensor data is typically interpreted with reference to a sensor's location. Data gathering/aggregation and sensor area coverage are described in Chapter 7 and Chapter 8, respectively.

The primary target audiences of this book are those who are interested in MANETs and WSNs and related issues. Typically they include scholars, researchers, developers and postgraduate students. The book could be a useful reference for university courses in wireless networks.

Finally, we would like to express our sincere appreciation to all the authors of the chapters in the book.

Hai Liu, Yiu-Wing Leung, Xiaowen Chu
Hong Kong Baptist University

CONTRIBUTORS

Guolong Chen	College of Mathematics and Computer Science, Fuzhou University
Hongju Cheng	College of Mathematics and Computer Science, Fuzhou University
Antoine Gallais	Computer Science and Remote Sensing Lab, University of Strasbourg
Wenzhong Guo	College of Mathematics and Computer Science, Fuzhou University
Majid Khabbazian	Computer Science and Artificial Intelligence Lab, Massachusetts Institute of Technology
Deying Li	School of Information, Renmin University of China
Zheng Li	School of Information, Renmin University of China
Yingshu Li	Dept of Computer Science, Georgia State University
Pascale Minet	Institut National de Recherche en Informatique
Stefan Ruhrup	Dept of Computer Science, University of Freiburg
Winston K.G. Seah	Networking Protocol Dept., Institute for Infocomm Research
Eddie B.S. Tan	Networking Protocol Dept., Institute for Infocomm Research
Jeffrey Tay	Tapper School of Business, Carnegie Mellon University
Feng Wang	Fujian Youtong Technologies Development Inc
Sau-Yee Wong	Networking Protocol Dept, Institute for Infocomm Research
Yiwei Wu	Dept of Computer Science, Georgia State University

CHAPTER 1

Topology Control for Wireless Ad Hoc and Sensor Networks

Deying Li [1], Zheng Li [1], and Feng Wang [2]

[1] School of Information, Renmin University of China, Beijing 100872, China

[2] Fujian Youtong Technologies Development Inc, China

Abstract: Topology control is one of the most fundamental issues in wireless ad hoc and sensor networks. In this chapter, we give a summary of our recently works for topology control problem. Firstly, we briefly summarize existing works and research activities. Secondly, we address QoS topology control problem in homogeneous and non-homogeneous ad hoc networks including minimizing the total energy cost and minimizing maximum transmitting power of nodes and give our results. Thirdly, we introduce strongly connected topology control including non-restricted and restricted topology control problem in the wireless sensor networks, and give the corresponding results.

1 INTRODUCTION

Wireless networks such as ad hoc networks and sensor networks have received significant attention of researchers in recent years due to their wide range of potential applications. Wireless networks consist of a number of wireless nodes that are deployed either inside or close to an application field without the aid of an established infrastructure of centralized administration. Wireless networks can be used in many areas such as military tactical communication, aircraft flight control, battlefield surveillance, environmental monitoring, home appliance control, and protection against bioterrorism [1-3].

There are several technical challenges related to wireless ad hoc and sensor networks. In such networks, the topology is highly dynamic with frequent changes, which may be difficult to predict. With the use of wireless links, the network suffers from higher loss rates, and can experience higher delays and jitter. Especially, as the nodes in such networks are powered by batteries, energy saving is an important system design criterion. The main design factors involved in ad hoc and sensor networks include power consumptions, topology control, fault tolerance, Quality of Service (QoS), etc.

Energy Efficiency: Wireless nodes composed of ad hoc networks or sensor networks are inherently resource constrained since they are powered by batteries. In many applications, wireless nodes are deployed in a remote or hazardous area, where replenishment of batteries might be impossible. Furthermore, the lifetime of batteries has not been improved as fast as processing speed of microprocessors, as network lifetime shows a strong dependence on battery lifetime. Therefore energy efficiency is a critical issue in wireless ad hoc and sensor network. Usually, there are two different optimization objectives for improving energy efficiency. One is to minimize the total power consumption of all nodes. The other objective is that minimizing the maximum transmitting power of nodes.

Topology Control: Topology control is one of the most important issues to sustain the network capacity for ad hoc and sensor networks, which attract a lot of attentions [4]. The topology of a wireless ad hoc/sensor network is a set of communication links between node pairs used explicitly or implicitly by routing mechanisms [5]. A network topology can be controlled by some "controllable" parameters such as transmission power, directional antennas and multi-channel communications. Topology control [6] has been proposed to save the power consumption of nodes: Each node, instead of using its maximal transmission power, sets its power to a certain level so that a good network topology can be formed to satisfy a certain constraint. Moreover, a wireless sensor network forms a dynamical topology and typically functions as sending data packets back to the data collectors. Basically, topology control is to sustain this data propagation topology and enhance the network connectivity to provide reliable QoS (Quality of Service) or prolong the network lifetime.

Connectivity: Especially, the most basic requirement of a network is that it be connected. Most prior researches on topology control assumed that the networks are modeled by undirected graph, i.e., the communication links are symmetric. However, the assumption of homogeneous nodes does not always hold in practice since even devices of the same type may have different maximal transmission power [7, 8]. Furthermore, the transmission power threshold [9] for a pair of network nodes depends on a number of impact factors including not only the Euclidean distance between the nodes, but also interference, surroundings, etc. Note that for any nodes pair u and v, transmission power threshold $p(u, v)$ may not be equal to $p(v, u)$ [10, 11]. In this scenario, the networks are modeled by directed graph, and the constructed topology should guarantee that the topology must be strongly connected.

Quality of Service (QoS): QoS guarantees some important requirements for the special applications such as fault tolerance, real-time or high-reliable transmission, etc. While a lot of researches have been done on some important aspects of ad hoc and sensor network such as energy efficiency, protocol design etc., supporting QoS in wireless ad hoc and sensor networks is still a largely unexplored research field [12, 13]. In multi-hop ad hoc networks and sensor networks, on-line QoS provisions such as end-to-end bandwidth and delay are highly dependent on the network topology. Without a proper configuration of the topology, some nodes in the network could be easily over-loaded and it might be impossible to find a QoS route during the operation of the network [14, 15].

In this chapter, we give a summary of our recent works for topology control problem. Several problems and their corresponding solutions related to QoS topology control and strongly connectivity topology control in wireless ad hoc and sensor networks are discussed. Specifically, topics discussed include: (1) QoS topology construction algorithms in both homogeneous and heterogeneous networks with respect to different optimization objectives; and (2) how to construct strongly connected network topology under both non-restricted and restricted maximum transmission power.

The rest of this chapter is organized as follows: In section 2, we summarize some existing research works. Section 3 presents the results on QoS topology control in ad hoc networks under several different system settings. Section 4 introduces the techniques on strongly connected topology control in wireless sensor networks under non-restricted and restricted scenarios. Finally, we conclude this chapter in Section 5.

2 RELATED WORK

Topology control is an important research issue in wireless ad hoc and sensor networks and a considerable amount of research works have been done regarding topology control problem. In this section, we give an overview of research related to topology control with energy efficiency, connectivity, fault tolerance and QoS (low interference).

The earlier works of topology control can be found in [16, 17]. In [16], a distributed algorithm was developed for each node to adjust its transmitting power to construct a reliable high-throughput topology. In [17], Hou *et al.* studied the relationship between transmission range and throughput. An analytic model was developed to allow each node to adjust its transmitting power to reduce interference and hence achieve high throughput. Minimizing energy consumption was not a concern in both works.

2.1 Topology Control based on Geometric Structures

There are some basic geometric structures used in various topology control protocols such as MST (Minimum Spanning Tree), LMST (Local Minimum Spanning Tree), RNG (Relative Neighbor Graph), GG (Gabriel Graph) etc. They create a chain since $MST \subseteq LMST \subseteq RNG \subseteq GG$ [18]. MST is a global structure, while LMST, RNG and GG are constructed based only on local knowledge. Li *et al.* [19] and Hou *et al.* [20] proposed a localized MST-based topology control algorithm, in which each node calculates local minimum spanning tree of itself and its 1-hop neighbors and then merge these local MSTs to construct entire topology. An edge (u, v) is in LMST if and only if u and v select each other in their respective trees. In [19], the authors showed that LMST is a planar graph and extended LMST to k-hop neighbors to achieve sparser network topology. RNG consists of all edges (u, v) such that (u, v) is not the longest edge in any triangle $\triangle uvw$. That is, (u, v) belongs to RNG if there is no node w such that $d(u, w) < d(u, v)$ and $d(v, w) < d(u, v)$, as shown in Fig. (1). (u, v) is not an edge in RNG. Cartigny *et al.* [21] showed that the LMST of a unit graph is a subgraph of RNG of the same graph. MST, LMST and RNG are used to construct sparse networks topology in many articles.

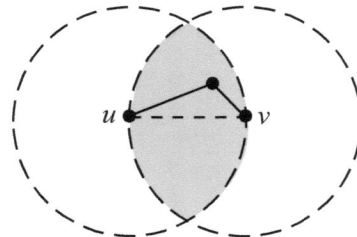

Fig. (1). (u, v) is not an edge in RNG.

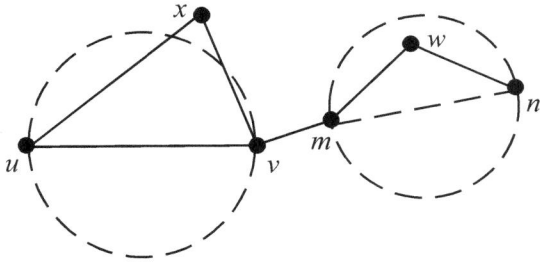

Fig. (2). (u, v) is a edge in GG while (m, n) is not.

The GG (Gabriel Graph) was proposed in [22], and it consists of all edges (u, v) such that the disk with diameter uv contains no other node inside it. Fig. (2) illustrates two examples. It is well-known that the GG is a planar graph and RNG is a subgraph of GG. Motivated by GG, the authors in [23] proposed a distributed topology control algorithm that offers provably salient performance guarantees with respect to energy efficiency and low level of interference. The authors formally proved that the networks topology constructed by their algorithm has good average performance on multiple design goals such as energy efficiency, low level interference, spatial reuse, sparseness, planarity and small nodal degree.

2.2 Energy Efficient Topology Control with Connectivity

Recently, energy efficient topology control becomes an important topic in wireless ad hoc and sensor networks. Most of the works have been focused on the construction and maintenance of a network topology with required connectivity by using minimal power consumption.

Lloyd *et al.* gave a good summary for energy efficient topology control [4]. The authors use a 3-tuple <*M*, *P*, *O*> to represent topology control problems, where *M* represents the graph model (either directed or undirected), *P* represents the desired graph property (e.g., 1-connected or 2-connected), and *O* represents the optimization objective, that is Min-max or Min-total transmission power. The NP-completeness of these kinds of problems has been analyzed and several algorithms have been proposed.

A cone-based distributed topology control method was developed in [24]. Basically, each node gradually increases its transmitting power until it finds a neighbor node in every direction (cone). As the result, the global connectivity is guaranteed a minimum power for each node. Huang *et al.* extended this work in [24] to the case of using directional antennas [25]. Marsan *et al.* [26] presented a method to optimize the topology of Bluetooth, which aims at minimizing the maximum

traffic load of nodes (thus minimizing the maximum power consumption of nodes). Melodia *et al.* [27] determined optimal local topology knowledge for energy efficient geographic routing in ad hoc and sensor networks. The authors provided different localized forwarding scheme to demonstrate that only a limited local knowledge is needed to take energy efficient decisions.

Ma *et al.* [28] constructed network with small number of coordinators while still maintaining the topology connectivity. It is assumed that all wireless links in a sensor network are bidirectional since 802.15.4 MAC has an ACK mechanism for every frame. They considered the problem as minimal connected dominated set problem. Three topology control algorithms had been proposed with different time complexity and power saving. Liu *et al.* [29] turned the random network into quasi-regular networks. The authors analyzed the network lifetime or regular, random, and quasi-regular networks in two operating modes, a monitoring mode and a reporting mode. In both cases, quasi-regular networks have substantial advantages over purely random ones.

In [5], two centralized optimal algorithms were proposed for creating connected and bi-connected static networks with the optimization objective of minimizing the maximum transmitting power used. Additionally, two distributed heuristics, LINT (Local Information No Topology) and LILT (Local Information Link-state Topology), were proposed for adaptively adjusting node transmitting power to maintain a connected topology in response to topology changes. But, neither LINT nor LILT can guarantee the connectivity of the network.

The works in literatures [9-11] dealt with the strongly connected minimum power restricted topology control problem. Chen *et al* [9] and Clementi *et al.* [30] proved the NP-completeness of the broadcast strong connectivity augmentation problem, and [9] revealed that the algorithm based on the minimum spanning tree (MST) has a performance ratio 2 for broadcast strong connectivity augmentation problem for *directed graph model* [4]. In [31], the authors proved the NP-completeness of the strong minimum energy topology problem (SMET) and proposed two heuristics: power assignment based on MST and incremental power, and the MST-based has a performance ratio 2.

2.3 Fault Tolerant Topology Control

Since wireless ad hoc and sensor networks are usually composed of a large number of unreliable terminals, fault tolerance is an important requirement for topology control [5]. In particular, the network connectivity should be preserved even when some nodes fail or deplete their power. One way to construct fault-tolerant topology is to construct a k-node connected network, that is, it can tolerate failure of at most k-1 nodes. As shown in Fig. (3), it is a 3-connected topology.

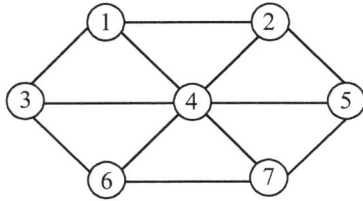

Fig. (3). A 3-connected topology.

The problem of finding a min-max cost k-connected subgraph can be solved optimally in general case [5], [32], but the problem of finding a minimum total cost k-connected subgraph has been proved to be NP-Hard; many approximation algorithms had been proposed [33].

Minimum total power k-connectivity problem: The works in [33-36] addressed the fault tolerant topology control with the objective of minimizing total power and majority of these algorithms are centralized. The authors [33] introduced three algorithms: one is centralized and gives an $O(kb)$-approximation, where b is the best approximation factor for the k-UPVCS problem. The second algorithm is also global and improves the approximation factor to $O(k)$ for general graphs. The third algorithm is distributed and gives an $k^{O(a)}$-approximation, where a is the exponent in the transmission model.

Minimum maximum power k-connectivity problem: The works in [5], [32] and [37] addressed the fault-tolerant topology control with the objective of minimizing the maximum transmission power. Ramanathan et al. [5] proposed a centralized greedy algorithm for assuring bi-connectivity ($k = 2$) that iteratively merges two bi-connected components until only one remains. Li and Hou [32] proposed two algorithms for the fault-tolerant topology control problem: FGSS$_k$ (Fault-tolerant Global Spanning Subgraph), is a generalized version of the Kruskal-MST algorithm and can optimally minimize the maximum transmission power used in the network among all k-connectivity networks. Based on this algorithm, the authors also proposed a distributed algorithm FLSS$_k$, in which each node applies the FGSS$_k$ algorithm to its 1-hop neighborhood and determines its neighbor set locally. FLSS$_k$ has also been proved to be optimal. Cardei et al. [37] addressed fault-tolerant topology control in a heterogeneous wireless sensor network consisting of several resource-rich supernodes used for data relaying and a large number of energy constrained wireless sensor nodes. The authors introduced the f_c-degree Anycast Topology Control (f_c-ATC) problem with the objective of selecting each sensor's

transmission range such that each sensor is f_c-vertex super-node connected and the maximum sensor transmission power is minimized, and proposed two solutions for the k-ATC problem: a greedy centralized algorithm that produces the optimal solution and a distributed and localized algorithm that incrementally adjusts sensors' transmission range such that the k-vertex super-node connectivity requirement is met.

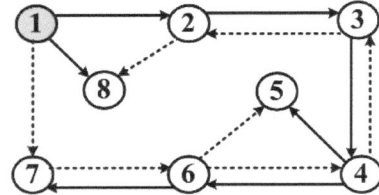

Fig. (4). A 2-connected one-to-all topology.

Furthermore, several works [38, 39] addressed k-connectivity in one-to-all and all-to-one communication models. As shown in Fig. (4), it is a 2-connected fault-tolerant one-to-all topology, where node 1 is the sink node. Frank and Tardos [38] studied k-connectivity from the root to any other node with the objective of minimizing the total weight of the edges. They proposed a polynomial time optimal solution using a maximum cost Submodular flow problem. Wang et al. [39] proposed an approximation algorithm with ratio k for k-connectivity from any node to the root, and an approximation algorithm with ratio $O(n)$ for k-connectivity from the root to any node. Both these two algorithms are centralized and their time complexities are high.

2.4 Topology Control with QoS

Low-Interference: A network topology with large interference has negative effects on throughput and energy consumption due to the excessive number of collisions at the MAC layer. Yet, only a few topology control schemes take into account low interference as a design goal. A common implicit assumption in traditional topology control methods is that low node degree implies small interference, which is not always true, as shown in [40].

Burkhart et al. [40] first raised a fundamental question: *Does Topology Control Reduce Interference?* The authors showed that traditional topology control methods will not always produce a subgraph whose interference is within a constant factor of the optimum. They proved that the average interference of RNG and LMST is $O(n)$ of the optimum in the worst case. Then they proposed several algorithms to construct topologies whose maximum link interference is minimized while the topology is connected or is a spanner for Euclidean length.

Li *et al.* [41] defined various criteria to measure the interference quality of a network topology and proposed several centralized or localized topology control algorithms to reduce interference under different criteria. Based on the MST and bisection search techniques, the authors presented several efficient centralized algorithms to construct network topologies such that the maximum link or node, or the average interference of the topology is either minimized or approximately minimized while the topology is connected or is a spanner for Euclidean length or transmission power. Then they proposed three distributed algorithms for the low-interference topology control problems and proved that the average interference of some widely used structures such as RNG and LMST is bounded by some constants for randomly deployed networks.

Delay constraints: In addition to connectivity, it is often desired that the resulting network topology should be a spanner of the given network. A spanner is a suitable network topology which supports efficient routing and prolongs the lifetime of the network. A *t-spanner* of a graph $G = (V, E)$ is a subgraph H of G such that for each node pair (u, v) in H, $d_H(u, v) \leq td_G(u, v)$, where $d_H(u, v)$ and $d_G(u, v)$ denote the Euclidean length (or the sum of hop and transmission power) of the shortest path between u and v in H and G, respectively.

With slight modifications, this definition can be extended to hop-spanner and transmission power-spanner. Constructing a spanner of a graph has been well studied by computational geometry community [42, 43]. Rodoplu and Meng [44] described a distributed protocol to construct a spanner, a connected subgraph of the unit disk graph, which is guaranteed to contain the minimum energy consumption path connecting any pair of nodes. However, the time and space complexity of this algorithm are high. Li and Wan [45] improved the result in [44] to construct a sparer spanner more efficiently. The constructed spanners have a linear number of edges and also preserve the path of the minimum power for any pair of nodes. M. Damian and N. Javali [46] presented an efficient distributed algorithm to construct a network topology, which can guarantee multiple optimal objectives: the result network topology is a $t(1+b)$-spanner of transmission graph G for any $t > 1$ and $b > 0$, and it has optimal interference among all *t*-spanner and $O(1)$ maximum degree. Especially, the result network topology can be implemented in $O(\log n)$ communication complexity and its total weight is within a factor of $O(\log n)$ of the weight of a minimum spanning tree for G.

3 QOS TOPOLOGY CONTROL IN WIRELESS AD HOC NETWORK

In this section, we introduce the energy efficient QoS topology control problem in both homogeneous and heterogeneous networks under different energy efficient optimization objectives [8], [14-15]. Given a set of wireless nodes in a plane and QoS requirements between node pairs, our problem is to find a network topology that can meet the QoS requirements and guarantee the energy efficiency for the network. The QoS requirements of our concern are traffic demands (bandwidth) and maximum delay bounds (in terms of hop counts) between end nodes at the application level. With the network configured in such a topology, as many as possible QoS calls can be admitted at run-time and the network life time can be prolonged.

We assume that the network topology can be controlled by the transmitting power at each node and the topology directly affects the QoS provisions of the network. If the topology is too dense (i.e., nodes have more neighbors), there would be more choices for routing, but the power consumption of the system would be high. On the other hand, if the topology is too loose (i.e., with less edges), there would be less choices for routing (hence, some nodes could be overloaded) and the average hop-count between end-nodes would be high. Our goal is to find a balance topology that can meet end-users QoS requirements and has minimal total transmission power or minimal maximum transmission power.

3.1 QoS Topology Control in Homogeneous Networks

3.1.1 System Model

Throughout this chapter, we adopt the widely used transmitting power model for radio networks: $p_{ij} = d_{ij}^a$, where p_{ij} is the transmitting power needed for node i to reach node j, $d(i, j)$ is the Euclidean distance between i and j, and a is a parameter typically taking a value between 2 and 4.

Since the network is homogeneous, it can be modeled by an undirected graph $G = (V, E)$, where V is the set of n nodes and E a set of undirected edges. Each node has a bandwidth capacity B, and a maximal level of transmitting power P. The bandwidth of a node is shared for both transmitting and receiving signals. That is, the total bandwidth for transmitting signals plus the total bandwidth for receiving signals at each node shall not exceed B. Let p_i denote the transmitting power of node i. We assume that each node can adjust its power level, but not beyond some maximum power P. That is, $0 \leq p_i \leq P$ for $1 \leq i \leq n$. The connectivity between two nodes depends on their transmitting power. An edge $(i,$

$j) \in E$ if and only if $p_i \geq d^n(i, j)$ and $p_j \geq d^n(i, j)$. $\lambda_{s,d}$ and $\Delta_{s,d}$ denote the traffic demand and the maximally allowed hop-count for node pair (s, d), respectively.

3.1.2 Objective with Minimizing Maximum Transmission Power

In this subsection, the optimization objective is to find a balanced topology that can meet end-users QoS requirements and have minimum maximum transmission power of nodes. From above discussion, we know that minimizing maximum transmission power can balance the energy consumption among all nodes and then avoid the situation that some nodes run out of energy faster than others. The network lifetime can be prolonged efficiently. Let $P_{max} = \max\{p_i \mid 1 \leq i \leq n\}$. We formally define the problem in [14] as follows:

Problem 1: The min-max QoS topology control problem in homogeneous networks: Given a node set V with their locations, $\lambda_{s,d}$ and $\Delta_{s,d}$ for node pair (s, d), find transmitting power p_i for $1 \leq i \leq n$, which is at most P, such that all the traffic demands can be routed within the hop-count bound, and P_{max} is minimized.

Ref. [14] considered two cases: (1) end-to-end traffic demands are not splittable, i.e., $\lambda_{s,d}$ for node pair (s, d) must be routed on the same path from s to d; (2) end-to-end traffic demands are splittable, i.e., $\lambda_{s,d}$ can be routed on several different paths from s to d. For the former case, the problem is formulated as an integer linear programming problem. For the latter case, the problem is formulated as a mixed integer programming problem, and an optimal algorithm has been proposed to solve the problem.

The authors in [14] assumed that each node can transmit signals to its neighbors in a conflict free fashion. Thus, signal interference had not been considered in [14]. There are many MAC (Medium Access Control) layer protocols or code assignment protocols [47] that have been proposed to avoid (or reduce) signal interference in radio transmissions.

A. QoS Topology Control with Traffics Non-Splittable

Suppose V is a set of n nodes with their locations. The bandwidth and maximally allowed transmitting power of each node are B and P, respectively. And $\lambda_{s,d}$ and $\Delta_{s,d}$ are the traffic demand and the maximally allowed hop-count for node pair (s, d), respectively. Since the topology control is to allow each node in the network to adjust its transmitting power (i.e., to determine its neighbors), so we must decide if there is a link between any two nodes. Let $x_{i,j}$ denote

whether there is a link from node i to node j or not, then $x_{i,j}=1$ if there is a link from node i to node j; otherwise, $x_{i,j}=0$. Because there is $\lambda_{s,d}$ traffic which must be routed from s to d, we need to determine which links these traffic routes go through. Let $x_{i,j}^{s,d}$ be Boolean variable, which denotes whether the route from s to d goes through the link (i, j). $x_{i,j}^{s,d} = 1$ if the route from s to d goes through the link (i, j); otherwise $x_{i,j}^{s,d} = 0$.

The QoS topology control for non-splittable problem can be formulated as following:

$$\text{Min } P_{max} \tag{1}$$

$$x_{i,j} = x_{j,i} \qquad\qquad \forall i, j \in V \tag{2}$$

$$x_{i,j} \leq x_{i,j'} \qquad d(i,j') \leq d(i,j) \quad \forall i, j, j' \in V \tag{3}$$

$$P \geq P_{max} \geq d_{ij}^{\alpha} \cdot x_{i,j} \qquad\qquad \forall i < j, i, j \in V \tag{4}$$

$$\sum_{(i,j)} x_{i,j}^{s,d} \leq \Delta_{s,d} \qquad\qquad \forall (s,d) \tag{5}$$

$$\sum_{(s,d)}\sum_{j} x_{i,j}^{s,d} \lambda_{s,d} + \sum_{(s,d)}\sum_{j} x_{j,i}^{s,d} \lambda_{s,d} \leq B \quad \forall i \in V \tag{6}$$

$$\sum_{j} x_{i,j}^{s,d} - \sum_{j} x_{j,i}^{s,d} = \begin{cases} 1 & \text{if } s = i \\ -1 & \text{if } d = i \\ 0 & \text{otherwise} \end{cases}$$
$$\forall i, j \in V, (s,d) \tag{7}$$

$$x_{i,j}^{s,d} \leq x_{i,j} \qquad\qquad \forall i, j \in V, (s,d) \tag{8}$$

$$x_{i,j} = 0 \text{ or } 1, x_{i,j}^{s,d} = 0 \text{ or } 1 \qquad \forall i, j \in V, (s,d) \tag{9}$$

Remarks:
- Constraint (2) ensures that each edge corresponds to two directed links.
- Constraint (3) ensures that nodes have broadcast ability. That is, the transmission by a node can be received by all the nodes within its transmitting range. This feature can be represented by the links in the network as: for node i, if there is a link to j (i.e., $x_{i,j} = 1$), then there must be a link to any node j' (i.e., $x_{i,j'} = 1$) when $d_{i,j'} \leq d_{i,j}$, which is constraint (3).
- Constraint (4) determines the maximum transmitting power among all nodes.
- Constraint (5) ensures that the hop-count for each node-pair does not exceed the pre-specified bound.
- Constraint (6) ensures that the total transmission and reception of signals at a node do not exceed the bandwidth capacity of this node. The first term at the right hand side of inequality (6) represents all the outgoing traffics at node i (transmitting) and the second term represent all the incoming traffics (reception).
- Constraints (7) and (8) ensure the validity of the route for each node-pair. Since traffics are not splittable,

$x_{i,j}^{s,d}$ represents that the entire traffics of (s, d) go through link (i, j) if it is in the route from s to d. The availability of bandwidth along the route is ensured by constraint (6).

The problem of QoS topology control for non-splittable has now been formulated as an integer linear programming problem (ILP) (1)-(9), which is NP-hard in general. When the size of the problem is not great, there are several tools that can be employed to compute the solution to this problem. After computing out $x_{i,j}$, the transmitting power of node i can be determined by the distance to its furthest neighbor.

B. QoS Topology Control with Traffics Splittable

When the network is in operation, the traffics between a node-pair may take different routes due to congestion or failures in the network. In this subsection, we introduce a general QoS topology control with traffics splittable problem, which increases delay constraints to [14].

Let $f_{i,j}^{s,d}$ be variables representing the amount of traffics of node pair (s, d) that go through link (i, j). Delay constraints can be changed as the following:

$$\frac{1}{\lambda_{s,d}} \sum_{(i,j)} f_{i,j}^{s,d} \leq \Delta_{s,d} \qquad \forall (s,d) \qquad (10)$$

This representation of the delay constraint is reasonable, because in splittable case, traffics between a node pair can be routed via several different paths and a bound on average delay provides a good delay guarantee for network applications.

The QoS topology control with traffics splittable problem can be formulated as following:

$$\text{Min } P_{\max} \qquad (11)$$

$$x_{i,j} = x_{j,i} \qquad \forall i,j \in V \qquad (12)$$

$$x_{i,j} \leq x_{i,j'} \quad d(i,j') \leq d(i,j) \quad \forall i,j,j' \in V \qquad (13)$$

$$P \geq P_{\max} \geq d_{ij}^{\alpha} \cdot x_{i,j} \qquad \forall i < j, i,j \in V \quad (14)$$

$$\sum_{(s,d)} \sum_{j} f_{i,j}^{s,d} + \sum_{(s,d)} \sum_{j} f_{j,i}^{s,d} \leq B \quad \forall i \in V \qquad (15)$$

$$\frac{1}{\lambda_{s,d}} \sum_{(i,j)} f_{i,j}^{s,d} \leq \Delta_{s,d} \qquad \forall (s,d) \qquad (16)$$

$$\sum_{j} f_{i,j}^{s,d} - \sum_{j} f_{j,i}^{s,d} = \begin{cases} \lambda_{s,d} & \text{if } s = i \\ -\lambda_{s,d} & \text{if } d = i \\ 0 & \text{otherwise} \end{cases}$$

$$\forall i,j \in V, (s,d) \quad (17)$$

$$f_{i,j}^{s,d} \leq f_{i,j}^{s,d} \cdot x_{i,j} \qquad \forall i,j \in V, (s,d) \quad (18)$$

$$x_{i,j} = 0 \text{ or } 1, f_{i,j}^{s,d} \geq 0 \qquad \forall i,j \in V, (s,d) \quad (19)$$

Constraint (16) is delay constraint for splittable problem. Constraint (17) is for flow conservation along all the routes for node pair (s, d). The QoS topology control problem with traffics splittable has now been formulated as a mixed integer programming problem in (11) – (19).

The problem is to find the network topology such that all traffics can be routed and the maximal node power is minimized. In the case, because traffics are splittable, we may first solve the QoS routing problem; based on the QoS routing problem, the energy efficient QoS topology control algorithm for the QoS topology control with non-splittable problem is proposed. The algorithm consists of two major steps: (1) increment node power to connect two nodes that have the shortest Euclidean distance among the unconnected node-pairs; (2) check if the traffics can be routed on the topology constructed in step 1. If so, the topology is found; otherwise steps 1 and 2 should be repeated.

The QoS routing problem in step 2 can be transformed to a variant of the multi-commodity flow problem, that is, for a given network topology, to route commodities on the network such that the maximal load of nodes is minimized. Since there is an assumption that all nodes have the same bandwidth capacity, the objective of minimizing the maximal node load would lead to the optimal routing to accommodate the traffics.

We first consider the QoS routing problem for a given network topology.

B1. QoS Routing Problem

Given a network graph G and traffic demands between node pairs, route these traffics in this graph, such that the maximum node-load in the system, denoted by L_{max}, is minimized. This problem can be formulated as the following:

$$\text{Min } L_{max} \tag{20}$$

$$\sum_j f_{i,j}^{s,d} - \sum_j f_{j,i}^{s,d} = \begin{cases} \lambda_{s,d} & \text{if } s = i \\ -\lambda_{s,d} & \text{if } d = i \\ 0 & \text{otherwise} \end{cases}$$

$$\forall i, j \in V, (s,d) \tag{21}$$

$$\sum_{(s,d)} \sum_j f_{i,j}^{s,d} + \sum_{(s,d)} \sum_j f_{j,i}^{s,d} \le L_{max} \quad \forall i \in V \tag{22}$$

$$\frac{1}{\lambda_{s,d}} \sum_{(i,j)} f_{i,j}^{s,d} \le \Delta_{s,d} \quad \forall (s,d) \tag{23}$$

$$f_{i,j}^{s,d} \ge 0 \quad \forall i, j \in V, (s,d) \tag{24}$$

$$L_{max} \ge 0 \tag{25}$$

Note that: $\forall (s,d), f_{i,j}^{s,d} = 0$, if $(i,j) \notin E(G)$

Function (20) is the objective, which is to minimize the maximum node load. Constraint (22) obtains the maximum node load in the network. When any request cannot be routed due to the disconnection of the network, it will report an error of disconnection. This is a linear programming (LP) problem. The optimal solution can be found in polynomial time $O((|E|t)^{3.5})$, where $|E|$ is the number of edges in graph G, and t is the number of node pairs which have non-zero traffic.

B2.   Energy Efficient QoS Topology Control Algorithm

The basic idea of the algorithm is to sort all node pairs (in fact, only the node pairs that can be reached within the maximal transmitting power P are considered) in ascending order according to their Euclidean distance. Each time the nodes pairs that have the shortest distance and have not yet had a link between the two nodes are picked and their power is increased until they can reach each other. Then, the QoS routing algorithm runs on the network to see if the requested traffics can be all routed. This operation is repeated until the QoS topology is found, or all nodes already reached their maximal power P (the topology that can meet the QoS requirements does not exist in this case).

The Energy Efficient QoS Topology Control Algorithm for homogeneous networks can be formally presented as following:

Input: Node set V with their locations, $\lambda_{s,d}$ for node-pair (s, d), and bandwidth capacity B.
Output: Power levels p for all nodes in V.

Begin:
1.   Sort all node-pairs with $d^t(i, j) \le P$ $(i < j)$ in ascending order according to $d(i, j)$.
2.   Pick up the node-pair with closest distance but not yet connected and increase the power to make it connected to get a new graph G.
3.   Run the QoS routing algorithm on G to obtain L_{max}. If $L_{max} \le B$, then do not proceed; otherwise repeat 2 and 3.
End.

The step 2 halts if all nodes already reach power P and an error of no solution is reported in this case. To reduce the number of times of calling the QoS routing algorithm in step 3, we use the binary search method to find the QoS topology, instead of adding an edge each time and running the routing algorithm.

In this algorithm, the node power is gradually increased until the required topology is formed. It is not difficult to see that the maximum node energy needed to form the required topology is minimal, provided the number of power-levels of a node is finite. Furthermore, the topology found in step (2) and (3) is minimized in the sense that it has the least number of edges that are added-in among all the possible topologies that can meet the QoS requirements. This is because the routing produced by the QoS routing algorithm (formulated in (20) – (25)) is also optimal in the sense that the maximum node-load in the topology is minimized. That is, given a topology, if the QoS routing algorithm cannot route all traffic demands without letting any node exceed its bandwidth capacity, there is no solution on this topology (i.e., the topology needs more edges to split traffics off). Therefore, when traffic demands are splittable, this algorithm can find the optimal solution to the QoS topology control with splittable problem.

We can use *lp_solve* (ftp://ftp.es.ele.tue.nl/pub/lp_solve) or Matlab 6.5 to solve the QoS topology control with non-splittable problem. For the QoS topology control with splittable problem, it can be solved by the energy efficient QoS topology control algorithm. In the following, we give an example of two problems.

Suppose there are 6 nodes with their positions shown in Fig.(5a). The bandwidth capacity of each node is set to 500. There are 6 pairs with their traffics. The details of the request and corresponding traffic are showed in Table 1. Fig.(5b) shows the QoS topology for non-splittable corresponding requests in Tab. (1). Tab. (2) shows the corresponding routings.

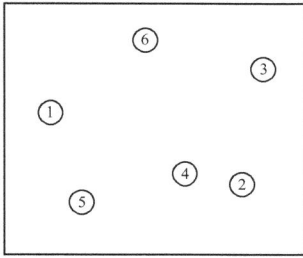

Fig. (5a). Original Network without topology control

s	d	$\lambda_{s,d}$
2	4	148.6403
3	4	142.2603
5	1	152.0183
5	3	137.8970
1	3	155.6549
6	2	163.5291

Tab. (1). Requests and their traffics

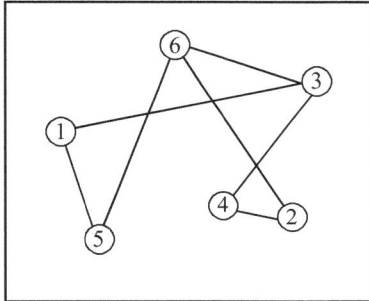

Fig. (5b). QoS topology for non-splittable case

s	d	$\lambda_{s,d}$	Route
2	4	148.6403	2→4
3	4	142.2603	3→4
5	1	152.0183	5→1
5	3	137.8970	5→6→3
1	3	155.6549	1→3
6	2	163.5291	6→2

Tab. (2). Routing for non-splittable

Fig. (5c).The QoS topology for splittable case

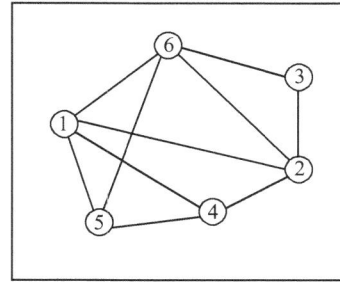

s	d	$\lambda_{s,d}$	Splitted $\lambda_{s,d}$	Route
2	4	148.6403	134.0611	2→4
			6.7199	2→1→5→4
			5.9452	2→1→4
			1.9141	2→3→4
3	4	142.2603	142.2603	3→4
5	1	152.0183	152.0183	5→1
5	3	137.8970	82.1792	5→6→3
			38.3595	5→4→3
			8.2598	5→1→2→3
			4.7424	5→1→6→3
			4.3561	5→1→4→3
1	3	155.6549	61.2726	1→2→3
			41.9292	1→6→3
			24.8259	1→4→3
			15.0018	1→5→6→3
			12.6254	1→5→4→3
6	2	163.5291	145.41	6→2
			7.3976	6→5→1→2
			6.5375	6→1→2
			4.1839	6→3→2

Tab. (3). Routing for splittable

For comparison, Fig.(5c) is the topology for the case where traffics are splittable and the topology is computed by using energy efficient QoS topology control algorithm. The requests are same as Table 1. Tab.3 shows the routing and traffic distribution in the topology of Fig.(5c). Comparing Fig.(5b) with Fig.(5c), we can see that the topology for non-splittable case has a long distance edge (1, 3) in Fig.(5b), which results in a much higher P_{max} than the splittable case. The topology for splittable case has more short edges, which helps splitting the traffic among multiple routes. Note that: Fig.(5b) and Fig.(5c) are topologies which remove the redundant edges, i.e., no traffic edges.

3.1.3 QoS Topology Control with Minimizing Total Transmission Power

The authors in [15] also discuss the energy efficient QoS topology control problem, where the objective is to minimize the total transmission power of nodes P_{total}, where $P_{\text{total}} = \sum_{i=1}^{n} p(i)$. The given is same as the above subsection, but it does not need that the topology is undirected.

The network model can be represented as a directed graph $G = (V, E)$, where V is the set of n nodes and E a set of directed edges. Let p_i denote the transmitting power of node i. We assume that each node can adjust its power level, but not beyond some maximum power P. That is, $0 \leq p_i \leq P$ for $1 \leq i \leq n$. The directed edge from i to j depends on i's transmitting power. An directed edge $(i, j) \in E$ iff $p_i \geq d^{\pi}(i, j)$.
We formally defined the problem in [15] as follows:

Problem 2: The min-total QoS topology control problem: Given a node set V with their locations, $\lambda_{s,d}$ and $\Delta_{s,d}$ for node pair (s, d), find transmitting power p_i for $1 \leq i \leq n$, such that all the traffic demands can be routed within the hop-count bound, and P_{total} is minimized.

If $\lambda_{s,d}$ are selected to ensure the network is strongly connected, and $\Delta_{s,d}$ are large enough, this problem is the topology control problem which was defined in [48], which had been proved to be NP-hard. Thus, this problem is NP-hard.

The authors also consider two cases of the problem: the traffic demands are not splittable and splittable. For the non-splittable case, the problem can be formulated as an integer linear programming:

$$Min \sum_{i=1}^{n} p(i)$$

Constraints: (3)-(9).
For the splittable case, the problem can be formulated as a mixed integer linear programming:

$$Min \sum_{i=1}^{n} p(i)$$

Constraints: (13)-(19).

Notice that the topology constructed by the above two formulations is directed. To make the topology undirected, we only need to add the constraint $x_{i,j} = x_{j,i}, \forall i, j \in V$, to the two formulations.

For the splittable case, a greedy algorithm and an approximation algorithm with ratio n are proposed to solve the problem 2, where n is the number of nodes.

The problem in [15] is to find the network topology such that all traffics can be routed and the total transmission power is minimized. In the case where traffics are splittable, the power of all nodes is adjusted to the minimal level firstly, i.e., $p(i)=0$, for $1 \leq i \leq n$. Then the QoS topology is computed in two

major steps: 1) pick a node and increase its power to reach a new neighbor. That is to add a new link to the network. 2) check if the traffics can be routed on the new topology obtained in step 1. If so, the QoS topology is found; otherwise steps 1 and 2 are repeated. The authors proposed two algorithms to construct the required topology. The first algorithm **LIPF** (Least Incremental Power First) is to minimize the incremental power in each step. The second algorithm **LPF** (Least Power First) is to add link with the least power in each step.

The two algorithms must use the same problem in the above subsection: the QoS routing problem: Given a network graph G and traffic demands from node directed pairs, these traffics are routed in the graph, such that the maximal node-load is minimized.

In LIPF algorithm, the least incremental power is computed for each node to reach its new neighbor firstly, and the node is picked with minimal incremental power and its transmitting range is increased to reach the new neighbor. Then QoS routing algorithm is run on this new topology to see whether the requested traffics can be all routed. The operation is repeated until the QoS topology is found, or all nodes already reach their maximal power P (the topology that can meet the QoS requirements does not exist in this case).

The LIPF algorithm can be formally described as follows:

Input: Node set V with their locations, $\lambda_{s,d}$ for node-pair (s, d), and bandwidth capacity B.
Output: Transmitting power $p(i)$ for each node i in V.

Begin:
1. Compute the least incremental power for each node to reach a new neighbor:
    $$\Delta_i = \min\{(d_{i,j})^{\alpha} - p(i) \mid 1 \leq j \leq n, (i, j) \notin E\}$$
    $\forall 1 \leq i \leq n$.
2. Pick up the node k that reaches a new neighbor j with the minimal incremental power:
    $\Delta_k = \min\{\Delta_i \mid 1 \leq i \leq n\}$, and add new link (k, j) to G.
3. Run the QoS routing algorithm on G to obtain $L_{\max}$. If $L_{\max} \leq B$ or all nodes reach their maximal power P, then do not proceed; otherwise repeat 2 and 3.
End.

In LPF algorithm, first of all, all node pairs (in fact, only the node pairs that can be reached within the maximal transmitting power P are considered) are sorted in ascending order according to their Euclidean distance. Each time the shortest link (the least power cost) which does not yet exist in the network is picked and the power of sender is increased until the other node is reached. Then, the QoS routing algorithm runs on the network to see whether the requested traffics can be all routed. Similarly, this operation is repeated until the QoS topology is found, or all nodes already reach their maximal power P.

The LPF algorithm can be formally described as follows:
Input: Node set V with their locations, $\lambda_{s,d}$ for node-pair (s, d), and bandwidth capacity B.
Output: Transmitting power $p(i)$ for each node i in V.

Begin:
1. Sort all node-pairs in ascending order according to $d_{i,j}$ (note that $p_{ij} = (d_{i,j})^a$ and $(d_{i,j})^a \leq P$).
2. Add the minimal $d_{i,j}$ which does not yet exist in the network and get a new graph G.
3. Run the QoS routing algorithm on G to obtain $L_{\max}$. If $L_{\max} \leq B$, or there is no available link left, then do not proceed; otherwise go to 2 and repeat.
End.

Theorem 1: LPF algorithm is $O(n)$-approximation algorithm with time $O(n^2 \log n + \log n(|E| \times t)^{3.5})$.
In step 3 of both algorithms, the process is stopped if all nodes already reach their maximal power P. An error of no solution is reported in this case. To reduce the number of times of calling the QoS routing algorithm in LPF algorithm, we use the binary search method to find the QoS topology, instead of adding a link each time and running the routing algorithm. The authors proved that approximation ratio of this algorithm is n and the time complexity is $O(n^2 \log n + \log n(|E| \times t)^{3.5})$, where $|E|$ is the number of edges in the network, and t is the number of node pairs which have non-zero traffic.

3.2 QoS Topology Control in Non-homogeneous Networks

Most of the existing works on topology control for wireless ad hoc networks assume homogenous network environment where nodes have the same bandwidth and energy capacities. However, this assumption on network homogeneity does not always hold in practice. In fact, even devices of the same type may have different maximal transmission power. Non-homogenous networks are more general, where nodes can have different bandwidths or energy capacities. In this subsection, the problem of QoS topology control in non-homogeneous networks was studied [8].

3.2.1 System Model

The network was modeled by a directed graph $G = (V, E)$, where V is the set of n non-homogeneous

nodes and E a set of directed edges. Each node i has a bandwidth capacity B_i, and a maximal level of transmitting power P_i. The bandwidth of a node is shared for both transmitting and receiving signals. It is also assumed that each node can adjust its transmitting power level. Let p_i denote the transmission power that node i chooses, $0 \leq p_i \leq P_i$. A directed edge $(i, j) \in E$ if $p_i \geq d_{ij}^{\ a}$, where a is a real number typically between 2 to 4. Let $\lambda_{s,d}$ denote the traffic demands and the maximum allowed hop-count for each node-pair (s, d), respectively. For node i, a power utilization ratio was defined by $R_i = p_i / P_i$. Let $R_{\max} = \max\{ R_i \mid 0 \leq i \leq n \}$. Then the QoS topology control problem in non-homogenous networks can be formally defined as:

Problem 3: The min-max QoS topology control problem in non-homogeneous networks: Given a node set V with their locations and each node i with B_i and P_i, and given $\lambda_{s,d}$ and $\Delta_{s,d}$ for each node-pair (s, d), find transmitting power p_i for $0 \leq i \leq n$, such that all the traffic demands can be routed within the hop-count bound, and $R_{\max}$ is minimized.

3.2.2 QoS Topology Control with Traffics Non-Splittable

Most of the constraints in this problem are the same as the constraints in subsection 3.1.3, but the constraints and methods in subsection 3.1.3 can not solve the similar problems in non-homogeneous networks. Additionally, since the network is non-homogeneous, we gave the new transmission power constraints [8]. Transmission power constraints are as follows:

$$P_i \geq p_i \geq d_{i,j}^{\alpha} \cdot x_{i,j} \qquad \forall i, j \in V \qquad (26)$$

$$R_{\max} \geq \frac{p_i}{P_i} \qquad \forall i \in V \qquad (27)$$

And then, just like the problems in subsections 3.1.2-3, the QoS topology control problem in non-homogenous networks with non-splittable traffic can be formulated as follows:

$$\text{Min } R_{max} \tag{28}$$

$$x_{i,j} \leq x_{i,j'} \qquad d(i,j') \leq d(i,j) \quad \forall i,j,j' \in V \tag{29}$$

$$P_i \geq p_i \geq d_{i,j}^{\alpha} \cdot x_{i,j} \qquad \forall i,j \in V \tag{30}$$

$$R_{max} \geq \frac{p_i}{P_i} \qquad \forall i \in V \tag{31}$$

$$\sum_{(i,j)} x_{i,j}^{s,d} \leq \Delta_{s,d} \qquad \forall(s,d) \tag{32}$$

$$\sum_{(s,d)}\sum_{j} x_{i,j}^{s,d}\lambda_{s,d} + \sum_{(s,d)}\sum_{j} x_{j,i}^{s,d}\lambda_{s,d} \leq B_i \quad \forall i \in V \tag{33}$$

$$\sum_{j} x_{i,j}^{s,d} - \sum_{j} x_{j,i}^{s,d} = \begin{cases} 1 & \text{if } s=i \\ -1 & \text{if } d=i \\ 0 & \text{otherwise} \end{cases}$$
$$\forall i,j \in V,(s,d) \tag{34}$$

$$x_{i,j}^{s,d} \leq x_{i,j} \qquad \forall i,j \in V,(s,d) \tag{35}$$

$$x_{i,j} = 0 \text{ or } 1, x_{i,j}^{s,d} = 0 \text{ or } 1, p_i \geq 0, R_{max} \geq 0$$
$$\forall i,j \in V,(s,d) \tag{36}$$

3.2.3 QoS Topology Control with Traffics Splittable

For the splittable case, the problem can be represented as a mixed integer linear programming:

$$\text{Min } R_{max} \tag{37}$$

$$x_{i,j} \leq x_{i,j'} \qquad d(i,j') \leq d(i,j) \quad \forall i,j,j' \in V \tag{38}$$

$$P_i \geq p_i \geq d_{i,j}^{\alpha} \cdot x_{i,j} \qquad \forall i,j \in V \tag{39}$$

$$R_{max} \geq \frac{p_i}{P_i} \qquad \forall i \in V \tag{40}$$

$$\sum_{(s,d)}\sum_{j} f_{i,j}^{s,d} + \sum_{(s,d)}\sum_{j} f_{j,i}^{s,d} \leq B_i \qquad \forall i \in V \tag{41}$$

$$\frac{1}{\lambda_{s,d}}\sum_{(i,j)} f_{i,j}^{s,d} \leq \Delta_{s,d} \qquad \forall(s,d) \tag{42}$$

$$\sum_{j} f_{i,j}^{s,d} - \sum_{j} f_{j,i}^{s,d} = \begin{cases} \lambda_{s,d} & \text{if } s=i \\ -\lambda_{s,d} & \text{if } d=i \\ 0 & \text{otherwise} \end{cases}$$
$$\forall i,j \in V,(s,d) \tag{43}$$

$$f_{i,j}^{s,d} \leq f_{i,j}^{s,d} \cdot x_{i,j} \qquad \forall i,j \in V,(s,d) \tag{44}$$

$$x_{i,j} = 0 \text{ or } 1, f_{i,j}^{s,d} \geq 0, p_i \geq 0, R_{max} \geq 0$$
$$\forall i,j \in V,(s,d) \tag{45}$$

We proposed an optimal algorithm for the QoS topology problem in non-homogenous network [8]. Let L_i denote the bandwidth utilization ratio of node i, defined as:

$$L_i = \frac{b_i}{B_i} = \frac{\sum_{(s,d)}\sum_{j} f_{i,j}^{s,d} + \sum_{(s,d)}\sum_{j} f_{j,i}^{s,d}}{B_i} \tag{46}$$

where b_i is the actual bandwidth usage of node i. Let $L_{max} = \max\{L_i | 1 \leq i \leq n\}$, the maximum bandwidth utilization. Firstly, we considered the *Load-balancing QoS routing problem*: Given a network topology, and traffic demands between node-pairs, route these traffics in the network such that the maximum bandwidth utilization L_{max} is minimized. Similar with the problem in [14], this problem also can be solved in polynomial time by transforming it to a variant of multi-commodity flow problem, where fractional flows are allowed. It can be formulated as follows:

$$\text{Min } L_{max} \tag{47}$$

$$\sum_{j} f_{i,j}^{s,d} - \sum_{j} f_{j,i}^{s,d} = \begin{cases} \lambda_{s,d} & \text{if } s=i \\ -\lambda_{s,d} & \text{if } d=i \\ 0 & \text{otherwise} \end{cases}$$
$$\forall i,j \in V,(s,d) \tag{48}$$

$$\sum_{(s,d)}\sum_{j} f_{i,j}^{s,d} + \sum_{(s,d)}\sum_{j} f_{j,i}^{s,d} \leq B_i \cdot L_{max} \quad \forall i \in V \tag{49}$$

$$\sum_{(i,j)} f_{i,j}^{s,d} \leq \lambda_{s,d} \cdot \Delta_{s,d} \qquad \forall(s,d) \tag{50}$$

$$f_{i,j}^{s,d} \geq 0 \qquad \forall i,j \in V,(s,d) \tag{51}$$

$$L_{max} \geq 0 \tag{52}$$

Note that: $\forall(s,d), f_{i,j}^{s,d} = 0$, if $(i,j) \notin E(G)$

The energy efficient topology control algorithm is based on the above *Load-balancing QoS routing* problem and the main idea is similar with the algorithm in subsection 3.1.2.2. But this algorithm may generate redundant links, i.e., some links that make no contribution in carrying traffic are added into the topology because they have low weights of R_{ij}. These redundant links will cause maintenance overhead of the topology. Thus the authors improved this algorithm by adding the final step to remove the links that have no traffic flowing through.

The energy efficient topology control algorithm for non-homogeneous network can be presented as following:
Input: Node set V with their locations, $\lambda_{s,d}$ for node-pair (s, d), and bandwidth capacity B.
Output: Power levels p for all nodes in V.

Begin:
1. Sort all node-pairs with $d_{i,j}^{\alpha} \leq P_i$ in ascending order according to R_{ij}.
2. Pick up the node-pair (i, j) that has the smallest R_{ij} but there is no link from i to j, and increase p_i to link j, making a new graph G.
3. Run the QoS routing algorithm on G to obtain $L_{\max}$. If $L_{\max} \leq 1$, then go to 4; otherwise repeat 2 and 3.
4. Remove redundant links from the obtained topology.
End.

The step 2, is stopped if all nodes already reach their maximal power and an error of no solution is reported in this case. To reduce the number of times of calling the QoS routing algorithm in step 3, the binary search method was used to din the QoS topology, instead of adding an edge each time and dunning the routing algorithm. From the analyses in 3.1.2, it was known that this algorithm can find the optimal solution to the energy efficient QoS topology control problem in non- homogenous networks.

4　STRONGLY CONNECTED TOPOLOGY CONTROL IN WIRELESS SENSOR NETWORK

The most basic requirement of a network is that it is connected, that is any two nodes that are connected in the transmission graph are also connected in the constructed topology. In wireless ad hoc and sensor networks, all communications among these devices are based on radio propagation, and controlled by their transmit powers. Each radio is equipped with Omni-directional antenna. For each order pair (u, v) of nodes, there is a transmission power threshold, denoted by $p(u, v)$. A signal transmitted by node u can be received by v only when the transmission power of u is at least $p(u, v)$. However, the transmission power threshold for a pair of sensors depends on a number of factors including the

distance between the sensors, attenuation, interference, etc. Note that for any pair of (u, v), $p(u, v)$ may not be equal to $p(v, u)$. In this section, we studied the strongly connected topology control problems.

Given transmission powers of the sensors, sensor network can be represented by a directed graph. The main goal of topology control is to assign transmission powers to all sensors so that the resulting directed graph satisfies some specific properties. We focus on the problem that adjusts the power level of each sensor to make the network strongly connected and to minimize the total amount of power used. We discuss this problem in two scenarios: one is that each node in network has the non-restricted maximum transmitting power; the other is that each node u has the restricted maximum transmitting power $p_{\max}(u)$. The authors in [10], [11] use different techniques to solve the problems involved with these two scenarios.

4.1 Non-restricted Topology Control

In this subsection, we focus on the problem of adjusting the power level of each sensor to make the network strongly connected and to minimize the total amount of power used. First of all, we give a formal definition of the problem in [10]:

Problem 4: Minimum Power Strong Connected Topology Control (MP-SCTC) Problem: Given n sensors in the Euclidean plane and transmission power threshold for each directed pair, find a power assignment for each sensor to reach a strongly connected directed graph with minimum total power.
Note that the problem in [10] is different from those in [4], [31], [9] and [30], which investigate symmetric weighted directed graph G. Ref. [4] addressed strong connectivity with only bi-directional links. Ref. [31], [9] and [30] pondered upon strong connectivity with all directed links. Ref. [10] addressed more general weight direct graph G, which must not be a symmetric weighted directed graph.

Suppose there are n sensors in 2-D plane, which form a set $V = \{v_1, v_2, ..., v_n\}$. Given a transmission power assignment $P: V \rightarrow R$, a sensor network can be represented by a directed graph $G = (V, E)$ where an arc (directed edge) (u, v) exists if $P(u) \geq p(u, v)$. A directed graph is strongly connected if for each directed pair (u, v) of V, there is a directed path from u to v.

Definition 2: Let $G = (V, E)$ be a directed graph, and $P(v_i)$ a transmission power assignment for each v_i in V. The total power $TP(G)$ of G is defined to be:

$$TP(G) = \sum_{i=1}^{n} P(v_i) \qquad (53)$$

Now, MP-SCTC problem can be described more clearly as follows: Given n sensors in the Euclidean plane and a transmission power threshold for each directed pair, find a power assignment $P(v_i)$ for each sensor v_i such that the resulting directed graph $G = (V, E)$ is strongly connected and total power $TP(G)$ is minimized.

The minimum power strong connected topology control problem is NP-hard because the special case was proved to be NP-hard [31]. Before solving problem 4, the authors firstly studied another problem [10] - the Minimum Directed Edge Augmentation Problem, to apply the result to design their heuristics for MP-SCTC problem.

Problem 5: Minimum Directed Edge Augmentation Problem (MDEAP): Given a directed graph $G = (V, E)$, which is a subgraph of the complete directed graph G_0, find a minimum set of directed edges $E_1 \subseteq E_0 - E$ such that adding E_1 to G would result in a strongly connected directed graph.

The authors proposed an optimal algorithm for MDEAP. We briefly describe the optimal algorithm for this problem as follows:

Input: A directed graph $G=(V, E)$.
Output: Such that $G'=(V, E \cup E')$ is strongly connected.

Begin:
1. Initially, set $E' \leftarrow \varnothing$
2. Find out all strongly connected components in G. Shrink each strongly connected component into a new node, and the resulting directed graph is still denoted by G. Suppose G has k weakly connected components. And then, If $k > 1$, go to Step 3; If $k = 1$, go to Step 4.
3. Find out one node with zero out-degree and one node with zero in-degree for each weakly connected component. Then add $k - 1$ arcs from a node with zero out-degree in a weakly connected component to one node with zero in-degree in another weakly connected component in order to connect all weakly connected components into one. Put all added arcs into E' and G go to Step 4.
4. If G is a single node, then G is strongly connected.
End.

This algorithm produces an optimal solution for MDEAP in time $O(n^2)$. The correctness of this algorithm was proved in [10], and then two greedy heuristics were also derived for MP-SCTC problem by applying this algorithm. Let $f(G)$ be the minimum number if arcs are added to G to get a strongly connected graph. Function $f(G)$ can be used as potential function to design the greedy algorithms. The greedy algorithm 1 starts with $|V|$ isolated nodes.

Then at each time, we find a node u and corresponding power w with maximum $(f(G) - f(G[u, w]))/w$, assign power w to node u, till all nodes have been assigned powers to get a directed graph G. Finally, add minimum number of arcs to G to get a strongly connected graph. The greedy algorithm 2, starts with $|V|$ isolated nodes as well. Then at each time, we find a node u and w', to adjust its power w to w' with maximum $(f(G) - f(G[u, w']))/(w' - w)$, ~~till~~ to get a strongly connected graph. These two greedy algorithms are represented as the following:

The Greedy Algorithm 1 for MP-SCTC problem (GA1-MP-SCTC):
Input: A set V of stations.
Output: A strongly connected topology for V with minimum power consumption.

Begin:
1. Initially, $U \leftarrow V$ and $G \leftarrow (V, \varnothing)$.
2. **While** $(U \neq \varnothing)$ **do**
3. Choose a station $u \in U$ and a power level w to maximize $(f(G) - f(G[u, w]))/w$, And set $U \leftarrow U - \{u\}$ and $G \leftarrow G[u, w]$.
4. Add minimum number of arcs to G to get strongly connected graph, where $G[u,w]$ is the resulting graph obtained from G by adding arcs from u to other nodes under power w.
5. **End-While.**
End.

In the following figures are examples for algorithm GA1-MP-SCTC. We randomly select 8 nodes in a 80×80 area and randomly produce transmission power threshold for each order pair. Then we get a graph shown in Fig. 6(a). Fig. 6 illustrates some steps for algorithm GA1-MP-SCTC. After four steps, we get Fig. 6(b). In the fifth step, we pick node K. In this time, the value of function $(f(G) - f(G[u, w]))/w$ is minimized to get graph (c) and (d).

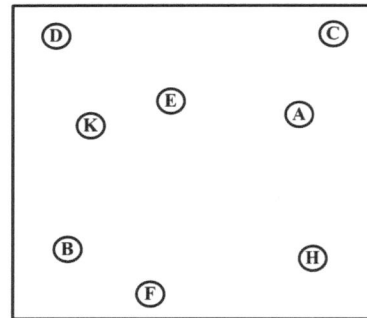

(a) The Initial Step for GA1-MP-SCTC.

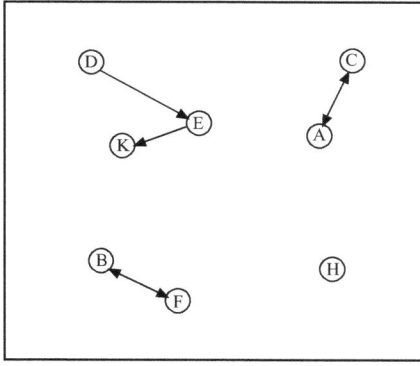

(b) The Fourth Step for GA1-MP-SCTC.

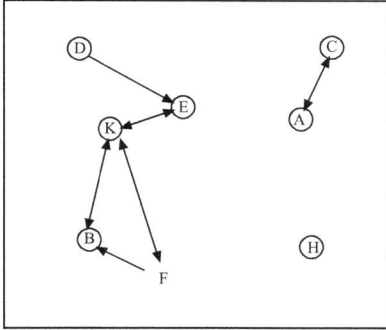

(c) The Fifth Step for GA1-MP-SCTC.

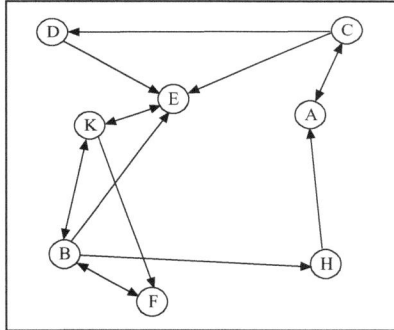

(d) The Final Graph for GA1-MP-SCTC.

Fig. (6). Example for GA1-MP-SCTC.

The Greedy Algorithm 2 for MP-SCTC problem (GA2-MP-SCTC):
Input: A set V of stations.
Output: A strongly connected topology for V with minimum power consumption.

Begin:
1.   Initially, $G \leftarrow (V, \varnothing)$.
2.   **While** ($f(G) > 0$) **do**
3.   Choose a station $u \in U$ and adjust u's power level from w to w' to maximize $(f(G) - f(G[u, w']))/(w' - w)$.
            // w is u's current power level in G.
4.   Set $G \leftarrow G[u, w']$.
5.   **End-While.**
End.

4.2 Restricted Topology Control

In this subsection, we also studied the problem of adjusting the power level of each sensor to make the network strongly connected and to minimize the total amount of power used. Furthermore, we add the constraint that each node has a restricted maximum transmission power, which is more practical for wireless sensor networks. Suppose there are n sensors in plane. $V = \{v_1, v_2, \ldots, v_n\}$ is defined as a set of sensors and each sensor v has a maximum power level $p_{max}(v)$. Let p be a transmission power assignment on V, i.e. for each node v, $p_{max}(v) \geq p(v)$. Given the transmission powers of the sensors, sensor networks can be represented by a directed graph $G = (V, E)$. A directed edge (u, v) is in this directed graph if and only if $p_{max}(u) \geq p(u) \geq p(u, v)$. $G_{max} = (V, E_{max})$ is the resulting directed graph by each sensor node using its maximum power level. The problem studied in [11] can be formulated as following:

Problem 6: Minimum Power Restricted Strong Connected Topology Control Problem (**MP-RSCTC**): Given n sensors in the Euclidean plane, and each sensor v having its maximum power level $p_{max}(v)$, and each directed pair (u, v) having a power threshold $p(u, v)$, find a power assignment $p(u)$ for each sensor u so that the resulting directed graph $G = (V, E)$ by p is a strongly connected directed graph and total power $TP(G)$ is minimized.

MP-RSCTC problem will be transformed to following problem: Given a weighted directed graph $G_{max} = (V, E_{max})$, which is strongly connected, to find a spanning subgraph $G = (V, E)$ of G_{max} such that G is strongly connected and $p(G)$ is minimized. This problem is proven to be NP-hard [9].

Three heuristics were derived in [11]. The main idea of the first two algorithms is to delete a maximum power such that it still remains strongly connected. Algorithm 1, starts with G_{max}. Then for each time we find a node with a maximum power, if the resulting graph still keeps strongly connected after deleting all out-edges under this maximum power, then delete this maximum power of the node, otherwise all power levels of the node are deleted.

For each sensor v, queuing transmitting power of v as $w_1^v, w_2^v, \ldots, w_{k(v)}^v$ from min to max, i.e., all out-directed edges of v along $p(v, u)$ can be queued as following: $p(v, u_1) \leq p(v, u_2) \leq \ldots \leq p(v, u_{k(v)})$, the different $p(v, u_j)$ is $w_1^v, w_2^v, \ldots, w_{k(v)}^v$ and $E_{w(j)}^v = \{(v, u) \mid$ if $w_j^v \geq p(v, u) > w_{j-1}^v\}$.

The Algorithm 1 for MP-RSCTC problem (A1-MP-RSCTC):
Input: n sensors and their maximum power.

Output: A strongly connected graph with minimized total power consumption.

Begin:
1. Initially, G ← G_{max} and
    $W \leftarrow \bigcup_{v \in V} \{w_1^v, w_2^v, ..., w_{k(v)}^v\}$.

2. **While** ($W \neq \varnothing$) **do**
3.   Choose a sensor $v \in V$ with maximum power w_j^v

        in W.

4.   If $G - E_{w(j)}^v$ is strongly connected, then

        $G \leftarrow G - E_{w(j)}^v$, $W \leftarrow W - \{w_j^v\}$.

5.   Otherwise, $W \leftarrow W - \{w_j^v, w_{j-1}^v, ..., w_1^v\}$.

6. **End-While.**
End.

In the following figures are examples for Algorithm 1. We randomly select 8 nodes in a 80×80 area and randomly generate transmission power threshold for each order pair. Then we get a graph shown in Fig.7(a) which illustrates some steps for A1-MP-RSCTC. After some procedure steps, we get Fig. 7(b). In the next step, we pick node 3 which has maximum power, after deleting (3, 4), it is still strongly connected and the resulting graph is shown in Fig. 7(c). The final resulting topology is Fig. 7(d).

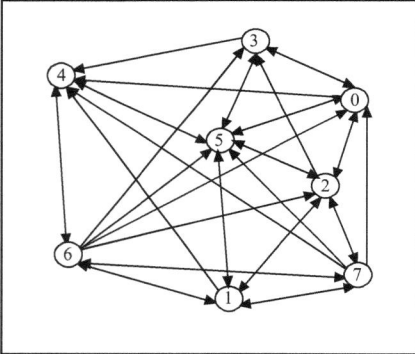

(a) The Initial Step for A1-MP-RSCTC.

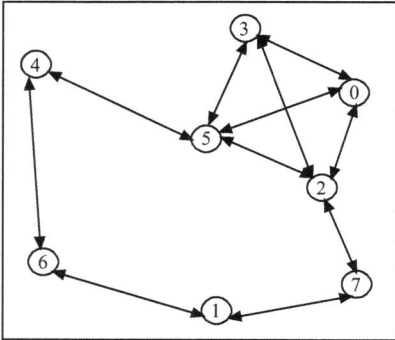

(b) After Some Step for A1-MP-RSCTC

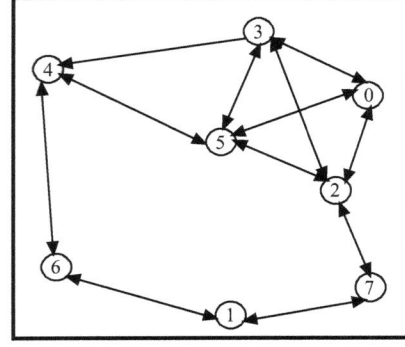

(c) The Next Step of (b) for A1-MP-RSCTC.

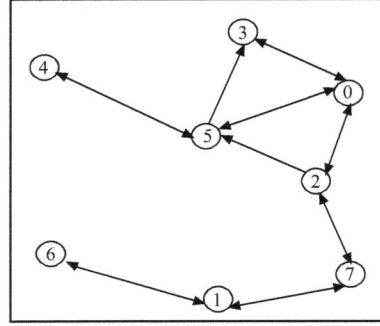

(d) The Final Topology for A1-MP-RSCTC

Fig. (7). Example for A1-MP-RSCTC.

The Algorithm 2 for MP-RSCTC problem (A2-MP-RSCTC):
Input: n sensors and their maximum power.
Output: A strongly connected graph with minimized total power consumption.

Begin:
1. Initially, $G \leftarrow G_{max}$ and
    $W \leftarrow \bigcup_{v \in V} \{w_1^v, w_2^v, ..., w_{k(v)}^v\}$.

2. **While** ($W \neq \varnothing$) **do**
3.   Choose a sensor $v \in V$ with maximum

        difference $w_j^v - w_{j-1}^v$, where w_j^v is maximum

        transmitting power of v in W.

4.   If $G - E_{w(j)}^v$ is a strongly connected, then

        $G \leftarrow G - E_{w(j)}^v$, $W \leftarrow W - \{w_j^v\}$.

5.   Otherwise, $W \leftarrow W - \{w_j^v, w_{j-1}^v, ..., w_1^v\}$.

6. **End-While.**
End.

The main idea of third algorithm is based on Minimum Spanning Tree. For $G_{max}=(V, E_{max})$, getting a weight undirected graph $G = (V, E)$. $(u, v) \in E$ if and only if $(u, v) \in E_{max}$ and $(v, u) \in E_{max}$, $w(u, v) = max\{p(u, v), p(v, u)\}$. Firstly, find a minimum spanning tree T on graph G, and then change each edge in T to two directed edges (u, v) and (v, u), to get a strongly connected subgraph of G_{max}.

The Algorithm 3 for MP-RSCTC problem (A3-MP-RSCTC):
Input: n sensors and their maximum power.
Output: A strongly connected graph with minimized total power consumption.

Begin:
1. Initially, construct an undirected graph G from G_{max}.
2. Find a Minimum Spanning Tree T of G, then get a strong connected subgraph of G_{max}.
End.

Note that the algorithm A3-MP-RSCTC can be accomplished only when G is a connected graph. Specially, when $p(u, v) = p(v, u) = d^r(u, v)$, the proposed algorithm is similar to MST algorithm in [2].

5 CONCLUSION

In this chapter, we investigate the current works on topology control problem in wireless ad hoc and sensor networks. We firstly focus on the most representative problems in each domain and present a comprehensive review of various existed algorithm and techniques. And then, we elaborately introduce the advanced techniques for QoS topology control and strongly connected topology control under different energy efficient criteria.

ACKNOWLEDGEMENTS

This research is partially supported by the National Natural Science Foundation of China under grant 10671208, and Key Laboratory of Data Engineering and Knowledge Engineering (Renmin University of China), MOE.

REFERENCES

[1]   J. Wu, Handbook of Theoretical and Algorithmic Aspects of Ad Hoc, Sensor, and Peer-to-Peer Networks, Auerbach Publications, 2006.

[2]   I. Chlamtac, M. Conti, and JN. Liu, Mobile Ad Hoc Networking: Imperatives and Challenges, Ad Hoc Networks, 2003, (1):13-64.

[3]   I.F. Akilydiz, W. Su, Y. Sankarasubramaniam, and E. Cayirci, A Survey on Sensor Networks, IEEE Communication Magazine, 2002, 102–114.

[4]   E. L. Lloyd, R. Liu, and M. V. Marathe, Algorithmic Aspects of Topology Control Problems for Ad Hoc Networks, Proc. of the ACM MobiHoc, 2002, 123-134.

[5]   R. Ramanathan and R. Rosales-Hain, Topology Control of Multihop Wireless Networks Using Transmit Power Adjustment, Proc. of the IEEE INFOCOM, 2000, 404-413.

[6]   R. Rajaraman, Topology Control and Routing in Ad Hoc Networks: a Survey, Proc. of ACM SIGACT, 2002, 60-73.

[7]   X. Li, W. Song, Y. Wang, Localized Topology Control for Heterogenous Wireless Ad Hoc Networks, ACM Transaction on Sensor Networks, 2006, 2(1):129-153.

[8]   D. Li, X. Jia, and H. Du, QoS Topology Control for Non-homogenous Ad Hoc Wireless Networks, EURASIP Journal on Wireless Communication and Networking, 2006, 1-10.

[9]   W. T. Chen, and N. F. Huang, The Strongly Connecting Problem on Multihop Packet Radio Networks, IEEE Transaction on Communication. 1989, 37(3):293-295.

[10]   D. Li, H. Du, and W. Chen, Power Conservation for Strongly Connected Topology Control in Wireless Sensor Networks, Proc. of the ACM FOWANC, 2008.

[11]   D. Li, H. Du, and L. Liu, Joint Toplogy Control and Power Conservation for Wireless Sensor Networks Using Transmit Power Adjustment, Proc. of the COCOON, 2008.

[12]   C. Zhu, and M. S. Corson, QoS Routing for Mobile Ad Hoc Networks, Proc. of the IEEE INFOCOM, 2002.

[13]   C.R. Lin, and J.S. Liu, QoS Routing in Ad Hoc Wireless Networks, IEEE Journal on Selected Areas in Communications, 1999, 17(8):1426-1438.

[14]   X. Jia, D. Li, and D. Du, QoS Topology Control in Ad Hoc Wireless Networks, Proc. of the IEEE INFOCOM, 2004, (2):1264–1272.

[15]   H. Liu, D. Li, and X. Jia, QoS Topology Control with Minimal Total Energy Cost in Ad Hoc Wireless Networks, Proc. of the MSN, 2006.

[16]   L. Hu, Topology Control for Multihop Packet Radio Networks, IEEE Transaction on Communications, 1993, 41(10):1474-1481.

[17]   T. Hou, and Victor O.K. Li, Transmission Range Control in Multihop Packet Radio Networks, IEEE Transaction on Communications, 1986, 34(1):38-44.

[18]   J. C. Hou, N. Li, and I. Stojmenovic, Topology Construction and Maintenance in Wireless Sensor Networks, Handbook of Theoretical and Algorithmic Aspects of Ad Hoc, Sensor, and Peer-to-Peer Networks, Auerbach Publications, 2006, 311-341.

[19]   X. Li, Y. Wang, P. Wan, and Ophir Frieder, Localize Low Weight Graph and its Applications in Wireless Ad Hoc Networks, Proc. of the IEEE INFOCOM, 2004.

[20]   N. Li, J. Hou and L. Sha, Design and Analysis of an MST-based Topology Control Algorithm, Proc. of the IEEE INFOCOM, 2003.

[21]   J. Cartigny, F. Ingelrest, D. Simplot-Ryl, and I. Stojmenovic, Localized LMST and RNG based Minimum Energy Broadcast Protocols in Ad Hoc Networks, Ad Hoc Networks, 2005, 3(1):1–16.

[22]   K. R. Gabriel and R. R. Sokal, A New Statistical Approach to Geographic Variation Analysis, Systemic Zoology, 1969, 18:259–278.

[23]   R. Banner, and A. Orda, Multi-Objective Topology Control in Wireless Networks, Proc. of the IEEE INFOCOM, 2008.

[24]   R. Wattenhofer, L. Li, P. Bahl, and Y.M. Wang, Distributed Topology Control for Power Efficient Operation in Multihop Wireless Ad Hoc Networks, Proc. of the IEEE INFOCOM, 2001, (1):1388-1397.

[25]   Z. Huang, C.C. Shen, C. Scrisathapornphat, and C. Jaikaeo, Topology Control for Ad Hoc Networks with Directional Antennas, Proc. of the IEEE ICCCN, 2002, 16-21.

[26]   M.A. Marsan, C.F. Chiasserini, A. Nucci, G.Carello, and L.D.Giovanni, Optimizing the Topology of Bluetooth Wireless Personal Area Networks, Proc. of the IEEE INFOCOM, 2002.

[27]   T. Melodia, D. Pompili, and Ian F. Akyildiz, On the Interdependence of the Distributed Topology Control and Geographical Routing in Ad Hoc and Sensor Networks, IEEE Journal on Selected Areas in Communications, 2005, 23(3):520-532.

[28]   J. Ma, M. Gao, Q. Zhang, and Lionel M. Ni, Energy-Efficient Localized Topology Control Algorithms in IEEE 802.15.4-Based Sensor Networks, IEEE Transactions on Parallel and Distributed Systems, 2007, 18(5):711-720.

[29]   X. Liu, and M. Haenggi, Toward Quasi-regular Sensor Networks: Topology Control Algorithms for Improved Energy Efficiency, IEEE Transactions on Parallel and Distributed Systems, 2006, 17(9):975-986.

[30] A.E.F. Clementi, P. Penna, and R. Silvestri, Hardness Results for the Power Range Assignment Problem in Packet Radio Networks, Proc. of the APPROX, 1999, 195-208.

[31] X. Cheng, B. Narahari, R. Simha and XY Cheng, Strong Minimum Energy Topology in Wireless Sensor Networks: NP-Completeness and Heuristic, IEEE Transactions on Mobile Computing, 2003, 2(3):248-256.

[32] N. Li, and J.C. Hou, FLSS: A Fault-Tolerant Topology Control Algorithm for Wireless Networks, Proc. of the ACM MOBICOM, 2004.

[33] M. Hajiaghayi, N. Immorlica, and V.S. Mirrokni, Power Optimization in Fault-Tolerant Topology Control Algorithms for Wireless Multi-hop Networks, Proc. of the ACM MOBICOM, 2003.

[34] M. Bahramgiri, M.T. Hajiaghayi, and V.S. Mirrokni, Fault-tolerant and 3-Dimensional Distributed Topology Control Algorithms in Wireless Multi-hop Networks, Proc. of the IEEE ICCCN, 2002.

[35] G. Calinescu, and P. Wan, Range Assignment for High Connectivity in Wireless Ad Hoc Networks, Proc. of the ADHOC-NOW, 2003.

[36] X. Jia, D. Kim, P. Wan, and C. Yi, Power Assignment for k-Connectivity in Wireless Ad Hoc Networks, Proc. of the IEEE INFOCOM, 2005.

[37] M. Cardei, S.Yang, and J. Wu, Fault-Tolerant Topology Control for Heterogeneous Wireless Sensor Networks, Proc. of the ACM MOBIHOC, 2007.

[38] A. Frank and E. Tardos, An Application of Submodular Flows, Linear Algebra and its Applications, 1989, 11(4):329-348.

[39] F. Wang, M.T. Thai, Y. Li, X. Cheng, and D.-Z. Du, Fault-Tolerant Topology Control for All-to-One and One-to-All Communication in Wireless Networks, IEEE Transaction on Mobile Computing, 2008.

[40] M. Burkhart, P.V. Rickenbach, R. Wattenhofer, and A. Zollinger, Does Topology Control Reduce Interference, Proc. of the ACM MOBIHOC, 2004.

[41] X. Li, K.M. Nejad, W. Song, and W. Wang, Low-Interference Topology Control for Wireless Sensor Networks, Proc. of the IEEE SECON, 2005.

[42] A. C.-C. Yao, On Constructing Minimum Spanning Trees in k-Dimensional Spaces and Related Problems, ACM SIAM J. Computing, 1982, 11:721-736.

[43] S. Arya, G. Das, D. Mount, J. Salowe, and M. Smid, Euclidean Spanners: Short, Thin, and Lanky, Proc. of the ACM STOC, 1995, 489–498.

[44] V. Rodoplu and T. H. Meng, Minimum Energy Mobile Wireless Networks, Proc. of the IEEE ICC, 1998.

[45] X. Li and P. Wan, Constructing Minimum Energy Mobile Wireless Networks, Proc. of the ACM MobiHoc, 2001.

[46] M. Damian and N. Javali, Distributed Construction of Bounded-Degree Low-Interference Spanners of Low Weight, Proc. of the ACM MOBIHOC, 2008.

[47] A. Muqattash and M. Krunz, CDMA-based MAC Protocol for Wireless Ad Hoc Networks, Proc. of the ACM MobiHoc, 2003, 153-164.

[48] A.E.F. Clementi, P. Penna and R. Silvestri, The power Range Assignment Problem in Packet Radio Networks in the Plane, Proc. of the 17th Annual Symposium on Theoretical Aspects of Computer Science(ATACS 2000), 651-660.

CHAPTER 2

Connected Dominating Sets

Yiwei Wu* and Yingshu Li*

Department of Computer Science, Georgia State University, {wyw,yli}@cs.gsu.edu

Abstract: Wireless sensor networks (WSNs) are now widely used in many applications. However, routing in WSNs is very challenging due to the inherent characteristics that distinguish these networks from other wireless networks. The concept of hierarchical routing is widely used to perform energy-efficient routing in WSNs. Thus, a Connected Dominating Set (CDS) has been recommended to serve as a virtual backbone for a WSN to reduce routing overhead. Fault tolerance and routing flexibility are necessary for routing since nodes in WSNs are prone to failures. Hence, it is important to maintain a certain degree of redundancy in a CDS. Therefore, the concept of k-connected m-dominating sets (kmCDS) is used to provide these redundancies. In this chapter, we present CDS based routing protocols and focus on how to construct CDS and kmCDS, including both centralized and distributed algorithms.

I. INTRODUCTION

Wireless sensor networks (WSNs), consist of small nodes with sensing, computation, and wireless communications capabilities, are now widely used in many applications, including environment and habitat monitoring, traffic control, *etc*. Although sensor networks share many common aspects with generic ad hoc networks, several important constraints in sensor networks introduce a number of research challenges [1] in designing routing protocols. Firstly, due to the relatively large number of sensor nodes, it is not possible to build a global addressing scheme for the deployment of a large number of sensor nodes as the overhead of ID maintenance is high. Thus, traditional IP-based protocols may not be applied to WSNs. Second, sensor nodes are tightly constrained in terms of energy, processing, and storage capacities. Thus, they require careful resource management. Finally, although position awareness of sensor nodes is important, it is not feasible to use Global Positioning System (GPS) hard ware for this purpose. GPS can only be used outdoors and not in the presence of any obstruction. Moreover, GPS receivers are expensive and unsuitable for the construction of small cheap sensor

nodes. Therefore, due to such differences, many new algorithms have been proposed for the routing problems in WSNs.

Almost all of the routing protocols can be classified according to the network structure as flat and hierarchical. A good survey is [1].

In flat networks, each node typically plays the same role and sensor nodes collaborate to perform the sensing task. A related set of problems known collectively as "broadcast storm" [2] should be considered in this kind of WSNs, since discovering a multi-hop route and connecting the source node to the destination from scratch usually require an expensive, global flooding of the network. Moreover, WSNs are very volatile because of nodes' mobility and unreliability. Thus, routing information gathered by a costly broadcast can quickly become out-of-date. There are some methods are proposed to deal with this flooding nature. Some terminologies such as DSR [3] and AODV [4] that are widely used in Ad-Hoc network are also used in WSNs. The on-demand nature of those reactive approaches can make them quick to detect and adapt to topology changes. However, the main disadvantageis that caching is less effective when nodes move and fail. In this situation, reactive algorithms will discover bad routes, and discovering new routes from scratch is extraordinarily costly. Other routing protocols are proposed for unicast, multicast or broadcast in WSNs, such as SPIN [5], COUGAR [6] and QoS-based [7]–[11], *etc*. However, almost all of these approaches have high protocol overhead and interference, or have high delays in propagation of data, or require synchronization among nodes, or adopt impractical topology of the network because of the flood nature, or is not suitable for sensor networks due to the limited bandwidth.

In this kind of flat routing protocol, Gossip-based [12]–[14] and probabilistic [15] protocols are considered as an efficient way of broadcasting or flooding of information in WSNs. For those gossip-based protocols, the simplicity in its probabilistic transmission behavior inspired its application towards wireless ad hoc networks. The parametric probabilistic sensor network routing scheme addresses the goal of reliability and scalability, where flooding is suppressed with a random probability similar to gossiping, but the parameter for the non-constant relaying probability is determined per packet in a distributed manner using a few readily-available topological parameters. This scheme is very simple, as it only requires the hop distance between the source and the sink and the hop distance a packet traveled. In a variety of realistic simulation scenarios [15], parametric probabilistic approach outperformed more established routing protocols, including AODV and Gossiping.

Another kind of flat routing protocol is Location-Based Routing, such as GPSR [16], GOAFR [17], *etc*, sensor nodes are addressed by means of their location. However, GPS can only be used outdoors and not in the presence of any obstruction. Moreover, GPS receivers are expensive and unsuitable for the construction of small cheap sensor nodes. Hence, there is a need to develop other means of establishing a coordinate system without relying on an existing infrastructure. Most of the proposed localization techniques depend on recursive trilat-

eration/multilateration techniques ([18], [19]), which would not provide enough accuracy in WSNs.

Hierarchical or cluster-based methods, originally proposed in wireline networks, are well-known techniques with special advantages related to scalability and efficient communication. As such, the concept of hierarchical routing is also utilized to perform energy-efficient routing in WSNs. In a hierarchical architecture, higher-energy nodes can be used to process and send the information, while low-energy nodes can be used to perform the sensing in the proximity of the target. The creation of clusters and assigning special tasks to cluster heads can greatly contribute to overall system scalability, lifetime, and energy efficiency.

II. CLUSTER-BASED ROUTING

There exist some cluster-based or hierarchical protocols such as LEACH [20], PEGASIS [21], HEED [22], *etc*. The main purpose of these protocols is to balance load on sensor nodes and increase lifetime. For example, Hybrid Energy-Efficient Distributed clustering (HEED) was proposed in [22] which introduces two variables. The first one is known as cluster radius which defines the transmission power to be used for intra-cluster broadcast. The second one is intra-cluster communication cost which is the function of cluster properties and whether or not variable power levels are permissible. The initial probability for each node to become a tentative cluster head depends on its residual energy and communication cost such as node proximity, and final heads are selected according to the intra-cluster communication cost. After the network is clustered, inter-cluster organization depends on the network application. For example, cluster heads can communicate with each other to aggregate their information via multiple hops. HEED terminates within a constant number of iterations, and achieves fairly uniform distribution of cluster heads across the network, thus prolong network lifetime by distributing energy consumption.

However, since the probability for becoming a cluster head is depend on the residual energy, this probability would become very small along with the decrease of residual energy. Thus, the number of iterations would increase significantly.

Mobility-Resistant, Efficient Clustering Approach (MRECA) is proposed in [25]. MRECA terminates without rounds of iterations as required by HEED which makes MRECA a less complex and more efficient algorithms. The MRECA is similar to HEED in that each node broadcasts its decision as the cluster head in the neighborhood based on some local information and score function. The main difference between MRECA and HEED lies in when and how the nodes make such decisions and how the score is computed. The score function in MRECA at each node is $w_1 E + w_2 C + w_3 I$, where E is the node residual energy, C is the node connectivity and I is the node ID. This score is used to compute the delay for a node to announce itself as the cluster head. MRECA also use local maintenance performed instead of re-clustering to deal with the node mobility. However, MRECA only calculate the clusters, no information is given about the inter cluster communication.

Since the cluster heads need to maintain the routing information, they bear heavy by-pass traffic especially for the cluster heads which close to the base station. In this situation, Chen *et al.* in [26] proposed an Unequal Cluster-based Routing (UCR) protocol. The main idea of UCR is that the clusters closer to the base station have smaller sizes than those farther from the base station, thus they can save more energy for the inter-cluster data forwarding. The UCR protocol consists of two parts: an energy-efficient unequal clustering algorithm (EEUC) and an inter-cluster greedy geographic and energy-aware routing protocol. In EEUC, several tentative cluster heads are randomly selected to compete for final cluster heads. Each tentative cluster head s_i has a competition range R_i which can be expressed as a linear

function of its distance to the base station and used to produce clusters of unequal sizes. The organization of intra-cluster is similar to LEACH. Since the distance of one node to another is computed based on the received beacon signal strength, this protocol is not very reliable due to the noise in the real environments.

Those clustering algorithms mentioned use the residual energy or other weight function of each node, which is the combination of many factors, in order to direct its decision about whether it will elect itself as a leader of a cluster or not. However, they ignore topological features of the sensor nodes. Other kind of hierarchical protocols are dominating set based protocols. A Connected Dominating Set (CDS) has been recommended to serve as a virtual backbone for a WSN to reduce routing overhead.

Definition 1. *For a graph $G(V, E)$, a Dominating Set S of G is defined as a subset of V such that each node in $V \setminus S$ is adjacent to at least one node in S.*

Definition 2. *A Connected Dominating Set (CDS) C of G is a dominating set of G which induces a connected subgraph of G. The nodes in a CDS are called dominators, the others are called dominatees.*

For example all black nodes in Figure 1(a) form a CDS according to the definition 2. Having such a CDS simplifies routing by restricting the main routing tasks to the dominators only. When a source node wants to deliver a packet to another destination node, it first forwards this packet to its dominator. And along this CDS, the packet will be delivered to one dominator neighbor of destination. Finally, this dominator neighbor forwards the packet to the destination node.

Fault tolerance and routing flexibility are necessary for routing since nodes in WSNs are prone to failures and nodes may have mobility and turn on and off frequently. Thus, it is important to maintain a certain degree of redundancy in a CDS. Unfortunately, a CDS

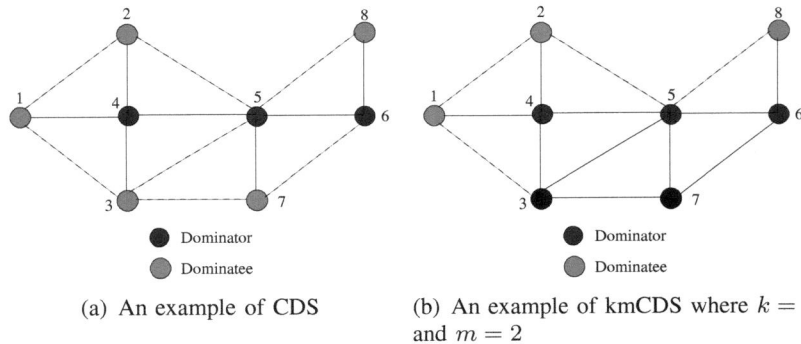

(a) An example of CDS   (b) An example of kmCDS where $k = 2$ and $m = 2$

Fig. 1.   CDS and kmCDS.

only preserves 1-connectivity and it is therefore very vulnerable. The concept of k-Connected m-Dominating Set (kmCDS) is also introduced to deal with those redundancies. We list some definitions as following.

Definition 3. *A graph G is said to be k vertex connected or k connected if for each pair of vertices there exists at least k mutually independent paths connecting them. In other words, the graph G is still connected even after the removal of any $k - 1$ vertices from G.*

Definition 4. *An m-dominating set D_m is a set $D_m \subset V$ such that every vertex in $V \setminus D_m$ is dominated by at least m vertices in D_m.*

Definition 5. *A set $C \subset V$ is a k-connected m-dominating set (kmCDS) of graph $G(V, E)$ if the induced subgraph $G'(C, E')$ is k-vertex connected and the set C is also an m-dominating set of G.*

For example, all black nodes in Fig. 1(b) form a kmCDS where $k = 2$ and $m = 2$. The requirement of k-connectivity guarantees that between any pair of dominators there exist at least k different paths. The requirement of m-domination takes care of fault tolerance and robustness for dominatees, which ensures that every dominatee has at least m adjacent dominator neighbors.

In this chapter, we focus on how to construct a CDS in WSNs, including both centralized and distributed algorithms. Theoretical analyses are also presented as well. Furthermore, some al-

gorithms for kmCDS are described in detail.

III. CONSTRUCTING CDSS

The problem of constructing a minimum CDS (MCDS) is NP-complete [27]. Some approximate algorithms (Table I) were proposed in literature to address the MCDS problem. According to the methods that all those algorithms are used, we classify them into two categories, Centralized and Distributed. Although the centralized approach can obtain a CDS with small size, it is not feasible to use in a real application since the topology of the whole network should be known in advance. Furthermore, for distributed algorithms we classify them into two subclasses, prune-based and MIS-based as [28] does. Almost all of the theoretical analyses are based on the Unit Disk Graph (UDG). The definition of UDG is given in [29] as following.

Definition 6. *A graph is a Unit Disk Graph if and only if its vertices can be put in one to one correspondence with equalized circles in a plane in such a way that two vertices are joined by an edge if and only if the corresponding circles intersection.*

Without loss of generality, the radius of each circle is assumed to be 1 in theoretical analysis. A UDG is widely used to model a homogeneous wireless network. Based on this UDG model, another important Lemma 1 is given in [29].

Lemma 1. *Let C be a circle of radio 1 and let*

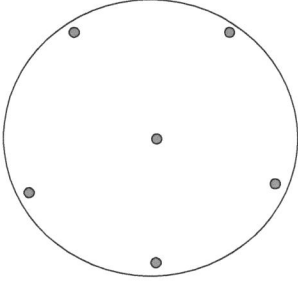

Fig. 2. A neighboring area with 5 independent nodes.

S be a set of circles of radius 1 such that every circles in S intersects C and no two circles in S intersect each other. Then, $|S| \leq 5$.

In another words, one node can only have at most five independent neighbors in a UDG graph as Figure 2 shows. This lemma is a fundamental fact when theoretical analysis is given especially for performance ratio.

Since many algorithms of construct CDS use the same strategy which needs to find a maximal independent set (MIS) first. Thus, we introduce the definition MIS here.

Definition 7. *Independent set is a set of vertices in a graph no two of which are adjacent. A maximal independent set (MIS) is an independent set that is not a subset of any other independent set.*

According to this definition, therefore an MIS is also a dominating set.

Another important definition we need to know is the performance ratio used in theoretical analysis for this kind of minimization problem. The smaller the performance ratio, the better the approximation algorithm.

Definition 8. *The performance ratio of a minimization problem is defined as $\max(\frac{A(I)}{opt(I)})$, where $A(I)$ is the solution obtained by an approximation algorithm A for any instance I and $opt(I)$ is the optimal solution.*

A. Centralized Algorithms

In this section, we survey some centralized algorithms. As we mentioned before, centralized algorithms can obtain a CDS with small size. However, it is not feasible to use in a large WSN because nodes need to know the topology of the whole network.

A heuristic Connected Domination (CDOM) algorithm is firstly introduced in [29] by Marathe *et al.*. In CDOM, a vertex v is picked arbitrarily as root. Rooted from v, a breadth-first spanning tree T is constructed. Let S_i be the nodes at level i. First, v is an MIS node and added to IS_i. Let DS_i be the nodes which can be dominated by some vertices in IS. Then in each level i, an MIS of $S_i - DS_i$ is constructed. For each node in this MIS, a connector need to added to NS_i. This procedure is executed from the lowest level to the highest level. Finally all nodes in IS and NS form a CDS. The performance ratio of CDOM is 10 based on Lemma 1.

Guha and Khuller [30] proposed two greedy heuristic algorithms. The first algorithm begins by marking all vertices white. Initially, the algorithm selects the node with the maximal number of white neighbors. The selected node is marked black and its neighbors are marked gray. The algorithm then iteratively scans the gray nodes and their white neighbors, and selects the gray node or the pair of nodes (a gray node and one of its white neighbors), whichever has the maximal number of white neighbors. The selected nodes are marked black, with their white neighbors marked gray. All the black nodes form a connected dominating set. The performance ratio of this algorithm is $2(1 + H(\Delta))$.

The second algorithm also begins by coloring all nodes white. A piece is defined to be either a connected black component, or a white node. The algorithm contains two phases. The first phase iteratively selects a node that causes the maximum reduction of the number of pieces. In other words, the greedy choice for each step in the first phase is the node that can decrease the maximum number of pieces. Once a node is selected, it is marked black and its white neighbors are marked gray. The first phase terminates when no white node left.

The second phase constructs a Steiner Tree that connects all the black nodes by coloring chains of two gray nodes black. The size of the resulting CDS formed by all black nodes is at most $ln\Delta + 3$. The distributed implementations of both algorithms were provided by Das *et al.* in [31]–[33].

Ruan *et al.* [34] proposed a one-step greedy approximation algorithm with performance ratio at most $3 + ln(\Delta)$. Let C be the set containing all black nodes. Given a connected graph $G(V, E)$, define $p(C)$ be the number of connected black components in the subgraph induced by $C \subset V$. Let $D(C)$ be the set of all edges incident to vertices in C. Define $q(C)$ be the number of connected components in the subgraph $G(V, D(C))$. Then the potential function is defined to be $f(C) = p(C) + q(C)$. Initially $f(C) = |V|$ since $C = \phi$ The first step chooses a node x with maximum degree. Every other step selects a node x such that $f(C) - f(C \cup \{x\})$ is maximized. Color node x black and color all its white neighbors gray. The algorithm ends when $f(C) = 2$, where C is the resultant CDS.

Both Min *et al.* [35] and Li *et al.* [36] use a Steiner tree with minimum number of Steiner nodes (ST-MSN) to connect a maximal independent set. These algorithms contain two phases. The first phase constructs an MIS. In the second phase, a node's color is changed from grey to black (or blue) if there exists a grey node adjacent to at least two black components (or black-blue components). The performance ratio are 6.8 and 5.8 respectively.

B. Distributed Algorithms

Distributed algorithms are preferred in WSNs since a large number of sensor nodes are randomly deployed in the monitored area and global information is not available for any single node even the base station. For those distributed algorithms we can classify them into two subclasses, Prune-based and MIS-based. In prune-based algorithms, all nodes are CDS nodes first, and then one node becomes dominatee according to some rules. The idea behind MIS-based algorithms is that find a maximal independent set (MIS) first, then find connectors to form a CDS. For MIS-based algorithms, we also divided them into two subgroups, Single Initiator and Multiple Initiators, as [28] does.

1) Prune-based Algorithms: The first prune-based algorithm was proposed by Wu *et al.* in [38], [39]. In this distributed marking process, firstly, every node v is assigned a marker F. Then a node assigns its marker to T if there exist two unconnected neighbors after it exchanges its open neighbors set with all its neighbors. Therefore, all nodes with marker T form a CDS. This method then prune certain redundant nodes from the CDS according two rules, Rule 1 and Rule 2, which are that a node u is redundant if it has either a CDS neighbor with larger ID which dominates all neighbors of u, or two adjacent CDS neighbors with larger IDs that together dominates all neighbors of u. The performance ratio is given by Wan *et al.* in [40] which is exactly $\frac{n}{2}$. That means this algorithm does perform extremely poorly over certain instances. After that, those two rules are extended to a generalized pruning rule in [41] named Rule k.

Definition 9. *Rule k: Assume that $V_k^{'} = \{v_1, v_2, \cdots, v_k\}$ is the vertex set of a strongly connected subgraph in G'. If $N_d(u) - V_k^{'} \subseteq N_d(V_k^{'})$ and $N_a(u) - V_k^{'} \subseteq N_a(V_k^{'})$ in G and $id(u) < \min\{id(v_1), id(v_2), \cdots, id(v_k)\}$, then change the marker of u to F.*

Probabilistic analysis is presented in [42], which shows that if $k > 3$ and $\ell_n \leq \sqrt{\frac{n}{10 \log n}}$, then expected size of the minimum CDS is $\Theta(\ell_n^2)$, where ℓ_n is the length of the square in which n nodes are randomly deployed.

Chen *et al* [43] proposed a distributed algorithm Span to find a MCDS. Span is a randomized algorithm where nodes make local decisions on whether to sleep, or to join a forwarding backbone as coordinators. Each node bases its decision on an estimate of how many of its neighbors will benefit from it being awake, and the amount of energy available to it. Span has two procedures, coordinator announcement and coordinator withdrawal. In the coordinator announcement, a non-coordinator node periodically determines if it should become a coordinator or not based on the coordinator eligibility rule which is a non-coordinator node should become a coordinator if it discovers that two of its neighbors cannot reach each other either directly or via one or two coordinators. Span resolves contention which occurs when multiple nodes discover the lack of a coordinator at the same time by delaying coordinator announcements with a randomized backoff delay. In the second procedure, each coordinator periodically checks if it should withdraw as a coordinator. If every pair of its neighbors can reach each other either directly or via one or two other coordinators, a node should withdraw and become a non-coordinator. Because of difficulty of finding two unconnected neighbors, the size of coordinator would become very large as the simulation shows.

2) MIS-based Algorithms: Recall that an MIS is also a dominating set. Since all dominators in a dominating set are disconnected with each other, we need to find some nodes, called connectors, to connect all dominators. Therefore, the basic idea of these kinds of MIS-based algorithms is that an MIS is first constructed. After that, all connectors are found. From here, we know that there are at least two phases to find CDS. However, some distributed algorithms merge those two phases together in which a connector is chosen whenever a dominator node is disconnected with others. Moreover, we also divide MIS-based algorithms into two groups, Single Initiator and Multiple Initiators. For the single initiator algorithms, a unique initiator is elected and becomes a CDS node firstly. Then CDS nodes are picked up according to their position in this tree. Actually, in this kind of algorithms, a tree is built implicitly or explicitly. In multiple initiators algorithms, many nodes claim themselves are

CDS nodes simultaneously at the first time based on their local information. Since a tree is need to maintain in the constructing procedure, some people argue that those single initiator algorithms are not total localized algorithms and also have high message complexities comparing with multiple initiator ones. However, from both theoretical analysis and simulation results, the size of CDS obtained by single initiator algorithms are smaller than ones obtained from multiple initiators algorithms in general.

a) Single Initiator Algorithms: There exist some Single Initiator algorithms such as [40], [44]–[49], *etc.* Although there are so many this kinds of Single Initiator algorithms, the basic idea behind them is almost the same. The main difference among all those kinds of algorithms is when and how to pick up MIS nodes and connectors.

Das *et al.* [31]–[33] proposed two single initiator algorithms that are distributed implementations of Algorithm I and II in [30]. Algorithm I first finds a small dominating set S by adding nodes to S in each rounds. The number of unmarked neighbors of a node u is its effective degree $\delta^*(u)$. Node u is added to S if u has the highest effective degree among its two hop neighbors. In the second phase, a rooted minimum spanning tree (MST) T is constructed which travels all the dominators in S, and all internal nodes in T form a CDS. Algorithm II dispenses with the MST used in the second phase of Algorithm I. Instead, algorithm II grows one fragment into a CDS. Let an extension to the fragment be either a one or two edge path consisting of one node in the fragment and one or two nodes not in the fragment. The effective combined degree of an extension is the number of unmarked nodes adjacent to the non-fragment nodes in the extension. Therefore, the best extension is the extension that has the highest combined effective degree. Algorithm 2 consists of rounds of adding the best extension to the current fragment.

Wan *et al.* [40], [44] proposed a Single

Initiator algorithm. They first choose a root by using distributed leader-election algorithm and build a spanning tree. The rank of each node is determined by a weight function which is the ordered pair (level, ID). After that, the root moves on the construction of the MIS by a color-marking process. All nodes are initially marked with white. The root first marks itself black and broadcasts a BLACK message. Upon receiving a BLACK message, a white node marks itself gray and broadcasts a GRAY message. If a white node receives all GRAY messages from its lower rank neighbors, it marks itself black and broadcasts a BLACK message. When a leaf node is marked with either gray or black, it transmits a MARK-COMPLETE message to its parent. When one node receives all MARK-COMPLETE messages from its children with high rank, it transmits a MARK-COMPLETE message to its parent. The second phase constructs a tree spanning all the MIS nodes, referred to as dominating tree. In this phase, the root first transfers it role to a gray neighbor which has the largest number of black neighbors. From this new root, a dominating tree is constructed. A gray node marks itself black when it can connect a black node to the dominating tree. All nodes in this dominating tree form a CDS.

The first algorithm Cheng et al. proposed in [46] is also a Single Initiator algorithm. This algorithm grows a spanning tree distributedly from the leader, with all non-leaf nodes form a CDS. Firstly, the leader colors itself black and broadcasts a dominator message. Upon receiving a dominator message, a white or yellow node colors itself gray and broadcasts a dominatee message, specifying itself as a dominatee. When a white node receives a dominatee message, it colors itself yellow. The yellow node whose id is the minimum among all of its one-hop yellow neighbors becomes a connector, colors itself black and broadcasts a dominator message.

A 2-phase distributed algorithm was proposed in [45] by Cardei et al.. This algorithm

improvements over the algorithms [40], [44] is that the root does not need to wait for the arrival of the COMPLETE messages from the furthest nodes. The leader colors itself black and broadcasts a message DOMINATOR. Each White node receiving a DOMINATOR message the first time colors itself gray and broadcasts a message DOMINATEE. A white host receiving at least one DOMINATEE message becomes active. An active white nodes with highest (d^*, id) among all of its active white neighbors will color itself black and broadcast a message DOMINATOR, where d^*, denoted as effective degree, is the total number of white neighbors. Each gray node broadcasts a message NUMOFBLACKNEIGHBORS whenever it detects that none of its neighbors is white. The root initiates the connecting phase right after it receives NUMOFBLACKNEIGHBORSs from all of its neighbors. The black nodes generated in the first phase are connected through a Steiner tree. The main idea is to pick those gray nodes which can connect to many black neighbors as connectors. This process begins from the leader to the furthest node of the leader. The time complexity and message complexity are $O(n)$ and $O(n\Delta)$ respectively.

Kim et al. in [50] proposed a CDS algorithm which is called Timer-based Energy aware Connected Dominating Set protocols. This algorithm has two phases. In the first phase an initiator is elected based on order pair (Energy, Degree) or (Degree, Energy). In the second phase, the CDS is constructed rooted from the initiator. In this phase, each node has a timer (DSTimer) whose time is determined by a function of uncovered neighbors and energy level. The initiator first broadcasts its status, and all the neighbors start DSTimers. When the DSTimer of one node expires, this node become a dominator node and also broadcasts its status. At the same time, one dominatee node becomes a dominator whenever it finds there exist at least two unconnected dominator neighbors.

Zeng et al. [47] also proposed a two phase

algorithm. In the first phase, the initiator colors itself black and broadcasts a BLACK message. A white neighbor that receives the BLACK message becomes grey and broadcasts a GREY message. Upon receiving a GREY message, a white node broadcasts an INQUIRY message toward its neighbors to inquire their stats and weights. If this white node has the highest weight among all neighbors based on the replies of INQUIRY, it becomes black and also broadcasts a BLACK message. In the second phase, a dominating tree is used to form a CDS. However, the different between [47] with [40] is that a localized approximation of minimum spanning tree is used. They take a greedy approximation algorithm that every MIS node selects the non-MIS node with the highest weight which are equivalent to 2-hop to interconnect two or more MIS nodes, as a connector.

Funke *et al.* [48] proposed their distributed Single Initiator algorithm. This algorithm also considers the message interference as well. They use the D2-coloring algorithm [51] to find the time slot for each node. The execution of this algorithm is divided into rounds. Each round consists of three phases. Initially, a leader is chosen by using a leader election algorithm and marks itself red. All other nodes are colored white. In each round red node u with minimum ID among its red neighbors joins a set I by sending APPLY-MSG. Then u marks itself black and broadcasts a CONFIRM-MSG(black) message. After that the colors of the relevant nodes are update accordingly. For example, all nodes that are the neighbors of nodes in I mark themselves blue. Therefore, whenever a red node joins I, its blue parent marks itself grey as a connector and joins I as well. Finally, all black nodes and grey nodes form a CDS.

Theoretical analysis of Single Initiator algorithms is very straightforward except [31]–[33]. Since each MIS node only need one connector, therefore, if the size of MIS M is bounded, the size of CDS $|C|$ is bounded by $|C| \leq 2|M|$ as

well. Since the performance of such algorithms highly depends on the relationship between the size of M and the size of opt in a UDG graph where opt is the optimal solution for a given graph, we briefly introduce some results here. The first one shows the relationship between $|M|$ and $|opt|$ is [29], in which $|M| \leq 5|opt|$ based on the fact that each node of CDS cannot dominate more than five independent nodes because no more than five independent nodes can lie in a unit disk area as Figure 2 shows. Later Wan *et al.* [40] shows that $|M| \leq 4|opt| + 1$. They claim that U_v lie in a sector of at most $240°$ within the coverage range of vertex v given two adjacent nodes v and u in a CDS. Thus, there exists at most 4 independent nodes can lie in this area as Figure 3(a) shows. [52] improves this result and shows $|M| \leq 3.8|opt| + 1.2$ based on the observation (Figure 3(b)) which is the neighboring area around two adjacent nodes in CDS cannot have more than 8 independent nodes. [48] shows that $|M| \leq 3.453|opt| + 8.291$ based on the fact that any placement of unit disk necessarily "wastes" some area besides the area π covered by the unit disk (Figure 3(c)). That is basically each placed unit disk "uses" up an area of at least $2\sqrt{3}$ (and not only π) with the only exception being disks near the boundary. Furthermore, [53] improve the result of [40] based on the fact that for all nodes in a CDS with $|U_i| = |U_j| = 4$ there exists a node CDS node k with $|U_k| < 3$ between i and j (Figure 3(d)). Thus, they decrease the previous ratio of 3.453 to 3.0, and also prove that this bound is tight and cannot be improved. Therefore, if we use α to represent the relationship between $|M|$ and $|opt|$, the performance ratio of the size obtained from Single Initiator algorithms can be shown as 2α.

b) Multiple Initiators Algorithms: Since a tree is build explicitly or implicitly in Single Initiator algorithms, some people argue that this kind of Single Initiator algorithms are not "totally localized". Therefore, they proposed some Multiple Initiators algorithms such as

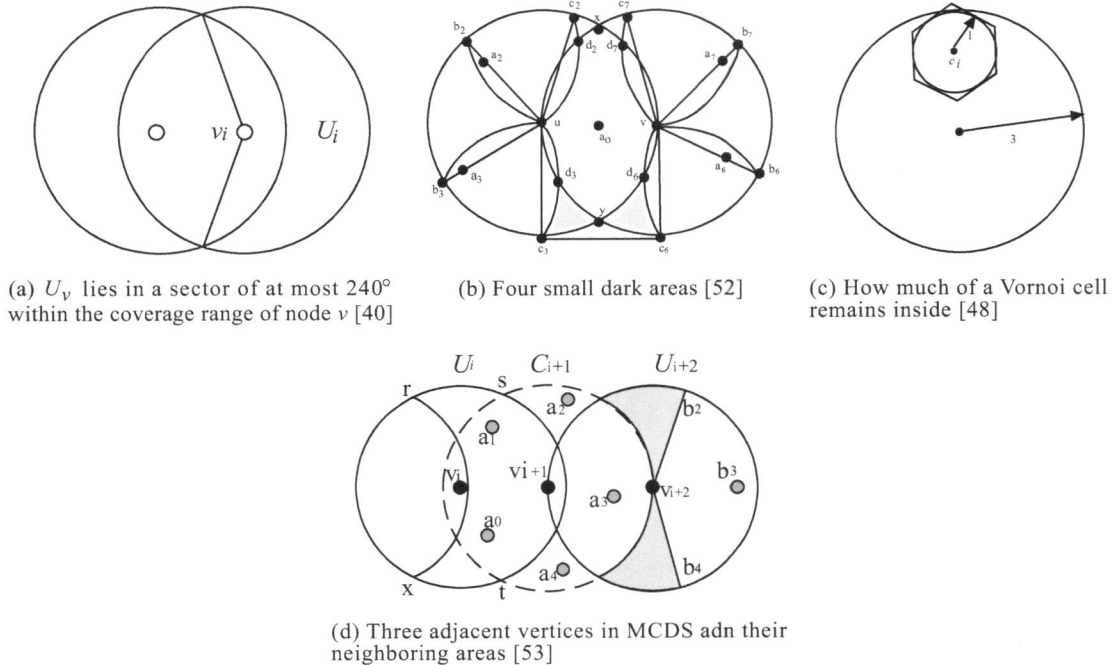

(a) U_v lies in a sector of at most 240° within the coverage range of node v [40]

(b) Four small dark areas [52]

(c) How much of a Vornoi cell remains inside [48]

(d) Three adjacent vertices in MCDS adn their neighboring areas [53]

Fig. 3. Some results of relation between the size of an MIS $|M|$ and the size of any optimal solution $|opt|$ for a given graph.

[46], [51], [55], [56] *etc*. The advantage of Multiple Initiators approach is that it is very simple. However, it need 3-hop neighbor information which significantly hurts the "totally localized" reputation.

Alzoubi *et al.* presented a distributed algorithm to construct a MCDS for UDG with a performance ratio 192, and linear time and linear message complexity in [55]. This algorithm also has two phases. Firstly, each node is in candidate status. In the first phase, all nodes (initiators) that have highest ID among their neighbors become dominators and broadcast DOMINATOR messages. Note that there exists at least one initiator at the very beginning. Upon receiving at least one DOMINATEE message, a candidate node with highest ID among all of its candidate neighbors becomes dominator and broadcasts a DOMINATOR message. In the second phase, each dominator in the MIS find a path to its three-hop dominators that have larger ID than its own ID and marks all intermediate nodes as connectors. Although

this algorithm does not need a construction of spanning tree, two-hop and three-hop neighbor information are need to find those connectors which makes it not fully localized as claimed.

Parthasarathy *et al.* proposed two distributed algorithms in [51]. The first one has three stages. The first stage involves D2-coloring the the nodes using a list of c colors. After that, all nodes in the network have a valid D2-coloring. An MIS is constructed in the second stage in which all nodes belonging to color i attempt to join the MIS during slot i. In the third stage, all MIS nodes exchange its information to all 3-hop neighbors by using PHASE-1 and PHASE-2 messages. Therefore, each MIS nodes can find the connectors to connect every other MIS node in its D3-neighborhood by using PHASE-4 and PHASE-5 messages. The main idea of the second algorithm is the same as the first one. However, the first one use D2-coloring to reduce the collision.

Li *et al.* in [56] proposed a one phase distributed algorithm, r-CDS, with constant performance ratio 172. The main idea is the same as [55]. The difference is the way to choose the MIS. In r-CDS, a novel variable r is introduced which is the number of 2-hop-away neighbors - the number of 1-hop-away neighbors. The node with highest (r, deg, ID) among its neighbors is claimed as MIS node and broadcasts a BLACK message. Upon receiving a BLACK message from its neighbors v, a white node u marks itself grey and broadcasts a GREY message. Upon receiving a GREY or BLACK message, a white node decrements its effective degree by 1. If a grey node finds that there exist two unconnected black nodes in its 2-hop neighbors, it marks itself as a connector. Although theoretical analysis about why r should be used is given, the simulation results show that r-CDS can obtain smaller CDS than others.

The second algorithm proposed in [46] by Cheng *et al.* is a distributed Multiple Initiators algorithm as [55] and [56]. In this algorithm, the node with smallest ID becomes an MIS node which is marked red. Then a node becomes black when it cannot be dominated by any red node. Therefore, all red and black nodes form an MIS. After exchanging at most two hops neighbor information, the connectors also are specified. They use different colors for different kinds of connectors. For example, blue color is used to specify a connector which has at least two MIS neighbors. Yellow color is used to specify a connector to connect two MIS nodes that are separated by 3 hops.

Theoretical analysis of Multiple Initiators algorithms are based on the Lemma list following.

Lemma 2. *Any subset of nodes in an MIS are separated by at most three hops away from its complement.*

Since the connectors are introduced at most 2 for each pair of MIS nodes, the performance ratio depends on how many independent nodes can have in a node's 3-hop neighbors in a UDG as Figure 4 shows. Therefore, if we use I to represent all the connectors, then

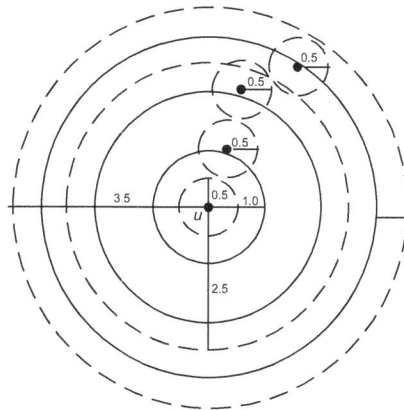

Fig. 4. The disks of radius 0.5 centered at the nodes in S that are within three hops away from u all lie within the annulus centered at u of radii 0.5 and 2.5 and are disjoint [55].

$|C| \leq |M| + |I|$. We also use β to represent the number of independent nodes one can have in it's 3-hop neighbors in a UDG. [55] shows that $\beta \leq 47$. [56] points out that $\beta \leq 42$. Furthermore, according to the Lemma 2, for each pair of independent nodes that are separated at most three hops, only two connectors are introduced. Therefore, according to those facts and the assumption that each pair of MIS nodes in a node's 3-hop neighbors can only has a unique path, then $|C| \leq |M| + 2\beta\frac{|M|}{2}$. From here, one can easy get performance ratio for this kind of Multiple Initiators algorithms by using the relationship between the $|M|$ and $|opt|$ as we mentioned before. The theoretical analysis in [46] is slightly different as the above analysis. They improve the performance ratio by considering two cases. One is two MIS nodes are separated exact 2 hops in which only one connector is required. The other is two MIS nodes are separated exact 3 hops. Thus, they slightly improve the performance ratio to 147.

IV. EXTENSION

In this section, we present other varieties of standard CDSs, include different network models and k-hop dominating sets or connected k-hop dominating sets.

TABLE I
COMPARISON OF THE PRESENTED CDS ALGORITHMS

Algorithms	Type	Time Complexity	Message Complexity	Performance ratio
[29]	Centralized	-	-	10
[30] (1)	Centralized	-	-	$2(1 + H(\Delta))$
[30] (2)	Centralized	-	-	$ln\Delta + 3$
[34]	Centralized	-	-	$3 + ln(\Delta)$
[35]	Centralized	-	-	6.8
[36]	Centralized	-	-	5.8
[49] (1)	Centralized	-	-	10.395
[49] (2)	Centralized	-	-	6.91
[38], [39]	Prune-based	$O(\Delta^3)$	$\Theta(n)$	$\frac{n}{2}$
[43]	Prune-based	-	-	-
[31]–[33]	Single Initiator	$O(n^2)$	$O(n^2)$	$3H(\Delta)$
[40], [44]	Single Initiator	$O(n)$	$O(nlogn)$	8
[45]	Single Initiator	$O(n)$	$O(n\Delta)$	8
[46] (1)	Single Initiator	$O(n)$	$O(nlogn)$	8
[50]	Single Initiator	-	-	-
[47]	Single Initiator	$O(n)$	$O(n)$	7.6
[48]	Single Initiator	$O(n)$	$O(n^2)$	6.91
[49] (3)	Single Initiator	$O(n^{1.6})$	$O(n^{1.6})$	6.91
[55]	Multiple Initiators	$O(n)$	$O(n)$	192
[51] (1)	Multiple Initiators	$O(\Delta log^2 n)$	$O(nlog^2 n)$	-
[51] (2)	Multiple Initiators	$O(log^2 n)$	$O(nlogn)$	-
[56]	Multiple Initiators	$O(\Delta)$	$O(n\Delta^2)$	172
[46] (2)	Multiple Initiators	$O(n)$	$O(n)$	147

A. Relaxing Network Model

In order to show the performance ratio for the proposed algorithms, a UDG is used to model the whole network. Actually, leaving the theoretical analysis, the network model can be relaxed to a general graph. All the algorithms mentioned above include centralized and distributed can still be used to generate a correct CDS. However, some works proposed their algorithms based on different network models.

Thai *et al.* [57] proposed two algorithms to construct CDS in a network which is modeled as a Disk Graphs with Bidirectional Links (DGB). In this kind of network, each node may have different transmission range and there is an edge between two nodes if and only if they can communication with each other. Therefore, this DGB is an undirected graph. The algorithms themselves are very similar with [35], [36]. The main contribution is that they find the relationship between MIS and optimal solution in a DGB graph.

Yang *et al.* [58] extends the network model from UDG to a directed graph. The CDS in this directed graph is called Directed Connected Dominating Set (DCDS). In this kind of network each node uses a directional antenna to communicate with each other. A DCDS is a subset of nodes and their selected sectors such that each node in the DCDS can reach any nodes in the original network through forwarding along the selected sectors. In addition, each node that is not in the backbone can select a sector to reach a DCDS neighbor. Two coverage conditions, Node and Edge, are used to determine the priority in Rule k [41] to generate a DCDS.

B. Connected k-hop Dominating Sets

Since CDS algorithms only work well in a dense network, some work tries to use connected k-hop dominating sets to obtain a small size of those kinds of dominators in general networks.

Definition 10. *A k-hop dominating set for a*

graph $G(V, E)$ *is a subset* $D \subseteq V$ *with the property that for every* v *in* $V \setminus D$ *there is some* $u \in D$ *at distance at most* k *hops from* v. *A Connected* k-*hop dominating set has an additional requirement that is the subgraph induced by* D *should be connected.*

Before we introduce the algorithms for connected k-hop dominating sets, we first present some algorithms [59]–[63] for constructing k-hop dominating sets. Since it is easy for one to construct the k-hop dominating set for a given graph because connectivity is not required, we will not talk about so many details here. The basic idea behind all these k-hop dominating sets algorithms especially for distributed ones is that one node claims itself as a cluster head and all its neighbors in its k hops join in this cluster. Different strategies use different priorities, such as ID, Degree, energy or a mix of those parameters to decide which one should become cluster head. For example, in [61], Amis *et al.* proposed a heuristic method to construct a k-hop dominating set. Each node maintains a variable WINNER used to determine the cluster head. Their heuristic has four logical stages. The first stage has k rounds of FloodMax in which each node locally broadcasts it WINNER value to all of its 1-hop neighbors. Therefore, at the end of first stage the surviving node IDs are the elected cluster heads in the network. Since FloodMax may result in an unbalanced loading for the cluster heads, k rounds of FloodMin are required in the second stage to allow the relatively smaller cluster heads the opportunity to regain nodes within their k-neighborhood. Finally, in the third and forth stages the gateway nodes begin a converagecast message to link all nodes of the cluster to the cluster head and link the cluster head to other clusters.

There exist some algorithms for constructing connected k-hop dominating sets such as [64]–[66]. Voung *et al.* [67] show that the problem of finding a minimum k-hop connected dominating set is NP-complete.

[64] proposed a distributed algorithm for connected k-hop dominating sets. Actually, this algorithm use the same idea as the Multiple Initiators CDS algorithms which also finds the dominator and then each dominator finds the connectors to connect other cluster heads in its $2k + 1$ hops. The difference is that $2k + 1$ hop neighbor information should be exchanged instead of just 3 in CDS. In order to find the connectors with minimum size, they use local minimum spanning tree algorithm (LMST) [68] for connecting adjacent cluster heads. However, this is not feasible for a large k or in a dense network, since for each node $2k + 1$ hop neighbor information are needed.

Yang *et al.* [66] proposed a prune-based algorithm to construct a connected k-hop dominating set. They first identify a sufficient condition that guarantees the connectivity of the virtual backbone. In this condition, each node x maintains a number denoted by $x.num$ which ranges from 0 to ∞. With the help of this condition, they propose a distributed algorithm to construct connected k-hop dominating sets. In this algorithm Rule k [41] is also used to prune some nodes. Whenever one node is pruned, the num is also updated according to some rules pre-defined and then make sure that the value of num of dominator is ∞. Then according to the sufficient condition, this algorithm can obtain a correct connected k-hop dominating set. This distributed algorithm is very efficient to construct and maintain connected k-hip dominating set in mobile network since the condition can be verified in a distributed manner by the node only having the link information of its neighbors.

C. Miscellany

Almost all of above algorithms try to minimize the size of CDSs. However, in many applications, it is desirable to construct a CDS with small cost. Different nodes may have different costs for serving as a coordinator due to some inherent characteristic such as power capacities, information loads to be processed, *etc*. Therefore, Wang *et al.* [69] try to construct a CDS with minimum cost. In their method an MIS is constructed first by using node weight as a selection criterion. Then for each node node v in MIS, find a set of nodes $GRDY_v$ with a total cost smaller than v to replace v if possible by running local greedy set cover method. After that, each node in MIS forms a VirtG which includes all 3-hops neighbors as the same procedure to find the connectors in the multiple initiators algorithms. After that, they transfer the weight in each node to the weight for each edge, and use LMST to find all connectors. They prove that the total cost of the constructed backbone is within a small constant factor of the optimum for homogeneous networks when either the nodes' cost are smooth or the network maximum node degree is bounded.

Other works address the problem of constructing CDS with several quality factors, such as diameter, risk factor and interference. Diameter is an important metric to evaluate the quality of CDS. According the routing scheme of using CDSs, the total energy consumption increases when a data packet is delivered through a longer path. Therefore, it is obvious that routing in a backbone with a larger diameter consumes more energy than in one with a smaller diameter. [70] first proposed a centralized algorithm RD-CDS to generate a quality CDS. The algorithm starts from a selected node as the root and use the procedure mimicking the breadth first search (BFS). All nodes at hop distance $i + 1$ are processed only after all nodes at hop distance i have been completed. Each nodes at level $i + 1$ computes the yield the one with maximum yield is picked as CDS node. However, no theoretical analysis is given for their algorithm.

Three algorithms in [49], [71] are proposed to construct a CDS with a bounded diameter. The first two, CDS-BD-C1 and CDS-BD-C2, are centralized algorithms. All of these two start BFS first and find an MIS for each level in the BFS tree as [29] does. After that, find connector to connect each node in MIS to its three or two hops dominator parent. Theoretical analysis shows that the diameter of CDS obtained from CDS-BD-C1 can be bounded by 3, and the diameter of CDS obtained from CDS-BD-C2 can be bounded by 4. The third one is a distributed algorithm CDS-BD-D. Although the basic idea is the same as other Single Initiator algorithm, the constructions of MIS nodes and connectors are merged in one phase. The root first builds a BFS tree. After that, the root marks itself black and broadcasts a BLACK message. After receiving either BLACK or WHITE messages from all parents, a node u who has the highest $W(N, ID)$ among its sibling nodes marks itself white if it receives at least one BLACK message from its parents or siblings. Otherwise, it sends a CONNECT message to its parent who has the highest $W(N, ID)$. Both of the parent node and u mark themselves black and broadcast BLACK messages. After all nodes decide their colors, all black nodes form a CDS. The diameter of CDS obtained from CDS-BD-D also can be bounded by 4.

V. CONSTRUCTING KMCDSS

Fault tolerance and routing flexibility are necessary for routing since nodes in WSNs are prone to failures and nodes may have mobility and turn on and off frequently. Moveover, nodes in the CDS consume more energy to handle various bypass traffics than dominatee nodes. Thus, it is important to maintain a certain degree of redundancy in a CDS. Unfortunately, a CDS only preserves 1-connectivity and it is therefore very vulnerable. In this section, we describe how to construct a k-Connected m-Dominating Set (kmCDS). The requirement of k-connectivity guarantees that between any pair of dominators there exist at least k different paths. The requirement of m-domination takes care of fault tolerance and robustness for dominatees, which ensures that every dominatee has at least m adjacent dominator neighbors.

Although CDS construction has been investigated extensively, not too much research for kmCDS construction has been conducted in the literature. There exist several algorithms, such as [72]–[77], including centralized and distributed ones to construct a kmCDS. Some of them only consider some special cases where $k = 1, 2$ or $k \leq m$, or are not easy to implement, or have high message complexity.

A. Centralized Algorithms

In [73], the 64-approximation centralized algorithm Connecting Dominating Set Augmentation (CDSA) to construct a 2-connected virtual backbone was proposed. This algorithm has three steps. In the first step a CDS C is constructed. In the second step all the blocks are computed. In the third step the shortest path is calculated and also should satisfy two requirements: 1) the path can connect a leaf block in C to other portion of C, 2) the path does not contain any nodes in C except the two endpoints. And then add all intermediate nodes in this path to C. Repeat step 2 and 3 till all the backbone nodes being in the same block. The authors also claim that at most 8 interconnecting nodes are necessary to connect a leaf block to other blocks at each augmenting step and all those intermediate nodes are neighbors to one cut vertex as Fig. 5(a) shows. Therefore, $|C_{21}| \leq 8(|C_{11}| - 1)$. By using a single initiator CDS algorithm in the step 1, they give the performance ratio 64. However, this work is also only for the case where $k = 2$ and $m = 1$.

Before we introduce some algorithms to construct a kmCDS for general k and m, we first introduce the basic idea of how to construct a 1mCDS in which $k = 1$. Almost all of the kmCDS algorithms construct 1mCDS first. In those kind of 1mCDS algorithms, a CDS C is build, and then sequentially choose an MIS of $G \backslash C$ $m - 1$ times and add all nodes in the MIS to C. The correctness of this algorithm is obvious since each dominatee can be dominated by one dominator in an MIS, and there

are totally m MISs. The performance ratio of this strategy depends on which algorithm is chosen to construct the CDS and the MIS. One important lemma about the relationship between a minimum m-dominating set with an MIS proved in [74] is list following.

Lemma 3. Let $G = (V, E)$ be a UDG and m a constant such that $\delta_G \geq m - 1$, where δ_G is the minimum degree of G. Let D_m^* be a minimum m-dominating set of G and M an MIS of G. Then $|M| \leq \max\{\frac{5}{m}, 1\}|D_m^*|$.

In [75], a centralized algorithm was proposed which is the extension of CDSA for general k and m. The main difference is that in this approach k-blocks are founded first rather than blocks in each iteration. First, a 1mCDS C_{1m} is built. Then C_{1m} is augmented to become a kmCDS sequentially. As Figure 5(b) shows in each augment step k', all k' connected block are computed. If there is more than one k'-block in C, find the shortest path in the original graph that satisfies the two requirements as CDSA does: (1) the path can connect a k'-leaf block in C to other portion of C. (2) the path does not contain any nodes in C except the two end points. Then add all intermediate nodes in this path to C. Although this algorithms construct kmCDS for general k and m, however, it is not easy to implement due to the difficulty in finding all the k-blocks or k-leaves from a given graph.

In [74], three centralized algorithms were proposed. One is for constructing a 1mCDS which use the same strategy as we mentioned before. Another one is for constructing a 2mCDS whose basic idea is that a 1mCDS C_{1m} is constructed firstly. Then use the same augment in [73] to achieve 2mCDS. The last one is for $3 \leq k \leq m$ which first constructs a kkCDS and then sequentially add an MIS $m - k$ times. Therefore, all of those proposed algorithms are special cases of general k and m.

Wu *et al.* [76] proposed a centralized greedy algorithm (CGA) to construct kmCDS for gen-

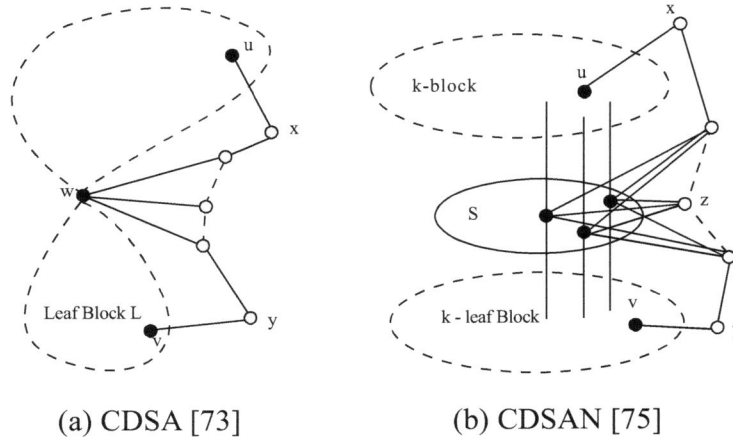

(a) CDSA [73]　　　　(b) CDSAN [75]

Fig. 5.　Augment steps in CDSA and CDSAN.

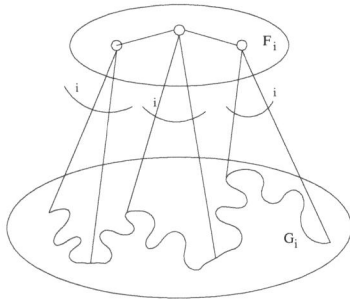

Fig. 6.　If G_i is i vertex-connected and F_i is a $(i+1)$-cover of G_i, then $G_{i+1} = \langle G_i \cup F_i \rangle$ is $(i+1)$ vertex-connected [77].

eral k and m. The main idea of CGA is to construct a m-dominating set first and then augment this set to be k-connected by adding enough number of connectors. In the augment step the nodes with maximum degree would be added first to make the result set k-connected. Since there is no matroid associated with this result set, CGA cannot always guarantee obtaining a solution unless the input graph is at least k-connected. Another centralized algorithm ICGA for general k and m proposed in [77] to improve CGA. The advantage of ICGA is that it can be easily implemented. The main idea of ICGA is based on two Lemmas.

Lemma 4. *If G is a k-connected graph, and G' is obtained from G by adding a new node x with at least k neighbors in G, then G' is also a k-connected graph.*

Therefore, from this lemma, they proposed another important Lemma list following.

Lemma 5. *Given a k vertex-connected graph G and a connected set F in which each node dominates at least k neighbors in G and all nodes in G can be dominated by at least one neighbor in F, the graph G' composed by $G \cup F$ is $k+1$ vertex-connected. F is said as $(k+1)$-cover of G.*

As Figure 6 shows, if G_i is i vertex-connected and F_i is a $(i+1)$-cover of G_i, then $G_{i+1} = \langle G_i \cup F_i \rangle$ is $(i+1)$ vertex-connected. Based on these two lemmas, ICGA includes two phases. In phase one a 1-connected m-dominating set C_{1m} is constructed. In phase two the set C_{1m} is augmented for k-connectivity sequentially according to Lemma 5 by adding F_i in each iteration i. Moreover, the performance ratio for ICGA is $5 + \frac{5}{m} + 7.6(k-1)$ when $m \leq 5$, and $7 + 7.6(k-1)$ when $m \geq 6$.

B. Distributed Algorithms

In wireless networks, especially for WSNs with a large number of nodes or a dense wireless network, it is more practical to employ distributed algorithms. By simultaneously executing a distributed algorithm at all the nodes, energy can be substantially conserved and a kmCDS can be formed faster compared with employing a centralized algorithm. This motivates us to design the distributed deterministic algorithm DDA for constructing a kmCDS.

In [72], three localized K-CDS construction protocols were proposed. This K-CDS is a

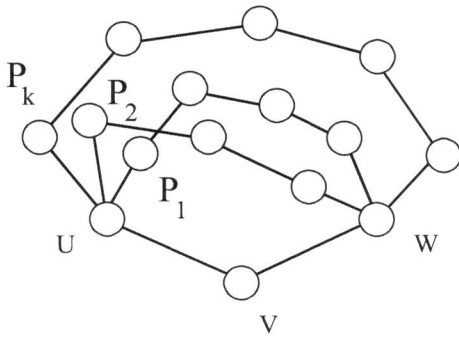

Fig. 7.   k-coverage condition [72].

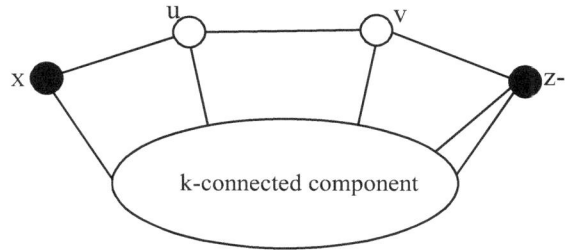

Fig. 8.   An example for phase 2 [76].

special case for $k = m$. The first one is a probabilistic approach which is based on K-Gossip. In K-Gossip algorithm, each node decides its color with a probability based on the network size, transmission range, the value of k, and *etc*. The second is a deterministic approach which is an extension from the k-coverage condition, which is

Definition 11. *k-Coverage Condition: Node v has a non-backbone status if for any two neighbors u and w, k node disjoint replacement paths exist that connect u and w via several intermediate nodes (if any) with higher ID's than v.*

Figure 7 shows that if there exist other k disjoint paths $P_1, P_2, \cdots, P_k$, then v can be removed from CDS. Thus, one node becomes dominatee whenever it satisfies this k-coverage condition. This approach is claimed that it depends on local information only, and no global information such as network size is required. However, at least two hop neighbors' information is need by one node to decide how many node disjoint paths exist between two neighbors. The last one is Color-Based K-CDS Construction. In Color-Based algorithm, each node randomly selects one of the k colors. Therefore, the whole network is divided into k-disjoint subsets based on colors. For each subset, a CDS is constructed. Then all CDS nodes in each subset form a K-CDS.

In [76], the first distributed algorithm DDA for general k and m was proposed. The behind scene idea of DDA is that an m-dominating set C can be obtained through superimposing m

disjoint 1-dominating sets. The k-connectivity of set C can be easily taken care of by adding more nodes to C based on Lemma 4. Therefore, DDA also include two phases. In the phase one a 1mCDS C is constructed. In the phase two C is augment to be k-connected. Since phase 1 is very straightforward, we focus on phase two here. We use an example (Figure 8) to show how phase two works.

Assume $k = 2$. Firstly, the root elected in phase 1 constructs a k-connected component based on its local information. After that each node in this k-connected component broadcasts a *KC* message. Upon receiving *KC* messages from the k-connected component, Node z has two black neighbors in the k-connected component. Then z turns to *Done* and broadcasts a *KC* message. However, node x only has one black neighbor in the k-connected component, x sends a *RC* message to u to request u to join the k-connected component. Node u also has only one neighbor in this k-connected component. So, u broadcasts a *RC* message. After receiving the *KC* message from z, v already has two black neighbors in the k-connected component. Then v sends an *AC* message to u, and u sends an *AC* message to x. After x receives this *AC* message, x can join the k-connected component. Node x sends a *CS* message to u, turns to *Done* and broadcasts a *KC* message. After u receives a *CS* message, u becomes black and sends a *CS* message to v. Then v also turns to black.

The theoretical analysis is also based on Lemma 2. The number of connectors added to C is at most k^2 for each black node in C in phase 2. After phase 2, the total number of

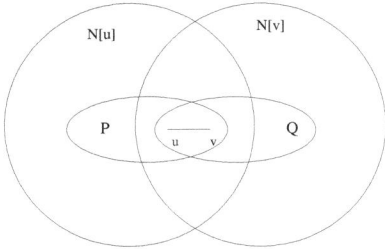

Fig. 9. $LVC(P \cup Q) = k$ if $\mid P \cap Q \mid \geq k$ and $LVC(P) = LVC(Q) = k$ [77].

black nodes in C is $|C| \leq (k^2 + 1)|C_{1m}| + (\Delta + 1)$, where $\Delta + 1$ is the size of the k vertex subgraph constructed by the root. Thus, the performance ratio of DDA is $(5 + \frac{5}{m})(k^2 + 1)$ for $m \leq 5$ and $7(k^2 + 1)$ for $m \geq 6$.

Although the DDA algorithm is a distributed algorithm, the message complexity of DDA is $O(m(|E| + |V|^{1.6} + \Delta|V|))$ which is a little high especially for very dense networks. Considering collisions at MAC layer, distributed algorithms with low message complexities are preferred. Therefore, in [77], another distributed algorithm LDA was proposed whose message complexity is much smaller compared with DDA. In LDA, the colors of nodes are decided based on their local graph information. Node v and all of its neighbors compose of node v's *local graph* denoted as $GL(v)$.

An important Lemma 6 [77] should be introduced before LDA algorithm is presented.

Lemma 6. *Given nodes u and v being neighbors, their closed neighbor sets are $N[u]$ and $N[v]$ respectively. For a node set P, $P \subseteq N[u]$, $v, u \in P$, $LVC(P) = k$ and a node set Q, $Q \subseteq N[v]$, $v, u \in Q$, $LVC(Q) = k$. If $|P \cap Q| \geq k$, then $LVC(P \cup Q) = k$. That means the graph superimposed by P and Q is k vertex-connected.*

Lemma 6 illumines us a distributed local decision way to make the whole graph k vertex-connected only using local graph information.

LDA has three phases. In the first phase 1-connected m-dominating set C_{1m} is constructed. In the second phase, a common black

node set is negotiated. Every black node in C_{11} negotiates with its parents or siblings who are also in C_{11} about the S_{cbn} to make $|S_{cbn}| \geq k$. Since $|S_{cbn}| \geq 2$ and according to Lemma 6, this step is unnecessary if $k = 2$. In the third phase, a local k vertex-connected subgraph is build. Every black node in C_{11} builds a local k vertex-connected graph G_k which includes all the black neighbors in C_{1m} and S_{cbn}s, and marks all the nodes in G_k black. After that, all black form a kmCDS. The advantage of LDA is that the global kmCDS can be obtained from local k-connected graphs. The message complexity of LDA is $O(\Delta|V|)$ which is much smaller than DDA's. The performance ratio of LDA is 7.6Δ, where Δ is the maximum node degree.

VI. CONCLUSION

In this chapter, we survey some existing cluster-based protocols which are well-known techniques with special advantages related to scalability and efficient communication. Especially, we focus on CDS-based algorithms including both centralized and distributed, to construct CDSs. The size of CDS obtained from the centralized algorithms is smaller than those from distributed algorithms. However, the topology of the whole network should be known in advance for those kinds of centralized algorithms. Distributed algorithms are well suitable for large scale WSNs, and they are very energy and time efficient. According to their characteristics, those distributed algorithms can be classified to prune-based and MIS-based. The prune-based algorithm is efficient to maintain a CDS in dynamic network. However, a MIS-based algorithm can obtain a CDS with small size. Having such a CDS simplifies routing by restricting the main routing tasks to the dominators only. Unfortunately, a CDS only preserves 1-connectivity and it is therefore very vulnerable. Fault tolerance and routing flexibility are necessary for routing since nodes in WSNs are prone to failures and nodes may have mobility and turn on and off frequently. Thus, it is important to maintain a certain degree of redundancy in a CDS. Therefore, the concept of k-connected m-dominating sets (kmCDS) is used to provide these redundancies. Even algorithms for constructing kmCDS are far more complexity than the ones for CDS, some centralized and distributed algorithms are proposed for constructing kmCDSs. However, not all algorithms present the sufficient and necessary conditions that are need for those algorithms to obtain a kmCDS.

REFERENCES

[1] J. N. Al-Karaki and A. E. Kamal, "Routing techniques in wireless sensor networks: A survey," *IEEE Wireless Communications*, vol. 11, pp. 6–28, 2004.

[2] S.-Y. Ni, Y.-C. Tseng, Y.-S. Chen, and J.-P. Sheu, "The broadcast storm problem in a mobile ad hoc network," *Wireless Networks*, vol. 8, pp. 153 – 167, 2002.

[3] D. B. Johnson and D. A. Maltz, "Dynamic source routing in ad hoc wireless networks," *Mobile Computing*, pp. 153–181, 1996.

[4] C. E. Perkins and E. M. Royer, "Ad-hoc on-demand distance vector routing," in *Proc. the Second IEEE Workshop on Mobile Computing Systems and Applications*, 1999.

[5] J. Kulik, W. R. Heinzelman, and H. Balakrishnan, "Negotiation-based protocols for disseminating information in wireless sensor networks," *Wireless Networks*, vol. 8, pp. 169–185, 2002.

[6] Y. Yao and J. Gehrke, "The cougar approach to in-network query processing in sensor networks," in *SIGMOD*, 2002.

[7] C. R. Lin and J.-S. Liu, "Qos routing in ad-hoc wireless networks," *IEEE Journal on Selected Areas in Communications*, vol. 17, 1999.

[8] P. Sinha, R. Sivakumar, and V. Bharghavan, "CEDAR: a core-extraction distributed ad hoc routing algorithm," in *INFOCOM*, 1999.

[9] S. Chen, K. Nahrstedt, and Y. Shavitt, "A qos-aware multicast routing protocol," in *INFOCOM*, 2000.

[10] D. Braginsky and D. Estrin, "Rumor routing algorithm for sensor networks," in *1st Wksp. of Sensor Networks and Apps.*, Atlanta, GA, Oct. 2002.

[11] C. Intanagonwiwat, R. Govindan, D. Estrin, J. Heidemann, and F. Silva, "Directed diffusion for wireless sensor networking," *IEEE/ACM Transactions on Networking*, vol. 11, pp. 2–16, 2003.

[12] D. Kempe, J. Kleinberg, and A. Demers, "Spatial gossip and resource location protocols," in *the 33rd ACM Symposium on the Theory of Computing (STOC)*, 2001.

[13] Z. J. Haas, J. Y. Halpern, and L. Li, "Gossip-based ad hoc routing," in *INFOCOM*, 2002.

[14] J. Luo, P. T. Eugster, and J.-P. Hubaux, "Route driven gossip: Probabilistic reliable multicast in ad hoc networks," in *INFOCOM*, 2003.

[15] C. L. Barrett, S. J. Eidenbenz, L. Kroc, M. V. Marathe, and J. P. Smith, "Probabilistic multi-path vs. deterministic single-path protocols for dynamic ad-hoc network scenarios," in *The 2005 ACM Symposium on Applied Computing (SAC'05)*, 2005.

[16] B. Karp and H. T. Kung, "GPSR: Greedy perimeter stateless routing for wireless networks," in *ACM MOBICOM*, 2000.

[17] F. Kuhn, R. Wattenhofer, and A. Zollinger, "Worst-case optimal and average-case efficient geometric ad hoc routing," in *the 4th ACM international symposium on Mobile ad hoc networking & computing*, 2003.

[18] N. Bulusu, J. Heidemann, and D. Estrin, "GPS-less low-cost outdoor localization for very small devices," *Personal Communications*, vol. 7, pp. 28–34, 2000.

[19] N. Bulusu, D. Estrin, L. Girod, and J. Heidemann, "Scalable coordination for wireless sensor networks: Self-configuring localization systems," in *the Sixth International Symposium on Communication Theory and Applications*, 2001.

[20] W. B. Heinzelman, "Application-specific protocol architectures for wireless networks," Ph.D. dissertation, MIT, 2000.

[21] S. Lindsey, C. S. Raghavendra, and C. S. Raghavendra, "PEGASIS: Power-efficient gathering in sensor information systems," in *Proceedings of Aerospace Conference*, 2002.

[22] O. Younis and S. Fahmy, "HEED: A hybrid, energy-efficient, distributed clustering approach for ad hoc sensor networks," *IEEE Transactions on Mobile Computing*, vol. 3, pp. 366–379, 2004.

[23] H. Luo, F. Ye, J. Cheng, S. Lu, and L. Zhang, "TTDD: Two-tier data dissemination in large-scale wireless sensor networks," *Wireless Networks Journal (WINET)*, vol. 11, pp. 161–175, 2005.

[24] C.-J. Lin, P.-L. Chou, and C.-F. Chou, "HCDD: Hierarchical clusterbased data dissemination in wireless sensor networks with mobile sink," in *Proceedings of the 2006 international conference on Wireless communications and mobile computing*, 2006.

[25] J. H. Li, M. yu, R. Levy, and A. Teittinen, "A mobility-resistant efficient clustering approach for ad hoc and sensor networks," *Mobile Computing and Communications Review*, vol. 10, 2006.

[26] G. Chen, C. Li1, M. Ye, and J. Wu, "An unequal cluster-based routing protocol in wireless sensor networks," *Wireless Networks*, 2007.

[27] M. R. Garey and D. S. Johnson, *Computers and Intractability: A guide to the theory of NP-completeness*. San Frncisco: Freeman, 1978.

[28] J. Blum, M. Ding, A. Thaeler, and X. Cheng, *Handbook of Combinatorial Optimization*. Springer US, 2005, ch. Connected Dominating Set in Sensor Networks and MANETs, pp. 329–369.

[29] M. V. Marathe, H. Breu, H. B. H. III, S. S. Ravi, and D. J. Rosenkrantz, "Simple heuristics for unit disk graphs," *Networks*, vol. 25, pp. 59–68, 1995.

[30] S. Guha and S. Khuller, "Approximation algorithms for connected dominating sets," *Algorithmica*, vol. 20, pp. 374–387, 1998.

[31] B. Das, R. Sivakumar, and V. Bharghavan, "Routing in

ad hoc networks using a spine," in *International Conference on Computers and Communications Networks*, Las Vegas, NV., 1997.

[32] B. Das and V. Bharghavan, "Routing in ad-hoc networks using minimum connected dominating sets," in *International Conference on Communications*, 1997.

[33] R. Sivakumar, B. Das, and V. Bharghavan, "An improved spine-based infrastructure for routing in ad hoc networks," in *IEEE Symposium on Computers and Communications*, 1998.

[34] L. Ruan, H. Du, X. Jia, W. Wu, Y. Li, and K.-I. Ko, "Agreedy approximation for minimum connected dominating sets," *Theoretical Computer Science*, vol. 329, pp. 325–330, 2004.

[35] M. Min, H. Du, X. Jia, C. X. Huang, S. C.-H. Huang, and W. Wu, "Improving construction for connected dominating set with steiner tree in wireless sensor networks," *Journal of Global Optimization*, vol. 35, pp. 111–119, 2006.

[36] Y. Li, M. T. Thai, F. Wang, C.-W. Yi, P. Wan, and D.-Z. Du, "On greedy construction of connected dominating sets in wireless networks," *Wireless Communications and Mobile Computing (WCMC)*, vol. 5, pp. 927–932, 2006.

[37] X. Cheng, X. Huang, D. Li, and D. zhu Du, "A polynomial-time approximation scheme for the minimum-connected dominating set in ad hoc wireless networks," *Networks*, vol. 42, pp. 202 – 208, 2003.

[38] J. Wu and H. Li, "On calculating connected dominating set for efficient routing in ad hoc wireless networks," in *the 3rd ACM international workshop on Discrete algorithms and methods for mobile computing and communications*, 1999, pp. 7–14.

[39] J. Wu, B. Wu, and I. Stojmenovic, "Power-aware broadcasting and activity scheduling in ad hoc wireless networks using connected dominating sets," *Wireless Communications and Mobile Computing (WCMC)*, vol. 3, pp. 425–438, 2003.

[40] P.-J. Wan, K. M. Alzoubi, and O. Frieder, "Distributed construction of connected dominating set in wireless ad hoc networks," in *Twenty-First Annual Joint Conference of the IEEE Computer and Communications Societies.*, 2002.

[41] F. Dai and J. Wu, "An extended localized algorithm for connected dominating set formation in ad hoc wireless networks," *IEEE Transactions on Parallel and Distributed Systems*, vol. 15, pp. 908–920, 2004.

[42] J. C. Hansen, E. Schmutz, and L. Sheng, "The expected size of the rule k dominating set," *Algorithmica*, vol. Volume 46, Issue 3, pp. 409 – 418, 2006.

[43] B. Chen, K. Jamieson, H. Balakrishnan, and R. Morris, "Span: an energy-efficient coordination algorithm for topology maintenance in ad hoc wireless networks," *Wireless Networks*, vol. 8, pp. 481–494, 2002.

[44] K. M. Alzoubi, P.-J. Wan, and O. Frieder, "New distributed algorithm for connected dominating set in wireless ad hoc networks," in *the 35th Hawaii International Conference on System Sciences*, 2002.

[45] M. Cardei, X. Cheng, X. Cheng, and D.-Z. Du, "Connected domination in multihop ad hoc wireless networks," in *International Conference on Computer Science and Informatics*, 2002.

[46] X. Cheng, M. Ding, D. H. Du, and X. Jia, "Virtual backbone construction in multihop ad hoc wireless networks," *Wireless Communications and Mobile Computing (WCMC)*, vol. 6, pp. 183–190, 2006.

[47] Y. Zeng, X. Jia, and Y. He, "Energy efficient distributed connected dominating sets construction in wireless sensor networks," in *International Wireless Communications and Mobile Computing Conference (IWCMC'06)*, 2006.

[48] S. Funke, A. Kesselman, U. Meyer, and M. Segal, "A simple improved distributed algorithm for minimum cds in unit disk graphs," *ACM Transactions on Sensor Networks (TOSN)*, vol. 2, pp. 444–453, 2006.

[49] D. Kim, Y. Wu, Y. Li, F. Zou, and D.-Z. Du, "Constructing minimum connected dominating sets with bounded diameters in wireless networks," *IEEE Transactions on Parallel and Distributed Systems (TPDS)*, 2008.

[50] B. Kim, J. Yang, D. Zhouy, and M.-T. Sun, "Energy-aware connected dominating set construction in mobile ad hoc networks," in *Proceedings. 14th International Conference on Computer Communications and Networks (ICCCN)*, 2005.

[51] S. Parthasarathy and R. Gandhi, "Fast distributed well connected dominating sets for ad hoc networks," University of Maryland, College Park, Tech. Rep. CS-TR-4559, 2004.

[52] W. Wu, H. Du, X. Jia, Y. Li, and S. C.-H. Huang, "Minimum connected dominating sets and maximal independent sets in unit disk graphs," *Theoretical Computer Science*, vol. 352, pp. 1–7, 2006.

[53] A. Vahdatpour, F. Dabiri, M. Moazeni, and M. Sarrafzadeh, "Theoretical bound and practical analysis of minimum connected dominating set in ad hoc and sensor networks," in *22nd International Symposium on Distributed Computing (DISC)*, 2008.

[54] I. Stojmenovic, M. Seddigh, and J. Zunic, "Dominating sets and neighbor elimination-based broadcasting algorithms in wireless networks," *IEEE Transactions on Parallel and Distributed Systems*, vol. 13, pp. 14–25, 2002.

[55] K. M. Alzoubi, P.-J. Wan, and O. Frieder, "Message-optimal connected dominating sets in mobile ad hoc networks," in *ACM MobiHoc '02*, 2002.

[56] Y. Li, S. Zhu, M. T. Thai, and D.-Z. Du, "Localized construction of connected dominating set in wireless networks," in *NSF International Workshop on Theoretical Aspects of Wireless Ad Hoc, Sensor and Peer-to-Peer Networks (TAWN04)*, 2004.

[57] M. T. Thai, F. Wang, D. Liu, S. Zhu, and D.-Z. Du, "Connected dominating sets in wireless networks with different transmission ranges," *IEEE Transactions on Mobile Computing*, vol. 6, 2007.

[58] S. Yang, J. Wu, and F. Dai, "Efficient backbone construction methods in manets using directional antennas," in *27th International Conference onDistributed Computing Systems (ICDCS 07)*, 2007.

[59] D. Kim, S. Ha, and Y. Choi, "K-hop cluster-based dynamic source routing in wireless ad-hoc packet radio networks," in *48th IEEE Vehicular Technology Conference*, 1998.

[60] S. Kutten and D. Peleg, "Fast distributed construction

Algorithms, vol. 28, pp. 40–66, 1998.

[61] A. D. Amis, R. Prakash, T. H. P, V. Dung, and T. Huynh, "Max-min d-cluster formation in wireless ad hoc networks," in *Proceedings of IEEE INFOCOM*, 2000.

[62] F. G. Nocetti, J. S. Gonzalez, and I. Stojmenovic, "Connectivity based k-hop clustering in wireless network," *Telecommunication Systems*, pp. 205–220, 2003.

[63] L. D. Penso and V. C. Barbosa, "A distributed algorithm to find k-dominating sets," *Discrete Applied Mathematics*, vol. 141, pp. 243–253, 2004.

[64] S. Yang, J. Wu, and J. Cao, "Connected k-hopclustering in ad hoc networks," in *Proceedings of the 2005 InternationalConference onParallelProcessing(ICPPŠ05)*, 2005.

[65] T. N. Nguyen and D. T. Huynh, "Connected d-hop dominating sets in mobile ad hoc networks," in *4th InternationalSymposium onModeling and Optimization in Mobile, Ad Hoc and Wireless Networks*, 2006.

[66] H.-Y. Yang, C.-H. Lin, and M.-J. Tsai, "Distributed algorithm for efficient construction and maintenance of connected k-hop dominating sets in mobile ad hoc networks," *IEEETransactions onMobileComputing*, vol. 7, pp. 444–457, 2008.

[67] T. Vuongand D. Huynh, "Connected d-hops dominating sets in wireless ad hoc networks," *SCI/ISAS*, vol. 4, 2002.

[68] N. Li, J. C. Hou, and L. Sha, "Design andanalysis of an mst-based topology control algorithm," in *Processing of IEEE INFOCOM*, 2003.

[69] Y. Wang, W. Wang, and X.-Y. Li, "Efficient distributed low-cost backbone formation for wireless networks," *Transactions on Parallel and Distributed Systems*, vol. 17, pp. 681–693, 2007.

[70] K. Mohammed, L. Gewali, and V. Muthukumar, "Generating quality dominating sets for sensor network," in *the Sixth International Conference on Computational Intelligence andMultimediaApplications(ICCIMA'05),*, 2005, pp. 204–211.

[71] Y. Li, D. Kim, F. Zou, and D.-Z. Du, "Constructing connected dominating sets with bounded diameters in wireless networks," in *InternationalConference onWirelessAlgorithms,Systems andApplications(WASA)*,2007.

[72] F. Dai and J. Wu, "On constructing k-connected k-dominating set in wireless networks," in *19thIEEEInternationalParallel andDistributedProcessingSymposium (IPDPS'05)*, 2005.

[73] F. Wang, M. T. Thai, and D.-Z. Du, "2-connectedvirtual backbone in wireless network," *IEEE Transactions on WirelessCommunications*, 2007, accepted with revisions.

[74] W. Shang, F. Yao, P.-J. Wan, and X. Hu, "Algorithms for minimum m-connected k-dominating set problem," in *the first International of ConferenceCombinatorial Optimization and Applications, COCOA 2007*, 2007.

[75] M. T. Thai, N. Zhang, R. Tiwari, and X. Xu, "On approximation algorithms of k-connected m-dominating sets in disk graphs," *Theoretical Computer Science*, vol. 358, pp. 49–59, 2007.

[76] Y. Wu, F. Wang, M. T. Thai, and Y. Li, "Constructing k-connected m-dominating sets in wireless sensor networks," in *2007 Military Communications Conference (MILCOM'07)*, 2007.

[77] Y. Wu and Y. Li, "Construction algorithms for k-connected m-dominating sets in wireless sensor networks," in *9thACMInternationalSymposium onMobile Ad Hoc Networking and Computing (Mobihoc 2008)*, 2008.

CHAPTER 3

Broadcasting In Wireless Ad hoc And Sensor Networks

Majid Khabbazian

Abstract: Broadcasting is the operation of disseminating a message originated by a source node to all reachable nodes in the network. This is a primary operation in wireless ad hoc and sensor networks and has many applications including route discovery in on-demand routing protocols. Broadcasting can be simply done through flooding, in which each node transmits/forwards the message to all its neighbors upon receiving it for the first time. However, it was shown that flooding can cause a large number of redundant transmissions particularly in networks with high average number of neighbors per node. Ideally, we would like to minimize the total number of transmissions. Unfortunately, this was proven to be NP-hard. Therefore, the aim of efficient broadcast algorithms is to reduce the total number of (redundant) transmissions as much as possible. In this chapter, we explain some of the existing classifications of broadcast algorithms and briefly describe their potentials and limitations in reducing the number of redundant transmissions.

I. INTRODUCTION

Broadcasting is a basic operation in wireless ad hoc networks with many applications including route discovery. In broadcasting, a node (called the source node) disseminates a message to all reachable nodes in the network. A straightforward method of achieving this is through flooding in which each node retransmits every message that it receives for the first time. As shown in [1], flooding can lead to a significant amount of redundant transmissions causing network performance degradation and waste of constrained resources such as power and bandwidth. This phenomenon is referred to as "the broadcast storm problem" [1]. As an example, consider a network in which all nodes are in the communication range of each other. In this case, only one transmission is sufficient to deliver a message to all the nodes in the network. However, in flooding all the nodes will transmit the message, which can result in a large number of redundant transmissions.

Many broadcast algorithms have been proposed to tackle the broadcast storm problem. One of the main objectives of the existing broadcast algorithms is to reduce the total number of required transmissions as much as possible. To theoretically analyze the performance of algorithms in terms of the number of required transmissions, a network is modeled by an undirected graph G (V, E), in which vertices represent nodes of the network and two vertices are connected by an edge if and only if the corresponding nodes are in communication range of each other. Two nodes are called 1hop neighbors if they are connected by an edge in G. In reality, the transmission range of each node can be of arbitrary shape as the wireless signal propagation can be affected by many unpredictable factors such as fading. However, when omni directional antennas are used, the transmission range of every node is often approximated by a disk of radius R centered at the node. This model is, up to scaling, identical to the Unit Disk Graph (UDG) model. In UDG, two nodes are connected by an edge if and only if their distance is at most one. To obtain strong theoretical results, UDG is typically used to model the network topology.

The problem of reducing the total number of transmissions can be translated to finding a small size connected dominating set in G. A set of nodes form a Dominating Set (DS) if every node in the network is either in the set or has a 1-hop neighbor in the set. A DS is called a Connected Dominating Set (CDS) if the sub graph induced by its nodes is connected. If the broadcast algorithm guarantees that every node in the network receives the message (full delivery), it can be shown that the set of nodes transmitting the message (including the source node) is a CDS. On the other hand, any CDS can be used as a backbone in broadcasting. In other words, if only the nodes in the CDS transmit the message upon receiving it, this guarantees that all the nodes in the network will receive the message.

Ideally, we are interested in eliminating all redundant transmissions. This translates to finding a CDS of minimal size in G. Such CDS is called the Minimum Connected Dominating Set (MCDS). Unfortunately, finding the MCDS was proven to be NP-hard in both general graphs and unit disk graphs [2], [3]. Therefore, the aim of the existing algorithm is to find a CDS whose size is at most a constant factor of the size of MCDS. In general graphs, it was proven that no polynomial time algorithm can achieve a constant approximation factor unless $NP \subset DTIME$ ($N^{O(\ln \ln N)}$), here N is the total number of nodes in the network [4]. However, using the UDG model, there are many broadcast algorithms that can generate a CDS whose size is a small factor of the size of MCDS. For example, the algorithm by [5] guarantees that the size of constructed CDS is at most 8 times the size of MCDS.

There are numerous broadcast algorithms in the literature. This chapter is not intended to be a comprehensive review, but aims to explain some of the existing classifications and highlight some of the results on the capabilities of broadcast algorithms in reducing the number of redundant transmissions.

II. CLASSIFICATIONS OF BROADCAST ALGORITHMS

There are several different classifications for broadcast algorithms. Following, some of these classifications are described.

A. Global vs. Local

The global broadcast algorithms assume that the global view of the network is available at a central node which uses this information to determine the broadcast backbone (i.e., members of CDS). Typically, the global algorithms are the most powerful algorithms in terms of reducing the size of CDS. For example, the global algorithm by Cheng et al. [6] achieves a $(1 + \frac{1}{s})$-approximation in UDG with running time $N^{\mathcal{O}((s \log s)^2)}$, where N is the total number of nodes in the network. This result implies that, in UDG, the approximation factor can approach one at the cost of more computing time.

In some broadcast algorithms (semi-global algorithms), the global view is not available at the source node. However, the construction of CDS is initiated by the source node and sequentially propagates to the whole network [7]. The broadcast algorithm by Alzoubi, et al. [5] is an example of a semi-global broadcast algorithm that can achieve an approximation factor of 8. Constructing and maintaining a CDS is costly in global and semi-global broadcast algorithms. For example, repairing local changes in the backbone may require global reconstruction [8]. Consequently, global and semi-global broadcast algorithms may not be suitable in ad hoc networks with frequent network topology changes.

In local broadcast algorithms, each node only has information about its k-hop neighbors, i.e. nodes that are within its k hops. Each node can achieve information about its k-hop neighbors through k rounds of information exchange. For example, when $k = 1$, every node can broadcast its ID in one round. Clearly, after the termination of this round, each node will have the ID of all its 1-hop neighbors. To obtain 2-hop neighbor information, each node can broadcast the list of its 1-hop neighbors in the second round (after termination of the first round). A large fraction of existing broadcast algorithms are local algorithms based on k-hop neighbor information, where k is at most two.

B. Deterministic vs. Probabilistic

Local broadcast algorithms can be divided into deterministic and probabilistic algorithms. Probabilistic algorithms [1], [9]–[13] cannot guarantee full delivery even in static networks with an ideal Medium Access Control (MAC) layer (i.e., there are no transmission errors such as collision and contention). An example of a probabilistic broadcast algorithm is the generalization of flooding in which each node forwards a message (received for the first time) with probability p. Theoretically, by increasing p, we can increase the fraction of nodes that receive the message [1] at the cost of adding to the total number of transmissions. Therefore, by adjusting p we can trade-off between the fraction of nodes that receive the message and the total number of transmissions. A suitable value of p may differ from one network to another (or from one node to another). For instance, in sparse networks, the value of p has to be larger than networks with high node density. Some probabilistic algorithms such as the counter or color based [1], [13] algorithms use some information provided by overheard broadcast packets. For example, in the counter-based algorithm, upon receiving a unique message, the node initiates a backoff timer and counts the number of

times it receives the same message during the backoff time. The node then transmits the message if and only if the value of the counter is less than a threshold. The counter based broadcast algorithm uses the fact that a transmission is most likely redundant if the value of the counter is large enough.

In contrast to probabilistic algorithms, deterministic algorithms [7], [14]–[27] are able to guarantee full delivery under some network assumptions. For example, many local algorithms can guarantee full delivery if the network is static during the broadcast process, there are no transmission errors such as collision and contention and the nodes' neighbor-information is up-to-date [2]. A generic framework that covers several existing deterministic algorithms was introduced in [20].

C. Static vs. Dynamic

The broadcast algorithms can also be classified as static and dynamic algorithms. In static algorithms, a backbone is constructed before any broadcast process. The constructed backbone is then used for every broadcast as long as no topology change occurs in the network.

In dynamic algorithms, a backbone is constructed "on-the-fly" as the message propagates in the network (i.e., during the broadcast process). The constructed backbone can change from one network-wide broadcast to another even if the source node (the node that initiates the broadcast) remains the same. As the result, dynamic broadcast algorithms can quickly adapt to network topology changes and are expected to be more robust to node failure and mobility than static algorithms [28]. Also, dynamic algorithms are generally stronger in terms of constructing a small size CDS [29]. On the other hand, the constructed backbone in static algorithms are relatively more stable and can facilitate both broadcasting and unicasting [20].

D. Neighbor-Designating vs. Self-Pruning

Dynamic broadcast algorithms can be divided into neighbor-designating (or sender-based), self-pruning (or receiver-based) and hybrid algorithms. In neighbor-designating algorithms [14], [15], [24], [30], [31], the status (within or outside the CDS) of each node is determined by its neighbors. In other words, every broadcasting node selects a subset of its k-hop neighbors to forward the message. The main design challenge for neighbor-designating algorithms is to choose a small subset of nodes to forward the message. For example, using the neighbor-designating algorithm proposed in [31], every broadcasting node selects a subset of its 1-hop neighbors with the maximum coverage area (outside its own coverage area), where the coverage area of a set of nodes is the union of their transmission coverages. It then piggybacks the list of the selected neighbors in the packet before transmitting it. Upon receiving a new message, a node schedules to transmit the message if and only if it was selected to forward the message. Of course, the new broadcasting node has to select a set of its own neighbors to forward the message.

---

[1] In practice, increasing p may lead to more packet collisions and reduce the total number of nodes that receive the message.

[2] In the lack of these or similar assumptions, even flooding cannot guarantee full delivery.

In self-pruning algorithms, each node determines its own status based on a self-pruning condition [17], [19], [21]–[23], [32]. When 1-hop neighbor information is available, a simple self-pruning condition is whether or not all the 1-hop neighbors have been covered by previous transmissions. Clearly, if this condition is satisfied, the node does not require to forward the message. As mentioned earlier, in neighbor-designating algorithms, each node has to include the list of selected neighbors in the packet. Self-pruning algorithms do not need to add extra information to the packet. However, when they are allowed to include some information in the packet, they can perform better than neighbor-designating algorithms (that use the same neighborhood knowledge) in terms of reducing the total number of transmissions [23].

Hybrid algorithms can be considered as a generalization of neighbor-designating and self-pruning algorithms. In hybrid algorithms, the status of each node is determined either by its own or by its neighbors. For example, in the hybrid algorithm proposed in [33], every broadcasting node selects at most one of its neighbors to forward the message. A node that has not been selected to forward must determine its status by its own.

E. Global/Semi-Global Broadcast Algorithms

In this section, we briefly describe a general approach used in several global/semi-global algorithms (e.g., [5], [34]) to construct a small size CDS in unit disk graphs. The aim of this section is to show that, global/semi-global algorithms can easily construct a small size CDS whose size is at most a constant factor of the size of MCDS.

The general approach consists of two phases. In the first phase, a Maximal Independent Set (MIS) is constructed. A MIS is a dominating set S such that no two nodes in S are neighbors. When the whole graph is known, a MIS can be easily constructed as follows. We start with an empty set S. At each step, we find a node $u \notin S$ such that

$$\forall v \in S: \quad u \text{ and } v \text{ are not neighbors.}$$

We then add u to the set S. This process continues until we cannot add any new node to the set. It is clear that the final set S is a maximal independent set.

In the second phase, the constructed MIS (which is a DS) is converted to a CDS by adding more nodes to it. Some simple algorithms [5], [35] can construct a CDS from a carefully-generated MIS by adding at most $|MIS|$ nodes, where $|MIS|$ denotes the size of MIS. In general, any dominating set DS can be converted to a connected dominating set by adding at most $2 \times |DS|$ nodes to it.

Recently, it was proven that [36]

$$|MIS| \leqslant 3|MCDS| + 3,$$

where $|MCDS|$ denotes the size of a MCDS in the graph. It is then clear that, using the aforementioned approach, any algorithm can construct a CDS whose size is at most a constant times the size of MCDS.

III. ON THE STRENGTH OF LOCAL BROADCAST ALGORITHMS

As mentioned earlier, the problem of computing MCDS is NP-hard even when the global network topology is known. However, some of the existing local broadcast algorithms can construct a small size CDS whose size, in the worst case, is less than a constant factor of the size of MCDS. In this section, we consider two general categories of local broadcast algorithms (i.e., static and dynamic algorithms) and show whether any broadcast algorithm in each category is capable of achieving a constant approximation factor to MCDS using the UDG model.

A. Dynamic Broadcast Algorithms

Many factors can affect the strength of dynamic broadcast algorithms in terms of reducing the total number of transmissions required to achieve full delivery. Some of these factors are:

- **Backoff delay:** upon receiving a message the receiver node can either immediately determine its status (forwarding or non-forwarding) or postpone the decision by a backoff delay. The backoff delay can be set randomly [21]–[23], [28] or based on, for example, location of neighbors [37]. During the backoff delay the node may receive the same message from other neighbors. This can help the node to make a more informed decision on whether or not its transmission is redundant. Consequently, dynamic algorithms based on backoff delay (also called "timer based" algorithms) can be more successful in constructing a smaller size CDS. Note that using backoff delay may increase the completion time of the broadcast process.

- **Position information:** Knowledge of position information, relative distance between nodes or directional information (angle-of-arrival) can greatly support constructing a small size CDS. However, to use this information, nodes may require specialized hardware. Also, position/distance/directional information is typically inaccurate.

- **Neighborhood knowledge:** In local broadcast algorithms, using k rounds of information exchange, each node can have a view of the nodes within its k-hop. Clearly, as k increases, an algorithm can perform better in terms of reducing the total number of transmissions. However, in practical broadcast algorithms, the value of k is often no more than 2. It is because the cost of collecting and updating k-hop neighbor information significantly increases as k increases. This is not desirable particularly in ad hoc and sensor networks with frequent topology changes.

- **Information piggyback:** The broadcast packet can carry some extra information as it is propagating in the network during the broadcast process. For example, the broadcast packet can piggyback the list of nodes recently visited or the list of 1-hop neighbors of the last visited node. Such information can be very valuable in determining the status of a node. For example, suppose all the nodes are located on a circle, and are in transmission range of each other. Assume that each node has only the list of its 1-hop neighbors. In this case, as will be explained later, all the nodes may transmit the message if no information is piggybacked. However, if the broadcasting node piggybacks the list of its 1-hop neighbors in the packet, every node can determine that its transmission is redundant.

1) Neighbor-Designating Algorithms: Algorithm 1, shows a general structure of neighbor-designating algorithms. Using Algorithm 1, upon receiving a packet, each node first extracts some information from the packet. The packet is then discarded if it has been received before. Otherwise, the node checks whether it has been selected by the previous node to forward the packet. If so, it removes the list of selected nodes (by the previous node) from the packet, adds its own list of selected nodes and schedules the packet for broadcast. Otherwise, the packet will be discarded.

Algorithm 1 A general neighbor-designating algorithm (1)

1: Extract the required information from the received message M
2: **if** *M has been received before* or does not contain node's ID **then**
3:   drop the message
4: **end if**
5: Select a subset of neighbors to forward the message
6: Attach the list of selected nodes to the message
7: Schedule a broadcast

In Algorithm 1, the main design challenge is to minimize the number of selected nodes such that full delivery is guaranteed. In neighbor-designating broadcast algorithms based on 1-hop neighbor information, it can be shown that full delivery is guaranteed if and only if any 2-hop neighbor of the broadcasting node is a 1-hop neighbor of at least one of the selected nodes. The problem of selecting the minimum number of 1-hop neighbors that cover all 2-hop neighbors is called the Minimum Forwarding Set Problem (MFSP) or Multi-Point Relay (MPR) [15], [38]. Note that if 2-hop neighbor information is not available, the selected nodes have to cover any potential 2-hop neighbor. For example, as shown in Figure 1, when 2-hop neighbor information is available, the smallest set of forwarding nodes by u is $\{v_2, v_4, v_6\}$. However, in the lack of 2-hop neighbor information, u has to select all its 1-hop neighbors, excluding v_3, to forward the message. It is because the coverage area of v_3 is covered by u, v_1, v_2 and v_4 and every other node has some coverage area that cannot be covered by even all other nodes. If a node is given a list of its 1-hop neighbors and their position information, the smallest set of 1-hop nodes that cover any potential 2-hop neighbor can be computed in $\mathcal{O}(n \log n)$, where n is the number of 1-hop neighbors [31]. Interestingly, when the list of 2-hop neighbor information is available, the problem of finding the smallest covering set (i.e., MFSP) becomes difficult. In [38], an approximation algorithm was proposed for MFSP. Recently, it was shown that MFSP can be solved in polynomial time [39]. However, as shown in [14], [23], even an optimal solution

to MFSP does not guarantee a good approximation factor to MCDS.

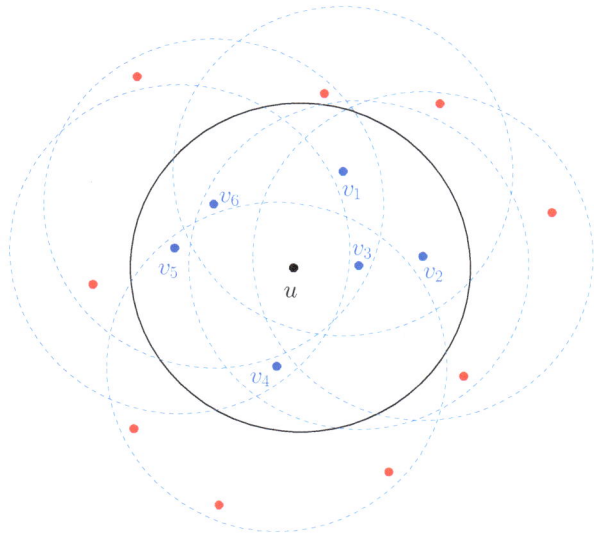

Fig. 1.   Selecting the minimum number of forwarding nodes.

Algorithm 2 shows another structure for neighbor-designating algorithms based on 1-hop neighbor information. Using Algorithm 1, each node may only schedule a broadcast when it receives a message for the first time. In contrast, in Algorithm 2, a message can be scheduled for a broadcast at any time provided that the node has been selected to forward the message and the message has not been scheduled before. For example, a message can be discarded after the first reception but scheduled for broadcast the second time. Note that in both structures, a message is scheduled for broadcast at most once.

Algorithm 2 A general neighbor-designating algorithm (2)

1: Extract the required information from the received message M
2: **if** *M has been scheduled for broadcast before* or does not contain node's *id* **then**
3:   drop the message
4: **end if**
5: Select a subset of neighbors to forward the message
6: Attach the list of selected nodes to the message
7: Schedule a broadcast

Suppose that only 1-hop neighbor information is available. Employing Algorithm 1, a broadcasting node may have to select a large fraction of its 1-hop neighbors to forward the message. For example, when all 1-hop neighbors are located on a circle, they all have to be selected in order to guarantee full delivery. In [24], the authors proposed a 1-hop based neighbor-designating broadcast algorithm using the structure of Algorithm 2 and proved that the maximum number of selected nodes is always less than or equal to 11. The proposed algorithm in [24] uses a slice-based selection scheme to choose the forwarding nodes. Let us define a bulged slice as the intersection area of three circles with radius R. Figure 2 shows a bulged slice around node u. A slice-based scheme, selects a set of 1-hop neighbors such that there is at least one selected node in every non-empty bulged slice around the broadcasting node. For example, as shown in Figure 2, node u has to select v_1 so there is at least one selected node in each non-empty bulged slice. The selection of node v_2 is not necessary as any bulged slice covering v_2 will include v_1 as well. Interestingly, full delivery may not be achieved if bulged slices are replaced with cones [24]. For example, suppose we use cones of degree $\frac{\pi}{3}$ instead of bulged slices. Therefore, the selection scheme computes a small (or the smallest) set of selected nodes such that there is at least one selected node in every non-empty cone (of degree $\frac{\pi}{3}$). As shown in Figure 2, this may not guarantee full delivery. It is because, node u may select node v_2 to forward the message. Similarly, when v_2 computes its forwarding neighbors, it may select u. These selections satisfy the requirement of having at least one selected node in each non-empty cone. However, node w will eventually miss the message sine node v_1 is the only node that can reach w. In [24], it was proven that the proposed slice-based scheme (based on bulged slices) guarantees full delivery and selects at most 11 nodes with running time $\mathcal{O}(n)$, where n is the total number of 1-hop neighbors. Unfortunately, similar to Liu's broadcast algorithm [31], the proposed algorithm in [24] cannot guarantee a good approximation factor to MCDS.

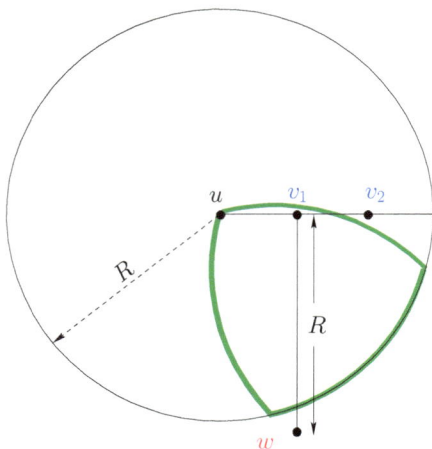

Fig. 2. Node selection based on bulged slices.

In [23], the authors proved that neighbor-designating algorithms based on 1-hop neighbor information cannot achieve a good approximation factor to MCDS, in the worst case, even when position information is available. The idea is based on the fact that, in any neighbor-designating algorithm based on 1-hop neighbor information, a node u will eventually broadcast if there is a point P such that $dist(u, P) \leqslant R$ and $dist(v, P) > R$ for every node $v \neq u$, where $dist()$ returns the Euclidean distance between its inputs. Note that, in neighbor-designating algorithms, a node does not broadcast a message if it is not selected to forward. Therefore, node u must be selected in order to guarantee full delivery since only u knows whether or not there is a node at point P. Thus, based on this idea, all the nodes in the network will broadcast if they are all located on a line segment of size R. It is because, as

shown in Figure 3, for every node u_i, $1 \leqslant i \leqslant N$ ($N = 11$ in this example), there is a point P_i such that $dist(u_i, P_i) = R$ and

$$\forall j \neq i, \quad dist(u_j, P_i) > R.$$

Clearly, since the length of the line segment is R, the size of MCDS is one and thus the approximation factor is N.

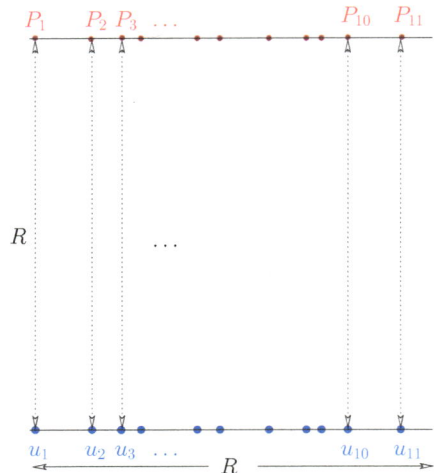

Fig. 3. Every node on the line segment has to broadcast.

2) Self-Pruning Algorithms: Algorithm 3 shows a general structure of a timer-based self-pruning algorithm. As mentioned earlier, in timer based algorithms, during the backoff delay each node may overhear packets from more nodes and thus can make a more informed decision on whether or not to broadcast. Therefore, timer-based broadcast algorithms are relatively more effective in reducing the number of redundant transmissions. The main step in designing a self-pruning algorithms is to find an effective self-pruning condition. One simple self-pruning condition is whether all the neighbors have received the message before the backoff timer expiration. For example, consider a network in which all the nodes are in transmission range of each other. Suppose every node has its 2-hop neighbor information. If a node receives a packet, it can easily find that its own transmission would be redundant as all its 1-hop neighbors have already received the packet. If each node has only 1-hop neighbor information, similar result can be achieved in the case where position information is available or the case where the broadcasting node piggybacks the list of its 1-hop neighbors in the packet. In both cases, a node can determine that all its neighbors have received the message by the previous transmission. This example, shows the effect of having more information such as the list of 2-hop neighbors and position information and piggybacking information on reducing the number of redundant transmissions.

It was proven that self-pruning algorithms based on 1-hop neighbor information cannot guarantee a good approximation factor to MCDS if no information is piggybacked in the packet [23]. The proof sketch is as follows. As shown in Figure 3, suppose that all the nodes are located on two circles $C_{O, \frac{R}{2}}$ and $C_{O, \frac{3R}{2}}$ centered at O with radii $\frac{R}{2}$ and $\frac{3R}{2}$, respectively. Suppose that for every node u_i on $C_{O, \frac{R}{2}}$, there is

Algorithm 3 A general self-pruning algorithm

1: Extract the required information from the received message M
2: **if** M has been received before **then**
3:     drop the message
4: **else**
5:     set a backoff timer
6: **end if**
7: When timer expires:
8: **if** the *self-pruning condition* is not satisfied **then**
9:     broadcast the message
10: **end if**

a corresponding node v_i on $C_{O, \frac{3R}{2}}$ such that $dist(u_i, v_i) = R$. Note that u_i and u_j do not have any common 1-hop neighbor. Since every node has only its 1-hop neighbor information and there is no information piggybacked in the broadcast packet, u_i (or v_i) cannot determine whether its corresponding node has received the message. Therefore, in order to guarantee full delivery, either u_i or v_i has to broadcast the message; thus the minimum number of transmissions would be $\frac{N}{2}$, where N is the total number of nodes in the network. Consequently, the approximation factor is $\Omega(N)$ because the size of MCDS can be shown to be $\mathcal{O}(1)$.

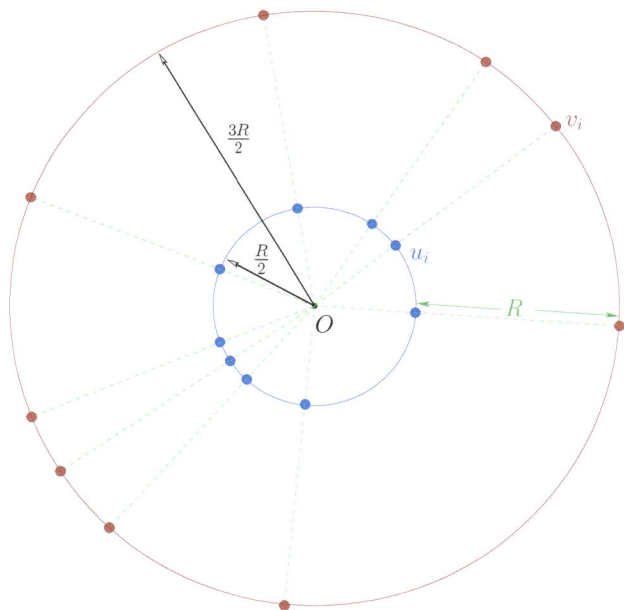

Fig. 4. At least half of the nodes must broadcast.

In the same work [23], the authors proposed a self-pruning algorithm based on 1-hop neighbor information and proved that the algorithm guarantee a constant approximation factor to MCDS if nodes are allowed to piggyback information in the broadcasting packet. Algorithm 3 is the basic structure of the proposed self-pruning algorithm in [23]. It is assumed that approximate position information is available. Each node periodically broadcasts a "hello" message including its ID and position. Therefore, every node has the list of its 1-hop neighbors as well as their positions. Using a carefully designed

self-pruning condition called the *responsibility condition* and allowing each broadcasting node to piggyback information in the packet, it was proven that Algorithm 3 guarantees to construct a CDS whose size is at most a constant factor of MCDS. Based on the responsibility condition, a node avoids broadcasting the message if and only if it is not responsible for any of its 1-hop neighbors. A node u is defined not to be responsible for its neighbor v if based on u's collected information, v has received the message from a previous transmission or there is another node w such that w has received the message (based on u's collected information) and $dist(w, v) < dist(u, v)$. For example, as shown in Figure 5, suppose that node u broadcast a message. Based on the responsibility condition, v_3 does not require to forward the message. It is because among v_3's 1-hop neighbors, v_1, v_2, v_4 have received the message from u and v_3 is not responsible for w_3 since v_4 has received the message and $dist(v_4, w_3) < dist(v_3, w_3)$.

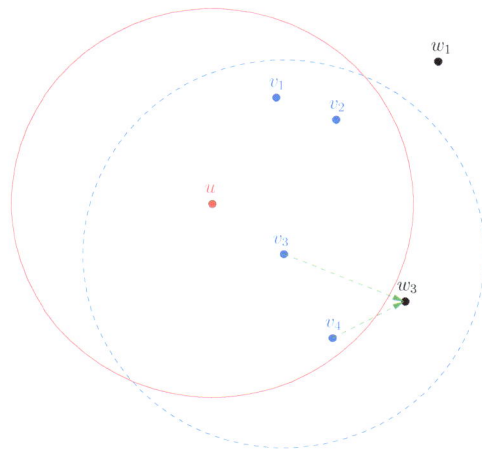

Fig. 5. An example of using the responsibility condition.

Figure 6 shows an example of using the proposed self-pruning algorithm in a network with 33 nodes. In this example, the node s initiates the broadcast. It is easy to see that the nodes $u_1 \ldots u_7$ are not required to broadcast based on the responsibility condition. Therefore, they can immediately drop the packet after they receive it from s. Other neighbors of s initiate a backoff timer with a random number. Thus, the next broadcasting node is random (it is v_1 in this example). Note that after v_1's transmission, some other nodes, which were previously set a backoff timer, may drop the packet. For example, node w_1 would be no longer responsible for any of its neighbors after v_1's transmission. At last, as shown in Figure 6, only 7 nodes (represented by stars) will broadcast the packet.

The significance of the proposed algorithm in [23] is that it shows dynamic broadcast algorithms are, indeed, able to guarantee a good approximation factor to the minimum number of required transmission. However, this result is achieved when approximate position information or relative distance between nodes is available. A remaining question, which will be answered in this chapter, is whether dynamic algorithms can achieve such a strong result (i.e. achieving a constant ap-

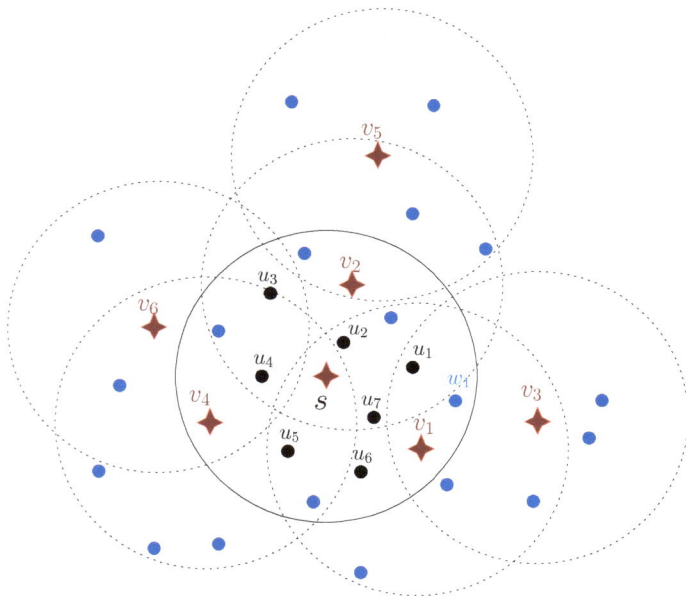

Fig. 6. An instance of using the proposed broadcast algorithm in [23].

proximation factor to MCDS) when position, relative distance and directional information is not available.

B. Hybrid Algorithms

Hybrid algorithms are a generalization of both neighbor-designating and self-pruning algorithms. In hybrid algorithms, a broadcasting node may select some of its neighbors to forward the message. If the message is received by a selected node, it will schedule a broadcast. Otherwise, it has to determine by its own whether or not to forward the message. A node which has not been selected to forward can use a self-pruning condition to determine its status.

In [33], the authors proposed a hybrid broadcast algorithm based on 2-hop neighbor information and proved that their algorithm guarantees a constant approximation factor to MCDS. The significance of their proposed hybrid algorithm is that it only uses topology information and does not require position, relative distance or directional information. Algorithm 4 shows the proposed hybrid algorithm in [33]. Since each node broadcasts the message at most once, the broadcast process will terminate. After the broadcast termination, a node has a forwarding status if it has broadcast the message and non-forwarding status, otherwise. However, during the broadcast, a node may have other intermediate statues represented by colors as follows:

- white: The node has not received the message;
- green: The node has received the message at least once;
- red: The node was selected to forward/broadcast the message;
- black: The node has broadcast the message.

There is a self-pruning condition called the *black condition* at the core of Algorithm 4. The black condition of a node is satisfied if and only if the node does not have any *sole neighbor*. A node v is called a *sole neighbor* of u if v is a 1-hop neighbor of u that has not received the message and

(based on u's collected information from overheard packets) there is no node $w \neq u$ such that w is a 1-hop neighbor of v and w's color is either red or black. If a node does not have a sole neighbor, it is assured that all its neighbors have either received the message (from a black neighbor) or will receive it (from a red neighbor). Based on Algorithm 4, any broadcasting node whose black condition is not satisfied must select one of its sole neighbors (if there is more than one) to forward the message. A selected node must forward the message regardless of its black condition. Figure 6 shows an instance of using the hybrid algorithm in a network with 9 nodes. Suppose that node u initiates the broadcast. Clearly, all 1-hop neighbors of u are sole neighbors. Thus, u can select any of them to forward the message. The selection of sole neighbors can be done randomly or based on a criteria. For example, a broadcasting node can select the sole neighbor with the highest degree (i.e., the maximum number of 1-hop neighbors). In this example, v_2 has the highest degree so it would be the selected node to forward. After u's transmission, only v_2 will broadcast the message because v_1, v_3, v_4 do not have any sole neighbors any more, thus their black conditions are satisfied.

Algorithm 4 The proposed hybrid algorithm in [33]

1: Extract information from the received packet
2: **if** color== black **then**
3:    Drop the packet
4:    Return
5: **end if**
6: **if** color==white **then**
7:    color ← green
8: **end if**
9: Update the *black condition* and the list of *sole neighbors*
10: **if** the black condition is not satisfied **then**
11:    Schedule the packet {(*only update the embedded sole neighbor if the packet is already scheduled*)}
12:    **if** the node is selected **then**
13:       color ← red
14:    **end if**
15: **else** {(*there is no sole neighbor in this case*)}
16:    **if** the node is selected **then**
17:       color ← red
18:       Schedule the packet {(*only remove the sole neighbor if the packet is already scheduled*)}
19:    **else**
20:       Cancel the schedule for broadcasting the packet
21:    **end if**
22: **end if**
23: Set the color to black when the packet is transmitted

C. Static Broadcast Algorithms

Recall that in static broadcast algorithms a backbone (i.e., a CDS) is constructed before any broadcast process. The constructed backbone can be used for any broadcast (or unicast) as long as the network topology remains unchanged. Upon any change in network topology, the backbone may need to be repaired. Local static algorithms are able to locally repair

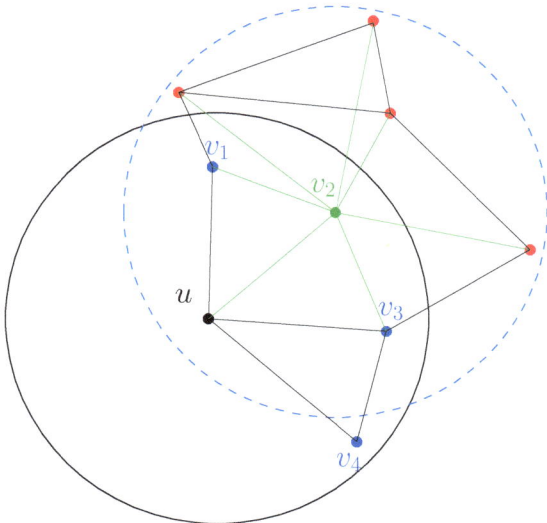

Fig. 7. An instance of using the hybrid broadcast algorithm proposed in [33].

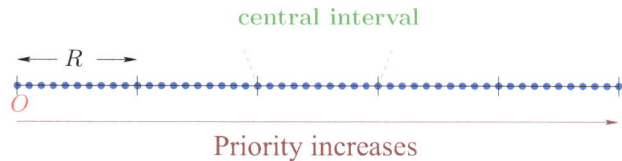

Fig. 8. An instance of using the hybrid broadcast algorithm proposed in [33].

the backbone if the network topology changes locally. In other words, any local topology change may only require repairing the backbone in the vicinity.

A local change in the backbone may require constructing a new backbone if the status (backbone membership) of each node depends on that of its neighbors. In local static algorithms, the status of each node typically depends on local topology information and a publicly known priority function. In [33], it was shown that local static algorithms may not be able to guarantee a constant approximation to MCDS if the status of each node is only determined by local topology information (not including position, relative distance or directional information) and a priority function. For example, suppose that the priority of node u is higher than that of node v if u's ID is larger than v's ID. Also, suppose that each node uses its 1-hop neighbor information to determine its status and all the nodes are located in a line segment of length $4R$ as shown in Figure 8. Assume that node IDs increase as their distance from O increase. Clearly, nodes in the central interval have the same view of their local topology so their status has to be the same. On the other hand, at least one of nodes in the central interval has to be in the backbone (otherwise the backbone is not connected). As the result, all the nodes in the central interval are in the backbone. Clearly, the minimum size of backbone in this example is not more than 10. However, the size of constructed backbone would be at least $\frac{N}{5}$ (N is the total number of nodes on the line segment) if all the nodes in the central interval are in the backbone. Similarly, it can be shown that the knowledge of k-hop neighbors does not guarantee constructing a small size backbone.

When position information is available, it can be shown that local static algorithms can guarantee a constant approximation factor to MCDS [33]. One solution, for example, is to divide the network into square cells as shown in Figure 9. Suppose that the side of each square is $\frac{\sqrt{2}}{2}R$. Therefore, all the nodes in a square cell are in transmission range of each other. If all the nodes in the network are located in a single cell, a CDS

can be easily constructed by, for example, selecting the node with the smallest ID. Assume that there are at least two non-empty cells in the network. Let us define two cells $\mathcal{C}_i$ and $\mathcal{C}_j$ as neighbors if

$$\exists u \in \mathcal{C}_i, v \in \mathcal{C}_j \text{ s.t. } dist(u,v) \leqslant R.$$

In this case, nodes u and v are called the connectors of $\mathcal{C}_i$ and $\mathcal{C}_j$. It can be shown that a set of nodes $\mathcal{S}$ is a CDS if any two non-empty neighboring cells have connectors in $\mathcal{S}$. The process of constructing $\mathcal{S}$ (hence a CDS) can be done locally if each node has the list of its 2-hop neighbors as well as their positions.

As suggested in [33], to construct $\mathcal{S}$, a node u selects itself as a connector (i.e. a member of $\mathcal{S}$) based on a selection criteria. The selection criteria has to be symmetric in the sense that node $u \in \mathcal{C}_i$ selects itself as the connector to cell $\mathcal{C}_j$ through the node v if and only if v selects itself as the connector to $\mathcal{C}_i$. For example, a node u can select itself as the connector of its cell $\mathcal{C}_i$ to a neighboring cell $\mathcal{C}_j$ trough node $v \in \mathcal{C}_j$ if and only if $dist(u,v)$ is minimum among all possible connectors of $\mathcal{C}_i$ and $\mathcal{C}_j$. As shown in Figure 9, each cell has at most 20 neighbors. This fact was used in [33] to show that the size of the constructed CDS is at most a constant factor of the size of MCDS.

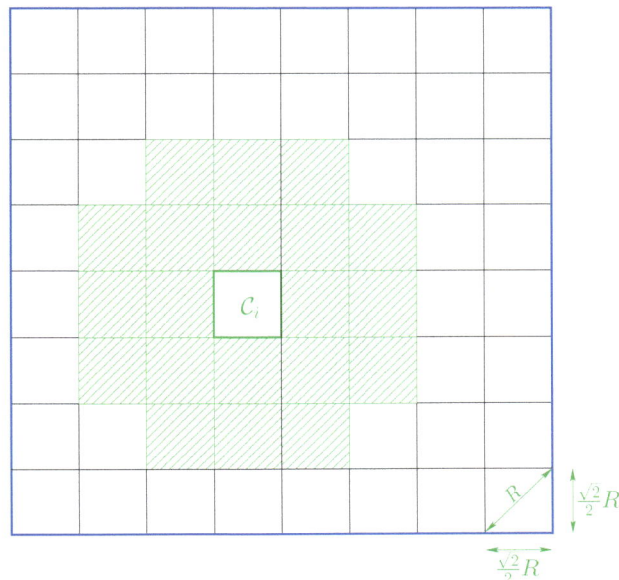

Fig. 9. A cell $\mathcal{C}_i$ has at most 20 neighbors.

References

[1]   S. Ni, Y. Tseng, Y. Chen, and J. Sheu, "The broadcast storm problem in a mobile ad hoc network," *ACM International Conference on Mobile Computing and Networking (MOBICOM)*, pp. 151–162, 1999.

[2]   M. Garey and D. Johnson, *Computers and Intractability; A Guide to the Theory of NP-Completeness*. New York: W. H. Freeman & Co., 1990.

[3]   B. Clark, C. Colbourn, and D. Johnson, "Unit disk graphs," *Discrete Mathematics*, vol. 86, pp. 165–177, 1990.

[4]   S. Guha and S. Khulle, "Approximation algorithms for connected dominating sets," *Algorithmica*, vol. 20, no. 4, pp. 374–387, 1998.

[5]   P. Wan, K. Alzoubi, and O. Frieder, "Distributed construction of connected dominating set in wireless ad hoc networks," *IEEE INFOCOM*, vol. 3, pp. 1597–1604, 2002.

[6]   X. Cheng, X. Huang, D. Li, and D. Du, "A polynomial-time approximation scheme for the m inimum-connected dominating set in ad hoc wireless networks," *Networks*, vol. 42, no. 4, pp. 202–208, 2003.

[7]   J. Wu and W. Lou, "Forward-node-set-based broadcast in clustered mobile ad hoc networks," *Wireless Communications and Mobile Computing*, vol. 3, no. 2, pp. 155–173, 2003.

[8]   Y. Chen and A. Liestma, "Maintaining weakly-connected dominating sets for clustering ad hoc networks," *Ad Hoc Networks*, vol. 3, no. 5, pp. 629–642, 2005.

[9]   Z. Haas, J. Halpern, and L. Li, "Gossip-based ad hoc routing," *IEEE INFOCOM*, pp. 1707–1716, 2002.

[10]   Y. Tseng, S. Ni, and E. Shih, "Adaptive approaches to relieving broadcast storms in a wireless multihop mobile ad hoc networks," *International Conference on Distributed Computing Systems (ICDCS)*, pp. 481–488, 2001.

[11]   J. Cartigny and D. Simplot, "Border node retransmission based probabilistic broadcast protocols in ad-hoc networks," *Telecommunication Systems*, pp. 189–204, 2003.

[12]   D. Y. Sasson and A. Schiper, "Probabilistic broadcast for flooding in wireless mobile ad hoc networks," *IEEE Wireless Communications and Networking Conference*, pp. 1124–1130, 2003.

[13]   A. Keshavarz-Haddad, V. Ribeiro, and R. Riedi, "Color-based broadcasting for ad hoc networks," *International Symposium on Modeling and Optimization in Mobile, Ad-Hoc and Wireless Networks (WiOpt)*, pp. 1–10, 2006.

[14]   J. Wu, W. Lou, and F. Dai, "Extended multipoint relays to determine connected dominating sets in manets," *IEEE Transactions on Computers*, vol. 55, no. 3, pp. 334–347, 2006.

[15]   A. Qayyum, L. Viennot, and A. Laouiti, "Multipoint relaying for flooding broadcast messages in mobile wireless networks," *International Conference on System Sciences (HICSS)*, vol. 9, p. 298, 2002.

[16]   J. Wu and H. Li, "On calculating connected dominating set for efficient routing in ad hoc wireless networks," *International Workshop on Discrete Algorithms and Methods for Mobile Computing and Communications (DiaLM)*, pp. 7–14, 1999.

[17]   F. Dai and J. Wu, "Distributed dominant pruning in ad hoc networks," *IEEE International Conference on Communications*, vol. 1, pp. 353–357, 2003.

[18]   J. Wu and F. Dai, "Broadcasting in ad hoc networks based on self-pruning," *IEEE INFOCOM*, pp. 2240–2250, 2003.

[19]   B. Chen, K. Jamieson, H. Balakrishnan, and R. Morris, "Span: An energy-efficient coordination algorithm for opology maintenance in ad hoc wireless networks," pp. 85–96, 2001.

[20]   J. Wu and F. Dai, "A generic distributed broadcast scheme in ad hoc

[21]   W. Peng and X. Lu, "On the reduction of broadcast redundancy in mobile ad hoc networks," *ACM Interational Symposium on Mobile Ad Hoc Networking and Computing (MobiHoc)*, pp. 129–130, 2000.

[22]   I. Stojmenovic, M. Seddigh, and J. Zunic, "Dominating sets and neighbor elimination-based broadcasting algorithms in wireless networks," *IEEE Transactions on Parallel and Distributed Systems*, vol. 13, pp. 14–25, 2002.

[23]   M. Khabbazian and V. Bhargava, "Localized broadcasting with guaranteed delivery and bounded transmission redundancy," *IEEE Transactions on Computers*, vol. 57, no. 8, pp. 1072–1086, 2008.

[24]   M. Khabbazian and V. K. Bhargava, "Efficient broadcasting in mobile ad hoc networks," *IEEE Transactions on Mobile Computing*, vol. 8, no. 2, pp. 231–245, 2009.

[25]   E. Pagani and G. Rossi, "Reliable broadcast in mobile multihop packet networks," pp. 34–42, 1997.

[26]   T. Kwon and M. Gerla, "Efficient flooding with passive clustering (PC) in ad hoc networks," *SIGCOMM Comput. Commun. Rev.*, vol. 32, no. 1, 2002.

[27]   W. Lou and J. Wu, "A cluster-based backbone infrastructure for broadcasting in MANETs," 2003.

[28]   A. Keshavarz-Haddad, V. Ribeiro, and R. Riedi, "DRB and DCCB: Efficient and robust dynamic broadcast for ad hoc and sensor networks," *Sensor, Mesh and Ad Hoc Communications and Networks (SECON)*, pp. 253–262, 2007.

[29]   "Virtual backbone construction in MANETs using adjustable transmission ranges," *IEEE Transactions on Mobile Computing*, vol. 5, no. 9, pp. 1188–1200, 2006, j. Wu and F. Dai.

[30]   W. Lou and J. Wu, "On reducing broadcast redundancy in ad hoc wireless networks," *IEEE Transactions on Mobile Computing*, vol. 1, no. 2, pp. 111–123, 2002.

[31]   H. Liu, P. Wan, X. Jia, X. Liu, and F. Yao, "Efficient flooding scheme based on 1-hop information in mobile ad hoc networks," *IEEE INFOCOM*, 2006.

[32]   M. Rieck, S. Pai, and S. Dhar, "Distributed routing algorithms for multi-hop ad hoc networks using d-hop connected d-dominating sets," *Computer networks*, vol. 47, no. 6, pp. 785–799, 2005.

[33]   M. Khabbazian, I. F. Blake, and V. K. Bhargava, "On the power of local broadcast algorithms," *Technical Report TR-2009-11, Department of Computer Science Technical Reports, UBC, Canada*, 2009. [Online]. Available: http://www.cs.ubc.ca/cgi-bin/tr/2009/TR-2009-11

[34]   K. Alzoubi, P. Wan, and O. Frieder, "Distributed heuristics for connected dominating sets in wireless ad hoc networks," *Journal of Communications and Networks*, vol. 4, no. 1, pp. 22–29, 2002.

[35]   M. Marathe, H. Breu, H. H. III, S. Ravi, and D. Rosenkrantz, "Simple heuristics for unit disk graphs," *Networks*, vol. 25, pp. 59–68, 1995.

[36]   A. Vahdatpour, F. Dabiri, M. Moazeni, and M. Sarrafzadeh, "Theoretical bound and practical analysis of connected dominating set in ad hoc and sensor networks," *DISC*, pp. 481–495, 2008.

[37]   M. Heissenbuttel, T. Braun, M. Walchli, and T. Bernoulli, "Optimized stateless broadcasting in wireless multi-hop networks," *IEEE INFOCOM*, pp. 1–12, 2006.

[38]   G. Calinescu, I. Mandoiu, P. Wan, and A. Zelikovsky, "Selecting forwarding neighbors in wireless ad hoc networks," *ACM Mobile Networks and Applications*, vol. 9, no. 2, pp. 101–111, 2004.

[39]   M. Baysan, K. Sarac, R. Chandrasekaran, and S. Bereg, "A polynomial time solution to minimum forwarding set problem in wireless networks under unit disk coverage model," *Accepted in IEEE Transactions on Parallel and Distributed Systems*.

[20]   ... wireless networks," *IEEE Transactions on Computers*, vol. 53, no. 10, pp. 1343–1354, 2004.

CHAPTER 4

Energy Efficient Routing

P. Minet

INRIA, Rocquencourt, 78153 Le Chesnay Cedex, France

Abstract: In wireless ad hoc and sensor networks, some nodes are battery operated. They have a limited amount of energy that can be difficult, expensive or even impossible to renew like in forest fire detection, nuclear plant monitoring or explorations in hostile environments. The challenge for these networks consists in maximizing network lifetime by means of energy efficient techniques. In this chapter, we first introduce basic concepts with regard to energy efficiency and present the four classes of energy efficient techniques: energy efficient routing, node activity scheduling, optimizing the transferred information and adapting transmission power to the topology. We then focus more particularly on energy efficient routing and classify existing protocols according different criteria: data centric, hierarchical, geographical, energy criteria used for route selection, multipath routing and support of sleeping nodes. We present EOLSR, the energy efficient extension of the OLSR routing protocol supporting different types of networks like IEEE 802.11 and IEEE 802.15.4. We compare its performance with multipath routing. Node energy consumption can be considerably reduced by scheduling node activity. We will briefly present SERENA that increases not only the network lifetime but also the amount of user data delivered. Hence, SERENA contributes to a more efficient use of energy and can be used with any routing protocol. To design a network protocol, two approaches have been traditionally used: a generic one that can lead to poor performance for some applications and the opposite one, specifically designed for a given application (e.g. data gathering). An in-between approach taking into account application specificities and environmental constraints by means of cross layering provides a very promising trade-off leading to improved performance and reactivity. We show how EOLSR benefits from cross layering with (1) the MAC layer by a better reactivity to topology changes and (2) the application layer by a reduced overhead. This induces an increased network lifetime.

1. MOTIVATIONS

Applications as various as environmental monitoring, nuclear plant monitoring, wildlife protection, emergency rescue, exploration of hostile environments are supported by wireless ad hoc and sensor networks. In these networks, some nodes can be battery-operated. It can be difficult, expensive or even impossible to renew their energy, when exhausted. Protocols operating in such networks should be designed with the target of maximizing network lifetime. We will first study how node energy is spent. We will define the states of a radio node and the consumption power in each state. Energy efficient techniques should take into account the specificities of these wireless networks to provide satisfying solutions.

1.1. States of a radio node

A wireless radio node can be in one of the following four states: *Transmit, Receive, Idle* or *Sleep*. Each state corresponds to a different power level (see Table 1):

· *Transmit*: node is transmitting a frame with transmission power $P_{transmit}$;

· *Receive*: node is receiving a frame with reception power $P_{receive}$. This frame can be decoded by this node or not, it can be intended to this node or not; · *Idle (listening)*: even when no messages are being transmitted over the medium, the nodes stay idle and keep listening the medium with power P_{idle};

· *Sleep*: the radio is turned off and the node is not capable of detecting radio signals: no communication is possible. The P_{sleep} power is largely the smallest one.

Table 1. Energy consumption in different states.

State	Power value (W)		Current (mA)
	802.11	**802.15.4**	**802.15.4**
Transmit	1.3	0.1404	33.1mA
Receive	0.9	0.1404	33.5 mA
Idle	0.74	0.0018	
Sleep	0.047	0.000018	0.005mA

Table 1 gives the energy consumption for different states of an IEEE 802.11 node [1] and a ZigBee node [2] implementing the IEEE 802.15.4 medium access. In both cases, we notice that the least consuming state is the *Sleep* state. The *Transmit* and *Receive* states consume the same amount of energy with ZigBee.

1.2. Specificities of wireless ad hoc and sensor networks

Wireless ad hoc and sensor networks have in common some specificities that have to be taken into account by energy efficient techniques:

∞ *Radio interferences*: Indeed, when a node N_1 is transmitting to a neighbor node N_2, no other node in the transmission range of N_1 can receive another frame. Similarly, no other node in the transmission range of N_2 can send another frame.

∞ *Radio link versatility*: as the propagation conditions change very frequently, the quality of a radio link varies strongly in the time.

∞ *Limited network resources*
  o Limited bandwidth: the wireless bandwidth has a capacity much smaller than a wired one (e.g. 11Mb/s for an IEEE 802.11b medium and 250 Kb/s for an IEEE 802.15.4 medium).
  o Limited memory: for a routing protocol, for instance, the routing table and the neighborhood table should be minimized.
  o Limited processing power: the protocol should be kept simple.

∞ *Battery operated nodes*: such nodes sleep to spare energy. Hence, sleeping nodes must be supported.

Depending on the considered application, additional requirements can be:
  ∞ *Mobility support*: it is an evident requirement for VANETs (Vehicular Ad hoc Networks), for instance. It is usually not required in data gathering applications.
  ∞ *Scalability*: in large (i.e. a high number of nodes) or dense (i.e. a high number of neighbors per node), such requirement is necessary.
  ∞ *Quality of Service (QoS) support*: multimedia applications for instance, require QoS support.

These specificities make difficult energy efficiency and lead to favor simple techniques. For instance, a routing protocol should meet the following requirements [3], as expressed by the 6LowPAN and ROLL working groups at IETF:
  ∞ It should induce a low overhead on routing packets as well as on data packets.
  ∞ It should have minimal memory and computation requirements.
  ∞ It should support sleeping nodes.

1.3. Chapter organization

In this chapter, we will first define the concept of network lifetime, and identify in section 2, four classes of energy efficient techniques, whose purpose is to increase network lifetime. Each of them uses different means that will be briefly described.

In section 3, we will focus on energy efficient routing. Energy efficient routing protocols can be analyzed according to different criteria such as: data centric, hierarchical, geographical, energy criteria used for route selection, multipath routing, and support of sleeping nodes. Examples of routing protocols will be given for each criterion.

In section 4, we will detail the EOLSR routing protocol, the energy efficient extension of OLSR [4]. We will see how this protocol selects the route minimizing the energy needed for an end-to-end transmission and avoids nodes with low residual energy. The EOLSR protocol [5] can be adapted to different types of networks: IEEE 802.11 or IEEE 802.15.4, with and without sleeping nodes, for instance. We will then compare the performance of EOLSR with other routing protocols such as OLSR and multipath routing. We will evaluate the increase in network lifetime and amount of user traffic delivered.

Section 5 will show that node energy can be more efficiently used and energy consumption considerably reduced by scheduling node activity. We will present SERENA, [6] an algorithm based on node coloring to schedule node activity and evaluate its benefit on the network lifetime. As expected, combining EOLSR with SERENA leads to cumulative benefits.

Another way to improve the performance of a routing protocol is given by cross-layering, the topic addressed in section 6. Cross-layering with the MAC layer will improve route stability and routing protocol reactivity to topology changes. Cross-layering with the application will spare network resources by meeting the application requirements and not a superset of them (e.g; maintaining routes only to the intended destinations and not to any other network node).

Finally we conclude in Section 7 and give some perspectives for further research.

2. CLASSIFICATION OF ENERGY EFFICIENT TECHNIQUES

All energy efficient techniques share the same goal: to maximize network lifetime. Unfortunately, there is no definition of network lifetime commonly agreed in the literature.

2.1. Definition of network lifetime

Several definitions of network lifetime exist, the most frequently used are:

∞ *Definition D1: Time to first node failure due to battery outage.* As sensor redundancy is generally used, a sensor failure can have no influence on the network and application functionalities. That is why, some authors prefer the time to the failure of a certain percentage of the sensors (e.g. 20%), in order to take into account possible redundancy.

∞ *Definition D2: Time to application failure*: an application functionality is no longer ensured (e.g. a vital parameter of a patient is no longer monitored). Definition D1 differs from definition D2 because of redundancy in sensor coverage. Indeed, if an area is covered by *k* sensors, the failure of *k-1* of them is perfectly tolerated.

∞ *Definition D3: Time to first network partitioning.* As soon as the network is no longer connected, vital information can no longer be transferred to its destination.

In the absence of knowledge of the application supported by the network, definitions D1 and D3 are the most useful ones to compare different energy efficient strategies.

2.2. Classification of energy efficient techniques

The energy constrained nature of wireless nodes requires the use of energy efficient strategies to maximize network lifetime. We can classify these strategies in four categories [7]:

1) **Topology control by tuning node transmission power**: these strategies have been proposed to reduce energy consumption and improve network capacity, while maintaining network connectivity. The key idea to topology control is that instead of transmitting using the maximal power, each node adjusts its power transmission. Thus, energy dissipated in transmission is reduced and a new network topology is created. These strategies like for instance [8], [9], [10], [11], [12] and [13] have the advantage of: (i) reducing energy consumption (power grows at least quadratically with distance), (ii) reducing interferences, (iii) improving spatial reuse and (iv) mitigating the medium access contention.

2) **Reducing information transfers**: these strategies consists in:

∞ aggregating information (e.g.; a node sends to its parent a single message containing the values transmitted by its children), with the use of clusters, like LEACH [14], [15] or without, like [16], [17] and SPIN [18];

∞ decreasing the frequency of information refreshment with distance according to the Fish Eye principle, like [19] and [20];

∞ tuning the refreshment period of control messages (e.g.; neighborhood discovery, topology dissemination, data gathering tree structure).

∞ avoiding to transfer information to uninterested nodes, like [21], [22], [23], [24], [25], [26] and [27].

3) **Node activity scheduling**: as seen in Table1, the power value in sleeping state is very small compared to the power value in any other state. Hence, allowing nodes to sleep saves energy. However, it is wasteful to send a message to a sleeping receiver, it is then necessary to coordinate neighbor nodes. Moreover, sleeping nodes must not prevent the application functionalities. That is why scheduling node activity is required. Such strategies allow nodes to sleep in order to spare energy, provided that the network and application functionalities are still ensured, like [28], [29], [30], [31] and [32].

4) **Energy efficient routing**: their goal is to minimize the energy consumed by the end-to-end transmission of a packet, to avoid nodes with a low residual energy and reduce the number of unsuccessful transmissions, like [33] to [52]. We will study these protocols in more details in the next section.

3. ENERGY AWARE ROUTING

Energy efficient routing is aware of energy dissipated during a transmission. In all cases, an energy consumption model is needed to conclude in favor of an increase in network lifetime. Indeed, this model can be used by the routing protocol itself to take decisions based on energy, and/or by the protocol designers to evaluate the performances of their protocol by simulation or mathematical modeling.

3.1. Energy consumption model

Let *Duration* denote the transmission duration of a packet and $P_{transmit}$ (respectively $P_{receive}$) be the transmission power (respectively the reception power). The energy dissipated in transmitting E_{trans} or receiving E_{rcv} a packet is evaluated as follows:

$$E_{trans} = P_{transmit} * Duration,$$

$E_{rcv} = P_{receive}$ *Duration.*

When a transmitter transmits a packet to next hop, because of the shared nature of wireless medium, all its neighbors receive this packet even it is intended to only one of them, we speak here about overhearing. Moreover, each node located between transmitter range and interference range receives this packet but cannot decode it. Hence, we can refine the *Receive* state in three substates:

- ∞ *Receive*: when this node is the packet destination,
- ∞ *Overhear*: when this node is an one-hop neighbor of the sender and is not the destination,
- ∞ *Interfere*: when this node is a two-hop neighbor of the sender.

Interference and overhearing generate loss of energy. Some protocols have taken into account both problems, others have considered only one of them. So energy dissipated by a transmission by sender i is calculated as follows [42]:

$$cost_{transmission}(i) = E_{trans} + n * E_{rcv}, \qquad (Eq.1)$$

where n represents:

- ∞ the number of one-hop non-sleeping neighbors of transmitter i, if the protocol takes into account only overhearing,
- ∞ or all non-sleeping nodes belonging to the interference zone of the transmitter i, if the protocol takes into account energy dissipated by overhearing and interferences.

This cost indicates the quantity of energy consumed by a packet of the flow to reach the next hop.

The energy dissipated by an end-to-end transmission over a path P can be computed as follows:

$$cost_P = \sum_{i \in sender(P)} cost_{transmission}(i). \quad (Eq.2)$$

3.2. Classification of energy efficient routing protocols

There exist many energy-aware routing protocols designed for wireless sensor networks. Our purpose is not to give an exhaustive list but rather to present a classification of these protocols. All of them aim at minimizing the energy consumed either in active communications, or in inactivity periods, or both. Some of them make assumptions on the application model (e.g. query of data meeting some attributes). Some build clusters to reduce the number of transmissions. Others use location based information to limit the broadcast of queries. Furthermore, some of them use multipath routing, in order to balance the energy consumption over the network nodes. They can also be distinguished according to the criteria used to select routes. Finally, we get the classification of Table 2 and organized according to the following criteria:

- ∞ data centric,
- ∞ hierarchical,
- ∞ geographical,
- ∞ energy criteria used for route selection,
- ∞ multipath routing,
- ∞ support of sleeping nodes.

A data centric routing protocol optimizes traffic by querying sensor nodes based on their data attributes or interests. It assumes a query driven model of data delivery and a routing based on data attributes. A generic routing protocol does not make such assumptions. Examples of data centric routing protocols are SPIN [18], and Directed Diffusion [44]. In SPIN, a node advertises the availability of data allowing interested nodes to query that data. However, this protocol does not ensure the end-to-end delivery of data if intermediate nodes are not interested in that data. In Directed Diffusion, the sink broadcasts an interest message to sensors, interested sensors reply with a gradient message. Both interest and gradient messages allow the sink to establish paths to sensor nodes. Then the sink reinforces the selected path to the sensor node. This protocol is efficient only with on demand query.

A hierarchical routing protocol improves scalability and minimizes traffic by building clusters. Each sensor transmits its data to its cluster head that is in charge of aggregating them and sending them to the sink. On the contrary, in a flat protocol, all sensor nodes can forward data to the sink if they are in communication range. The most famous hierarchical routing protocol is LEACH [14], where the cluster head is chosen according to its signal strength. Energy consumption is balanced by a random change of cluster heads. Initially, LEACH supports only single hop routing between both a sensor node and its cluster head and between a cluster head and the sink. TEEN [46], is another example of hierarchical protocol. TEEN is also data centric. It builds clusters of different levels until reaching the sink node. The cluster head broadcasts two thresholds to the nodes: only a value of the sensed attribute higher than the hard threshold can force the sensor node to transmit, and if this sensor was already transmitting only changes higher than the soft threshold should be transmitted. This mechanism considerably reduces the number of transmissions. However, TEEN is not adapted to periodic queries. An extension called APTEEN [47] has been proposed.

A geographical routing protocol improves routing by using location information. Each sensor node is assumed to know its location (e.g. with GPS for instance). Hence, the broadcast of a query can be limited to a given region, as in GEAR [49]. In this protocol, a node forwards a packet to its neighbor that is the closest one to the destination. If all neighbors are at the same distance, some neighbor is randomly selected. GAF

[48] is another example of geographical routing protocol energy aware. Indeed, each node uses the knowledge of its location provided by its GPS to determine its region in the virtual grid. Nodes located in the same region of the grid are considered equivalent from the routing point of view. Moreover, GAF allows nodes to sleep as long as the existence of an active node per region in the virtual grid is achieved.

Energy criteria taken into account for route selection enable to distinguish between protocols selecting (i) the minimum energy path like [37], (ii) the path avoiding nodes with low residual energy like REAR [39] and (iii) the path of minimum energy while avoiding nodes with low residual energy, like EOLSR. The protocols [38] and [39] are presented in more details in section 3.3, whereas EOLSR is described in section 4.

Multipath routing protocols maintain several paths for the same couple (source, destination). As energy is taken into account, the path minimizing the energy consumed by an end-to-end transmission is usually selected as the primary path. Another path, called the secondary one, is used less frequently, with a probability inversely proportional to its energy cost. The source selects for each data packet to transmit, the path to use according to this probability. Source routing is generally used to force the data packet to follow the path selected by the source. Protocols described in [33] to [36] are multipath routing protocols. They are presented in more details in subsection 3.4. On the contrary, with a hop-by-hop routing protocol, a data packet does not contain its path and is routed to the next hop, at each visited node. EOLSR, presented in section 4, is an example of such a protocol.

A routing protocol can support sleeping nodes. As the sleep state is the least consuming state, making nodes sleep during their inactivity period spares energy. Such protocols have to maintain both network connectivity and application functionalities. As examples, we can cite GAF [48], SPAN [50] and PEN [51]. In SPAN, nodes build a connected backbone such that only nodes belonging to this backbone are active. These nodes are called coordinators. A node decides to become a coordinator using a random backoff delay, function of its residual energy and the number of neighbors it can bridge.

Table 2 summarizes this classification and provides examples of energy-aware routing protocols in wireless sensor networks. In the route selection column, we distinguish different criteria used to select the route:

∞ *residual* means that the residual energy of nodes is taken into account,

∞ *overhear* means that the route minimizing the energy dissipated during a transmission is selected, taking into account the energy lost in overhearing.

∞ *interfere* means that the route minimizing the energy dissipated during a transmission is selected, taking into account the energy lost in interferences.

Other classifications exist, like for instance this given in [43] that does not take into account the support of sleeping nodes.

Table 2. Classification of energy aware routing protocols.

Protocol	Data centric	Hier	Geo	Multi path	Route Select.	Sleep node
SPIN [18]	yes					
Directed Diffusion [44]	yes					
LEACH [14]		yes			residual	
TEEN [46]	yes	yes				
EAP [52]		yes				yes
GAF [48]			yes			yes
GEAR [49]			yes			
REAR [39]					residual	
Ganesan [34]				yes		
Srinivas [35]				yes		
Sha [33]				yes	residual	
Kwon [38]					residual overhear interfere	
EOLSR [5]					Residual overhear interfere	yes with Serena[6]

Residual means that the residual energy of nodes is taken into account, whereas *overhear* (respectively *interfere*) means that the route minimizing the energy dissipated during a transmission is selected, taking into account the energy lost in overhearing (respectively interferences).

Table 3. Impact of routing protocols on network resources.

Reduces the use of	Data centric	Hier	Geo	Multi path	Route Select.	Sleep node
bandwidh	yes	yes	yes			
memory	yes	yes	yes			
processing	yes	yes	yes			
energy	yes	yes	yes	yes	yes	yes

An energy-aware routing protocol can exhibit several criteria. For instance, EAP [52] is hierarchical and allows nodes to sleep, while ensuring the coverage of the monitored region as well as network connectivity. GAF [48] is geographical and supports sleeping nodes.

Table 3 shows the impact of routing protocols on bandwidth, memory, processing and energy capacities.

3.3. Computation of an energy efficient route

Energy aware routing protocols establish energy efficient routes to maximize network lifetime. These protocols run in wireless sensor networks subject to radio interferences. In such networks, a very interesting complexity result has been established in [40]: because of radio interferences the selection of a unicast route ensuring that each node has sufficient residual energy is NP-hard. This result is still valid, even if radio interferences were limited to a single hop.

We now focus on the criteria used by energy aware routing to select energy efficient routes. We can distinguish three families of energy aware routing protocols [7]:

• *the protocols selecting the path consuming the minimum energy*. The advantage is that each transmission of a packet from its source to its destination minimizes the energy consumed. We can cite for instance [37] and a more sophisticated protocol [38]. This routing protocol computes the additional energy dissipated by one flow when routed on a given path, taking into account the SINR and the energy lost by radio interferences. Then, it uses the Dijkstra algorithm to find the path which minimizes this additional energy. This protocol takes into account the impact of the flow transmission in the interference area. However, this protocol is complex and requires that all nodes know the global topology of the network. Furthermore, such protocols use always the same nodes (those minimizing the energy consumed) without any consideration on their residual energy. Consequently, these nodes will

exhaust their battery more quickly than the others and the network lifetime may not be maximized.

· *the protocols selecting the path visiting the nodes with the highest residual energy*, such as [39]. REAR (Reliable Energy Aware Routing) ensures that each flow is ensured to have enough energy on the selected path: nodes with low residual energy are avoided. REAR is a reactive protocol triggered by the data sink. To achieve its goal, the amount of energy needed by the end-to-end transmission of the flow must be reserved in each intermediate node. Besides, to improve reliability a second path is computed to route a flow in case of first path failure. This path is disjoint from the first path and has enough energy to route the flow. But, there is no energy resource reservation on this second path. This protocol ensures the energy necessary to route a flow in the intermediate nodes but it does not take into account energy dissipated by the reception of packets and the interferences. However, the path selected does not minimize the energy needed to transmit a flow packet from its source to its destination. Hence, the network lifetime may not be maximized.

• *the hybrid protocols selecting the path with the minimum cost*, where the cost takes into account the residual energy of each visited node (and possibly its neighbors) and the energy consumption of a packet on this path. These protocols avoid the problems encountered by the protocols of the two previous categories by weighing the factors used in the cost computation. We can cite for instance [41]. In the next section, we present an energy efficient extension of OLSR belonging to this category.

3.4. Multipath routing protocols

Multipath routing protocols rely on the following observation: using the lowest energy path leads to energy depletion of nodes along this path and in the worst case may lead to network partition. To avoid this problem and improve network lifetime, these protocols use multipath routing instead of minimum energy path.

In [33], a multipath routing, energy aware, is proposed to maximize network lifetime. It is a reactive routing protocol triggered by the data sink. It consists in finding all paths between source and destination according to a metric which takes into account 1) the energy consumed by the transmission and reception of the packet and 2) the residual energy of nodes. Paths that have a cost higher than a given threshold are discarded. At each path kept is assigned a probability inversely proportional to its cost. To route a flow packet, one path is randomly chosen by the source according to its probability. This protocol ensures load balancing by using multipath routing. Moreover, considering residual energy of nodes to compute paths enables to avoid nodes with low energy capacity.

In [35], two variants of minimum energy multipath routing are considered to improve network lifetime and reliability against nodes and links failures. These two variants are: 1) multipath with disjoint links, 2) multipath with disjoint nodes. The authors show that link disjoint path routing is more energy efficient and node disjoint path routing is more reliable. However, their model does not take interferences into account.

Performance evaluations in [35] and [36] show that the relative benefit of maintaining one additional path strongly decreases with the number of maintained paths, whereas the complexity considerably increases. Hence, maintaining two paths is generally considered sufficient.

We will now focus on EOLSR, a routing protocol that is neither data centric, nor hierarchical, nor geographical, selects the path consuming the least energy while avoiding nodes with low residual energy, maintains only one route and supports sleeping nodes, when used in combination with SERENA.

4. EOLSR: THE ENERGY EFFICIENT EXTENSION OF OLSR

4.1. Why OLSR is not energy efficient

The OLSR (Optimized Link State Routing) protocol, RFC 3626 [4], has been optimized for MANETs (Mobile Ad Hoc Networks). It can also be used in wireless sensor networks. OLSR is a proactive routing protocol where nodes periodically exchange topology information in order to establish a route to any destination in the network. It is an optimization of a pure link state routing protocol, based on the concept of *multipoint relays* (*MPRs*). First, using *multipoint relays* reduces the size of the control messages: rather than declaring all its links in the network, a node declares only the set of links with its neighbors that have selected it as "*multipoint relay*". The use of *MPRs* also minimizes flooding of control traffic. Indeed only *multipoint relays* forward control messages. This technique significantly reduces the number of retransmissions of broadcast messages.

OLSR provides two main functionalities:

∞ *Neighborhood discovery*: An OLSR node detects its one-hop and two-hop neighbors by means of periodic Hello messages. This node independently selects its own set of MPRs among the one-hop neighbors in such a way that the MPRs cover all two-hop neighbors.

∞ *Topology dissemination*: Each node also maintains information about the network topology obtained from Topology Control (TC) messages, periodically generated by MPRs and disseminated by MPR flooding. The routing table is computed using Dijkstra's algorithm. This table provides the shortest route (i.e. the smallest hop number) to any destination in the network.

We can notice that with OLSR, intermediate nodes along a route are MPR nodes. As MPR selection does not take energy into account, the route selection is not energy aware. Hence, OLSR does not maximize network lifetime, even if network flooding is optimized by means of MPRs.

4.2. Principles of EOLSR

EOLSR [5] is the energy efficient extension of OLSR. Like OLSR, it consists of two main functionalities Neighborhood discovery and Topology dissemination. Some changes have been brought (1) in the MPR selection in order to avoid nodes with low residual energy and (2) in the route selection where the route of smallest energy cost is chosen. The energy cost is computed according to equations (Eq.1) and (Eq.2), as presented in section 4.2.2.

Unlike OLSR, two types of relay multipoint are used with EOLSR:

∞ EMPR, energy multipoint relays, used to build energy efficient routes. We will detail the EMPR selection in section 4.2.1.

∞ MPR to optimize broadcasts in the network, like in classical OLSR.

From these principles it follows that EOLSR selects the route minimizing the energy cost and avoids nodes with low residual energy.

We recall that in EOLSR, like in OLSR, only links of good quality are used for routing. For this purpose, two thresholds have been introduced:

∞ *LINK_QUALITY_PWR_HIGH* which is the minimum quality to accept a new link;

∞ *LINK_QUALITY_PWR_LOW* which is the minimum quality of an already accepted link. A previously accepted link whose quality becomes lower than this threshold is rejected.

4.2.1. Selection of EMPR in EOLSR

To enable a selection of multipoint relays energy-aware, additional information about energy has to be included in the *Hello* message. We adopt the usual assumption that interferences are limited to two hops from the transmitter.

The policy used to select EMPRs takes into account the residual energy of the EMPR candidate as well as the residual energy of its 1-hop neighbors. Its goal is to select the EMPRs such that each 2-hop node is covered by the EMPR able to support the highest number of transmissions.

Let *N* be the node selecting its EMPRs.
Let *M* be a 1-hop neighbor of *N* covering at least one 2-hop neighbor of *N*, hence *M* is an EMPR candidate of *N*.

If *M* is selected as EMPR, it will propagate the message received from *N* toward the next hop on the route. Hence, it will dissipate the energy corresponding to a transmission and a receipt.

That is why, the EMPR selection algorithm weighs the residual energy of an EMPR candidate *M*, denoted $E_R(M)$, by the energy dissipated in a transmission and a receipt. This quantity represents the number of transmissions that *M* is able to support.

Algorithm of EMPR selection:

Let *N* be the considered node.
. *N* inserts in the set *Uncovered* all its 2-hop neighbors,
. *N* orders its one-hop neighbors *M* by decreasing order of :

min
$$\left(\frac{E_R(M)}{P_{transmit} + P_{receive}}, \min_{D \in N1(M)} (\frac{E_R(D)}{2 * P_{receive}}) \right),$$
where $E_R(M)$ denotes the residual energy of node *M*.
Let *Neighbor* be this ordered set.

. *N* selects *M* the first node in *Neighbor* allowing to reach at least one node in *Uncovered* as EMPR and removes from *Uncovered* all nodes covered by *M*.

. If the node after *M* in *Neighbor* covers nodes in *Uncovered*, this node is selected as EMPR and all nodes covered by this node are removed from *Uncovered*

Let *N* be the considered node.

. *N* inserts in the set *Uncovered* all its 2-hop neighbors,
. *N* orders its one-hop neighbors *M* by decreasing order of :

$$\min \left(\frac{E_R(M)}{P_{transmit} + P_{receive}}, \min_{D \in N1(M)} (\frac{E_R(D)}{2 * P_{receive}}) \right),$$
where $E_R(M)$ denotes the residual energy of node *M*.
Let *Neighbor* be this ordered set.

. *N* selects *M* the first node in *Neighbor* allowing to reach at least one node in *Uncovered* as EMPR and removes from *Uncovered* all nodes covered by *M*.

. If the node after *M* in *Neighbor* covers nodes in *Uncovered*, this node is selected as EMPR and all nodes covered by this node are removed from *Uncovered*.

. And so on until *Uncovered* is empty.

We can notice that the algorithm of EMPR selection tends to share the energy consumption between the different nodes. This selection avoids that nodes deplete their battery more quickly than others.

However, with regard to the native MPR selection algorithm, this new algorithm introduces more frequent route changes. To limit these changes, we recommend to change the EMPR selection, only if the two following conditions are met:

(1) there is at least one 2-hop neighbor such that :
$$\frac{E_R(newEMPR) - E_R(oldEMPR)}{E_R(oldEMPR)} \geq ThresholdChange$$

Where *ThreshlodChange* limits the frequency of EMPRs changes. It can be set equal to 10%, for instance.

(2) the residual energy of the new EMPR is sufficient:
$$E_R(newEMPR) \geq ThresholdMinEnergy$$
This avoids frequent changes when the residual energy of an EMPR tends to 0.

Each node computes its EMPRs and its MPRs before sending its periodic *Hello*.

4.2.2 Route selection in EOLSR

As previously said, EOLSR selects the route of minimum energy cost. This cost depends on the network type. EOLSR distinguishes the networks where:

∞   *Nodes do not sleep*: we distinguish two cases:

○ *Nodes are in the idle state when the medium is idle,* like in IEEE 802.11. In this case, the energy dissipated in receiving + overhearing + interferences takes into account the number of nodes in the 1-hop and 2-hop neighborhood of each sender of the considered flow.

$$Cost(flow) = \sum_{i \in Sender(flow)} \left(E_{transmit}(i) + \sum_{j \in N1(i) \cup N2(i)} E_{receive}(j) \right) (Eq.3)$$

○ *Nodes stay in the receive state when the medium is idle,* like in ZigBee. In order to select the route maximizing network capacity, we take the smallest route.

$$Cost(flow) = \sum_{i \in Sender(flow)} E_{transmit}(i) \quad (Eq.4)$$

∞ *Nodes sleep as with SERENA,* an algorithm that will be described in section 5. A node is allowed to sleep when neither itself nor its 1-hop neighbors have a message to transmit. Hence, only 1-hop neighbors have to be taken into account in the energy cost, leading to:

$$Cost(flow) = \sum_{i \in Sender(flow)} \left(E_{transmit}(i) + \sum_{j \in N1(i)} E_{receive}(j) \right) (Eq.5)$$

If several routes dissipate the same energy, the shortest one is chosen.

4.2.3. Optimized broadcasts

EOLSR keeps the optimization of network broadcasts, as in OLSR. Multipoint relays are used in OLSR to optimize network flooding by means of the following forwarding rule:
OLSR forwarding rule: a node forwards once a broadcast message with a non-null time-to-live only if it has received this message for the first time from a node that has selected it as MPR.

We will see why in section 4.3.4, that MPRs and not EMPRs optimize network flooding.

We notice that this extension of OLSR does not need additional messages. Existing messages of OLSR include additional information related to energy.

4.3. Comparative performance evaluation of energy efficient routing protocols

We now compare the performances of OLSR, EOLSR, multipath routing with disjoint links, denoted *DL* and multipath routing with disjoint nodes, denoted *DN*. With *DN* and *DL* two paths are maintained, as it has been proved generally sufficient.

4.3.1. Simulation parameters

We use the NS2 simulation tool. We consider that nodes are uniformly distributed in the network area. The number of nodes ranges from 50 to 200. The network density is set to 10, it represents the average number of neighbors per node. Each node implements the IEEE 802.11b PHY-MAC layers, the IP network layer with the energy efficient extension of OLSR. Network bandwidth is set to 2Mbps. The transmission range is equal to 250m, interferences are limited to 2-hop. We consider 30 point-to-point CBR flows, whose sources and destinations are randomly chosen. The packet size is set to 512 bytes and the interarrival time

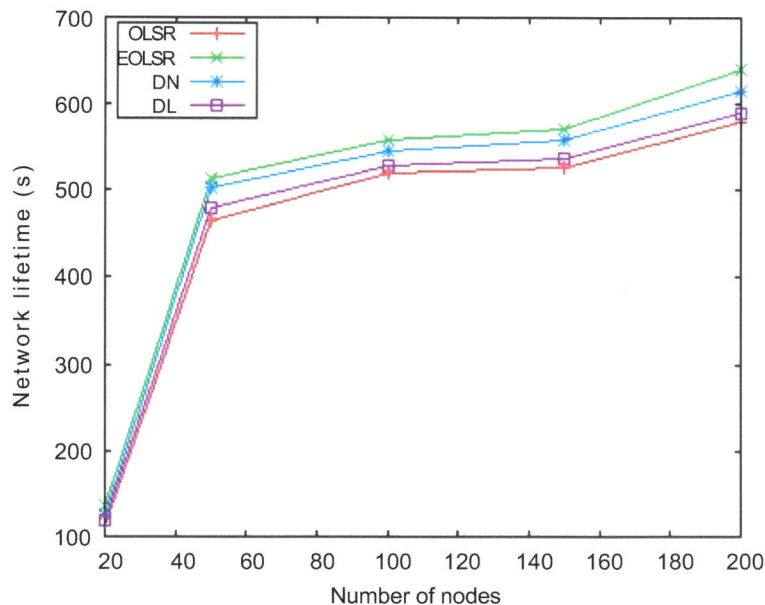

Fig. (1). Network lifetime.

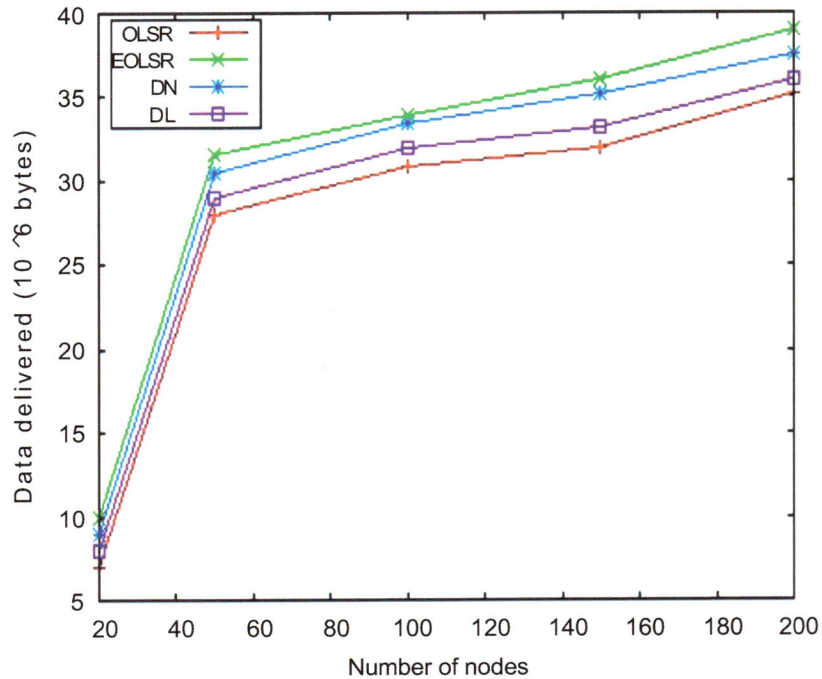

Fig. (2). Amount of data delivered to the user.

is 250ms. Initially, each node has a residual energy of 60 Joules. Energy consumption computation is done according to the model presented in Section 3.1. Results are the average of ten simulations.

4.3.2. Network lifetime

We compare the network lifetime obtained with OLSR, EOLSR, *DN* and *DL*. Simulation results are depicted on Figure 1.

As expected, OLSR provides the smallest network lifetime. This is not surprising since it does not take energy into account. Moreover, it shows that the selection of the shortest path is not sufficient to save energy. Concerning the two 2-path source routing strategies, *DN* provides better results than *DL*. Indeed, energy is dissipated per nodes and not per wireless link. Hence, *DL* that allows common nodes in the two paths can exhaust the energy of these common nodes more quickly. The main conclusion of these experiments is that EOLSR significantly outperforms *DN* and *DL* whatever the number of nodes. Moreover, the gain is increasing with the network size. EOLSR prolongs the network lifetime of 33% compared with OLSR for a network of 200 nodes. Notice that in the same conditions, *DN* prolongs the network lifetime of only 10%. Indeed, the two paths chosen by the source of the flow are used for all flow packets independently of the residual energy of these nodes. So the intermediates nodes exhaust their energy more quickly.

4.3.3. Amount of user data delivered

From the user point of view, an increased network lifetime can present no interest if the amount of user data is not higher. That is why, we evaluate the data amount delivered to the user. Simulation results are depicted on Figure 2.

We observe that the benefit obtained with EOLSR in terms of increased network lifetime is followed by an increase in the amount of user data delivered. In other words, this benefit is a real one that can be perceived by the application. Indeed, a higher amount of user data is delivered.

4.3.4. Overhead of EOLSR

We now evaluate the overhead induced by EOLSR. For this purpose, we evaluate the number of retransmissions per TC. We compare the number of retransmissions of a TC in OLSR, EOLSR and in a variant where EMPRs are used instead of MPRs to optimize network flooding. Simulation results are depicted on Figure 3.

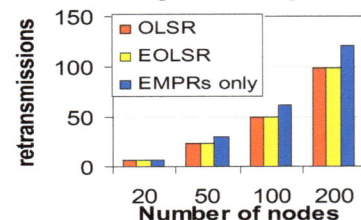

Fig. (3). Number of retransmissions per TC.

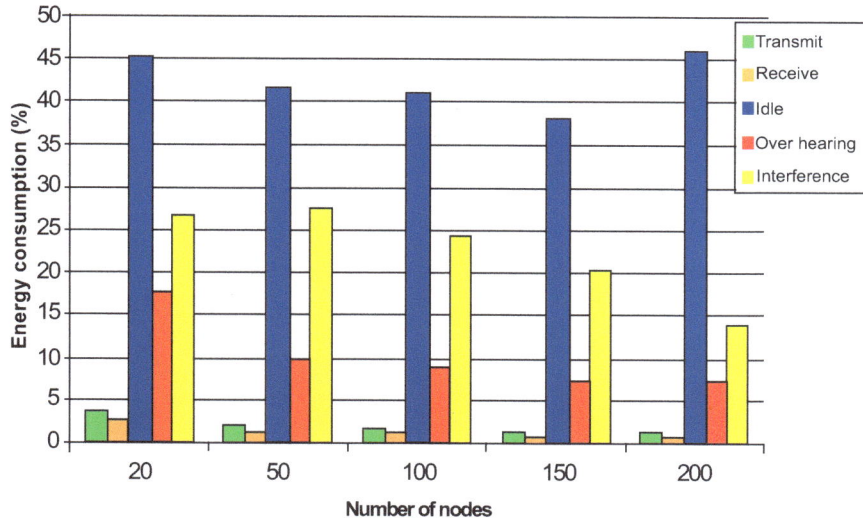

Fig. (4). Distribution of energy consumption with OLSR.

Figure 3 shows that the number of retransmissions is minimized when MPRs are in charge of optimizing the broadcast. EMPRs induce a higher overhead. This difference increases with the number of nodes and the density.

5. A MORE EFFICIENT ENERGY USE

5.1. Energy consumption distribution

We now focus on how a node uses its energy. We always consider the simulation parameters given in subsection 4.3.1 and study the distribution of energy consumption in the states previously defined in subsection 3.1, obtained with OLSR (see Figure 4) and EOLSR (see Figure 5).

Figure 4 depicts the average on all network nodes of the energy consumption in the different states, when the OLSR routing protocol is used. It appears that in the conditions of the simulation, the highest part (about 50%) of energy consumed in a network of 100 nodes is dissipated in the *Idle* state. Then come the *Interferences* (with 30%). *Overhearing* arrives in third position (with 10%). Finally, the energy dissipated in the two useful states *Transmit* and *Receive* is very small (about 3%). These results show that the highest energy cumulative consumptions are due to the *Idle* and *Interference* states. An energy aware routing protocol can limit the energy spent in *Interferences*, as we will see on Figure 5.

With EOLSR, we observe an improvement (see Figure 5): less energy is lost in interferences. However, the least important part of energy is dissipated in the *Receive* and *Transmit* states that are the only states that matter from the application point of view. Too much energy is spent in the *Idle* state. That is why, node

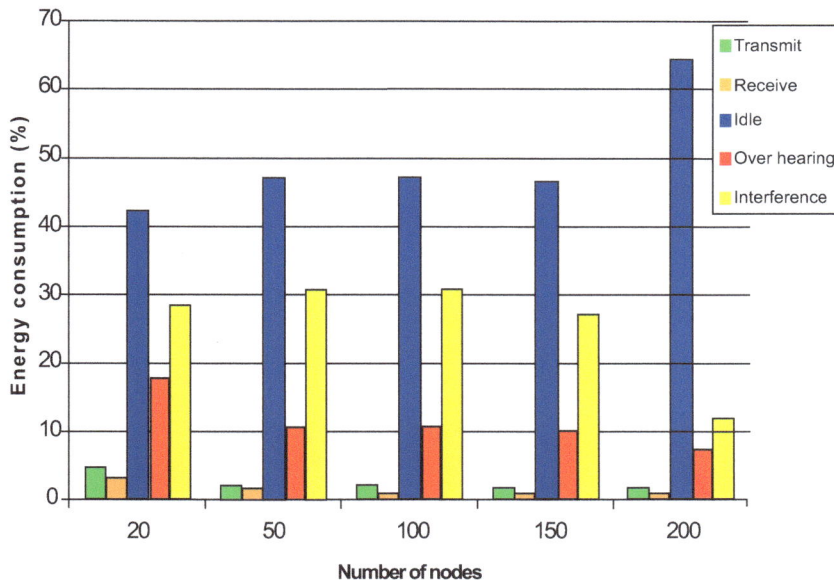

Fig. (5). Distribution of energy consumption with EOLSR.

activity scheduling is introduced: nodes that have nothing to transmit and receive can enter the S*leep* state. These results allow us to conclude that the most energy efficient techniques are those allowing nodes to sleep. Energy aware routing techniques come after.

5.2. Node activity scheduling

Node activity scheduling alternates node activity and sleeping periods. As it is wasteful to transmit a message to a sleeping node, node activity must be coordinated. As an example of node activity scheduling, we present SERENA [6], an algorithm to SchEdule RoutEr Nodes Activity. It allows nodes to sleep, while ensuring end-to-end communication in the wireless network. It is a localized and decentralized algorithm assigning time slots to nodes.

Sleeping rule: Any node stays awake only during its slots to transmit its messages and during the slots assigned to its one-hop neighbors to receive their messages. It sleeps the remaining time.

SERENA proceeds in two steps:

∞   First it performs three-hop coloring. It assigns a color to each node in the network such that two nodes that are one, two or three hops neighbors have two different colors. Hence, a color is reused four hops away. Three hop coloring has been shown NP-hard.

∞   Second, it assigns time slots to nodes according to their color. These slots are used to transmit in unicast or broadcast.

We now justify the choice of three-hop coloring. Generally, in wireless ad hoc and sensor networks, interferences are assumed to be limited to two hops. Hence, two transmitters at a distance strictly higher than two transmission ranges can transmit simultaneously. For this reason, at least two hop coloring algorithm is necessary to prevent collisions. However, if we consider a unicast transmission, immediate acknowledgement is used to confirm the correct receipt of the message by its destination. In this case, two-hop coloring does not suffice to prevent collisions as we can see on node $N3$ in Figure 6 where we consider four nodes $N1$, $N2$, $N3$ and $N4$. Nodes $N1$ and $N4$ have the same color. When the slot

assigned to this color arrives, node $N1$ sends a frame to node $N2$ that acknowledges, while node $N4$ sends a frame to its neighbour node $N3$. The acknowledgement sent by $N2$ enters in collision on node $N3$ with the frame sent by $N4$ to its neighbor $N3$. That is why three-hop coloring is used.

The idea of the three hop coloring is to assign one color to each node in the network such that the following requirements are met:

• two nodes that are one, two or three-hop neighbors have distinct colors,
• the number of colors used is as small as possible,
• the complexity of the algorithm is minimized,
• the algorithm is distributed and localized: only information about one, two and three-hop neighbors is used to run the algorithm.

First, each node in the network computes its priority. The priority of a node N is defined as the cardinality of *Neighbor3(N)*, where *Neighbor3(N)* denotes the set of one-hop, two-hop, three-hop nodes of N. The node with the highest cardinality receives the highest priority. If several nodes have the same cardinality, the node with the smallest identifier wins. Nodes color themselves according to the order given by their priority.

Coloring rule: For any node N, if all nodes in Neighbor3(N) with a higher priority than N, are already colored, N selects the smallest color unused in Neighbor3(N). Colors are assumed to be positive integers.

Each node N sends to its one-hop neighbors, a message *Color* containing its identifier, its priority, its color if already assigned, its list of one-hop neighbors, their priority and the list of colors already used by them, its list of two-hop neighbors, their priority and the list of colors already used by them. Hence, each node N in the network can build its neighborhood up to three hops and knows all the colors already assigned to nodes in *Neighbor3(N)*.

Slots are then granted to each color. Each node behaves according to the sleeping rule.

5.3. Performance evaluation

5.3.1 Performance and complexity of the coloring algorithm

The performance of a coloring algorithm is given by the number of colors needed to color all network nodes and the time complexity. Simulations have been run for different network topologies. Each network topology is characterized by a number of nodes and a density. The number of nodes ranges from 50 to 200 and the

Fig. (6). Collision on node N3 in case of immediate acknowledgement.

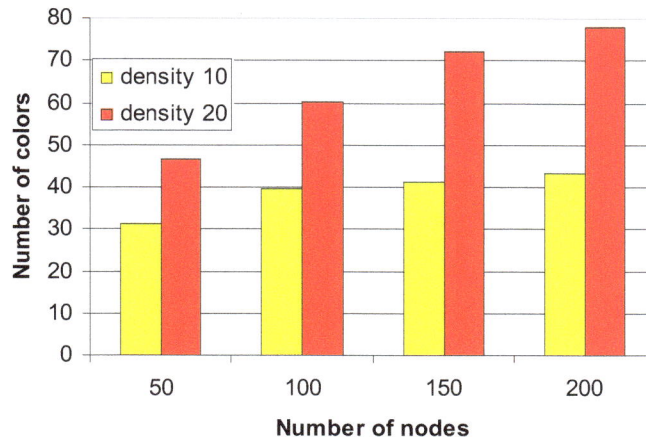

Fig. (7). Number of colors with SERENA.

density is either 10 or 20. Each result is the average of 100 simulations. The number of colors is depicted on Figure 7. We observe that the number of colors strongly depends on the density and in a less extent of the number of nodes.

This distributed coloring algorithm does not require a synchronous system. However, for simplicity reasons, we use the term round to evaluate the time complexity of this algorithm.

A round is defined such that each node can:

- ∞ send a message to all its one-hop neighbors,
- ∞ receive the messages sent by them,
- ∞ perform some local computation based on the information contained in the received messages.

Figure 8 depicts the number of rounds needed to color all network nodes. We observe that the number of rounds needed to color all network nodes is close

to the number of nodes, whereas the worst theoretical case is three times this number.

5.3.2 Network lifetime and amount of user data delivered

We now consider a network whose number of nodes varies from 50 to 200, whereas the density is equal to 10. There is a number of CBR flows at 4 kb/s equal to half of the number of nodes. The sources and destinations of these flows are randomly selected. The initial energy of each node is equal to 100 Joules. A time slot of 15 ms is assigned to each color.

We evaluate the benefit brought by SERENA by comparing the lifetime obtained with and without SERENA. It appears on Figure 9 that for a network of 100 nodes, the network lifetime is doubled with SERENA.

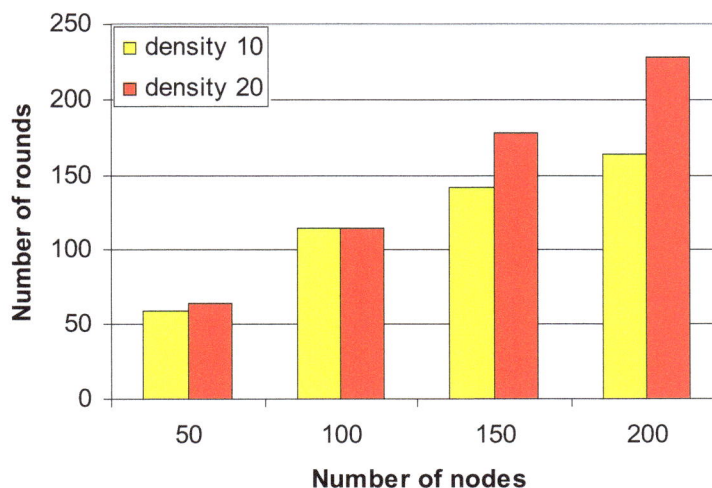

Fig.8. Number of rounds with SERENA.

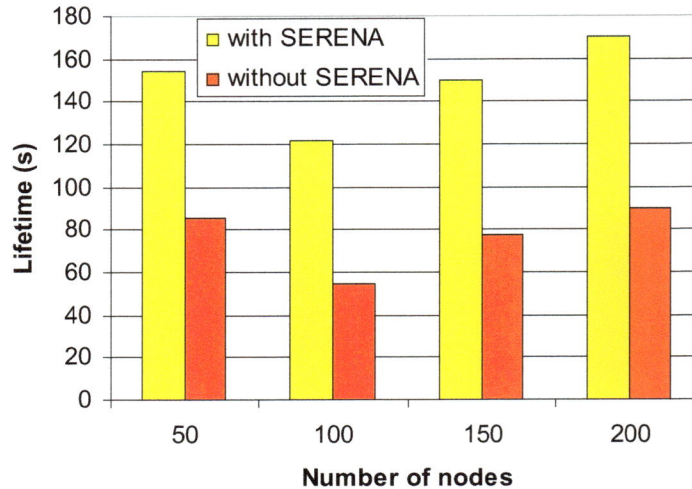

Fig. (9). Network lifetime with and without SERENA.

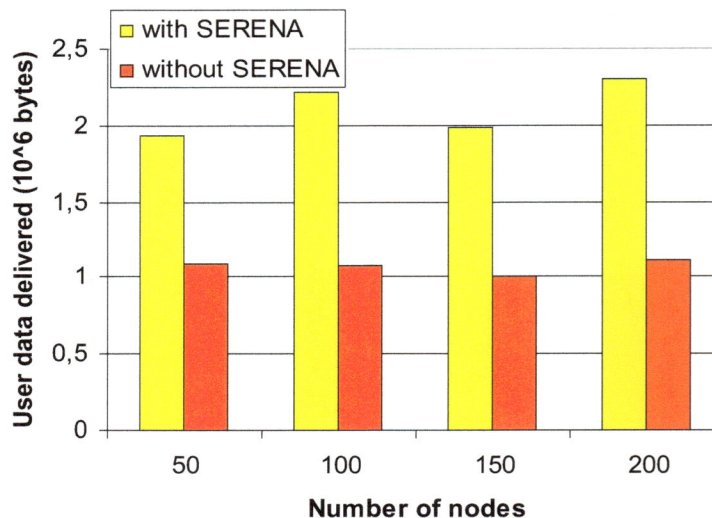

Fig. 10. Amount of user data delivered with and without SERENA.

Figure 10 shows that the increase of network lifetime is a true benefit for the application, insofar as being alive a longer time, the network can transmit and deliver more user data.

5.3.3. Comparative benefits of SERENA and EOLSR

We now compare the benefits brought respectively by SERENA and EOLSR, used alone or in combination. We consider a network of density 10. The simulation parameters are those given in subsection 4.3.1. Notice however that in these simulations a 2-hop coloring is used instead of a 3-hop coloring.

Figure 11, [58] shows that EOLSR increases the network lifetime of about 40% with regard to OLSR in a network of 150 nodes. This is due to the choice of energy efficient routes. However, the major improvement is brought by SERENA that ensures a better use of the bandwidth, limited in wireless sensor networks. All nodes colored with the same color can transmit simultaneously without collision and without interference, leading to a good spatial reuse. EOLSR and SERENA, used separately or in combination, contribute to a more efficient use of node energy and hence a higher network lifetime.

We now study the distribution of energy consumption. Simulation results are illustrated on Figure 12. We

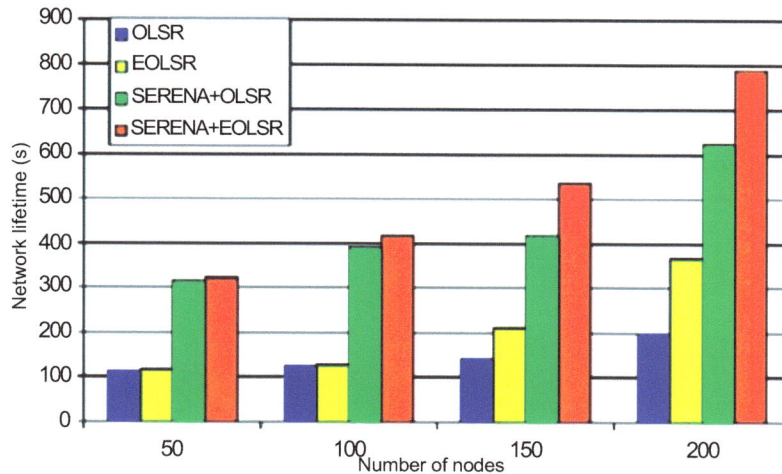

Fig. (11). Network lifetime.

notice a big improvement with regard to Figures 4 and 5. More energy is spent in the useful states *Transmit* and *Receive*. The energy dissipated in *Interferences* is very low and can be neglected. SERENA can be improved in order to minimize the energy lost in *Overhearing*. This can be done easily by locally sorting messages to transmit according to their destination: broadcast messages will be transmitted first and then unicast messages according to the destination address order. In conclusion, SERENA leads to a more efficient energy use.

Figure 11 shows the interest of using SERENA with EOLSR, leading to a more efficient use of energy.

5.3.4. SERENA in a real environment

Until now, we have considered an ideal environment, assuming that there is no message loss and all links are bidirectional. This is not true in the real world,

where messages can be lost and some radio links are unidirectional. Due to the existence of unidirectional links, color conflicts are possible.

Definition of a color conflict: a color conflict occurs between two nodes having the same color when these nodes prevent each other or some neighbor destination from correctly receiving an intended message.

Notice that this definition takes advantage of the capture effect to decrease the number of color conflicts detected. Color conflicts can also result from node mobility or late node arrivals in the network. Indeed, two nodes that have the same color and were neither 1, 2 or 3-hop neighbors can become 1, 2 or 3-hop neighbors because of node mobility or late arrivals. Such conflicts are detected by a cross-layering with the MAC layer and solved by SERENA as follows: If the node detecting the conflict can reach the conflicting node with the smallest priority, this conflicting node will take another

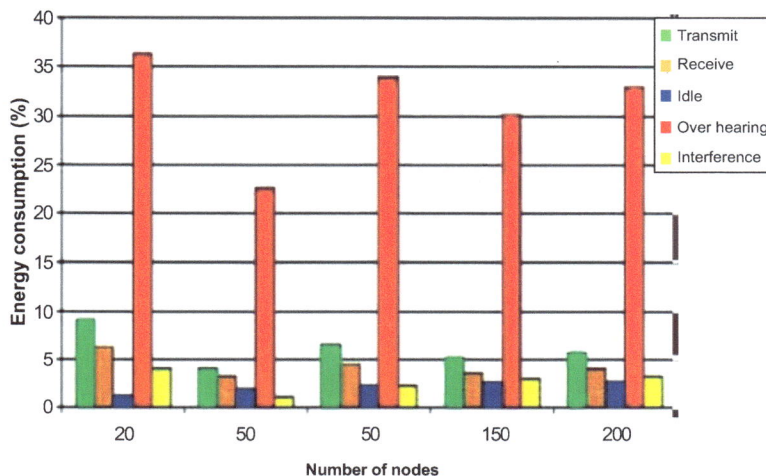

Fig. (12). Distribution of energy consumption with SERENA.

color. Otherwise, the other conflicting node will take another color.

SERENA and EOLSR are implemented in the OCARI project, (see http://ocari.lri.fr), funded by the ANR. A presentation of the architecture adopted in the OCARI project can be found in [59].

5.3.5. Applicability statement of SERENA

SERENA enables any routing protocol to support nodes that sleep while they and their one-hop neighbors have nothing to transmit. Indeed, the sleeping mode is kept transparent to the routing protocol operating on top of SERENA.

SERENA is based on three-hop node coloring for the following reasons:

- ∞   Unlike link coloring, node coloring enables both unicast and broadcast transmissions.
- ∞   Three-hop coloring enables the immediate acknowledgement of unicast transmissions.

SERENA can be clearly applied in TDMA networks. It can also be applied in CSMA networks where a network synchronization is provided. For instance, in the OCARI project, the PAN coordinator synchronizes all network nodes by means of its beacon that is broadcast multihop. More decentralized solutions are also possible, where the broadcast of the synchronization message in the network can be optimized by means of multipoint relays for instance.

6. CROSS LAYERING

6.1. Cross layering to optimize network performances

With the increasing number of applications in many domains (detection of forest fire or seismic event, wild life protection, building and bridge monitoring, emergency rescue, target tracking, exploration mission in hostile environments and home monitoring to mention only some of them), wireless sensor networks have a promising future. However, the characteristics of the layered architectures are not sufficiently flexible to cope with the specificities of wireless networks [58]. These specificities include:
• dynamically changing network conditions due to mobility or versatility of the propagation conditions on the physical medium,
• network resources of limited capacity: limited bandwidth, limited amount of energy for battery operated nodes…
• radio interferences...

They bring new constraints in designing protocols for wireless sensor networks. These protocols must be energy efficient and dynamically adaptive. Moreover, they must satisfy the quality of service desired by the applications. To meet these requirements, there were two classical approaches to design new protocols:

- ∞   Either the generic one that design protocols to suit a very high number of applications. The drawback is that it can lead to poor performances for some applications or can be too much expensive in terms of network resources. We can cite for instance [31] for scheduling node activity in sensor networks.

- ∞   Or, at the opposite, the specific approach consists in designing protocols optimized for a given type of application (e.g. data gathering by a sink node). This results in very good performances, however it provides no flexibility. As soon as the real application differs a little bit from the one considered, it can no longer be applied. Hence, this approach is not largely adopted.

Now a hybrid approach is possible, keeping the genericity of the first approach and some optimizations of the second one. This third approach, based on cross layering, optimizes the performance of communication, taking advantage of some knowledge about the application and its environment. Different cross layering architectures have been proposed:

- ∞   *Non-layered architectures* [55] are very flexible. However, their inherent complexity makes them difficult to maintain and evolve when new requirements appear.

- ∞   *Layered architectures* are favored for their ease of use, maintenance and evolution. These layered architectures can be distinguished according to the communication scheme of non-adjacent layers:
  - o   *Each layer can communicate directly with any other layer*, like in [53] and [54]. This scheme does not easily adapt to changes in a layer.

  - o   *Non adjacent layer communicate via an intermediate cross layer entity*, like in [56] and [57]. The advantage of this architecture relies on its genericity that adapts to different types of applications. This architecture is used in the OCARI project, where SERENA and EOLSR are implemented [59].

We will now focus on cross layering and detail the benefits obtained by a routing protocol when it uses cross layering.

6.2. Cross-layering between MAC and routing

With cross layering, the routing protocol can use the received signal power to decide whether a link is of acceptable quality or not. Only links with a quality higher than a given threshold will be used for routing. This feature considerably increases route stability and thus improves the quality of service perceived by the user.

Moreover, the MAC layer is the first layer to detect the breakage of a radio link presently in use. Notifying quickly the routing layer will gain time and enable a quick reaction to this breakage.

In SERENA algorithm, the cross-layering with the MAC layer is used to schedule node transmission in slots according to node colors and to identify the conflicting nodes in case of a color conflict.

6.3. Cross layering between routing and energy management

It is obvious that EOLSR requires the knowledge of the residual energy of the local node. This information is provided to the routing by the energy management of the considered node. It is used for EMPR selection as described in section 4.2.1.

6.4. Cross layering between application and routing

6.4.1 Tuning the refreshment period

In EOLSR, control information sent by *Hellos* and *TCs* is periodically refreshed. Some applications consist of different phases, each phase having its own requirements. It could then be useful to adapt the refreshment periods to these phases.

Another approach that provides very interesting results in large and dense networks is the use of the Fish Eye extension [19]. The refreshment period of an information decreases with the distance to the information source. Applied to TC messages, it means for instance that the TC is propagated once per TC period in the first zone, once per two TC periods in the second zone and once per four TC-periods in the third zone. The first zone comprises all nodes up to three hops from the TC originator, the second zone contains all nodes between four and six hops and the third zone all the remaining nodes. The overhead induced by the routing protocol can be considerably reduced, see [20] for a quantitative evaluation.

6.4.2 Maintaining routes to strategic nodes

In data gathering applications, for instance or in more general applications, we can identify *strategic* nodes

such as sink nodes, supervision nodes.... The other nodes in the network only need to know a route to these strategic nodes [58]. It will be profitable to the routing protocol to build and maintain only such routes instead of a route to any other node in the network. In such a case, we recommend that only the strategic nodes periodically broadcast a TC message.

- ∞ This TC message would contain the originator of the TC (i.e. a strategic node), a sequence number, the cost from the strategic node to the receiver.
- ∞ Upon receipt of such a message with a sequence number higher than this maintained in the local table, a node would take the node from which the TC has been received as the next hop to the strategic node, originator of the TC.
- ∞ Upon receipt of a TC with the same sequence number, the next hop to the TC originator is changed only if the received cost is smaller.
- ∞   If the next hop has been changed, the cost in the TC is updated and the TC message propagated.

The benefit in terms of number of TC messages sent is illustrated by Figure 13 for a network of 100 nodes and a density of 10, with a radio range of 250m and interferences limited to two transmission ranges. Simulation results are averaged over 5 runs [58]. We evaluate the number of TC sent per EMPR node and per TC period. This number includes the TC generated by this node and the TCs forwarded by this node. The average number of EMPRs is equal to 82 in the considered simulations. We can see that as long as the number of strategic nodes is smaller than the number of EMPRs, the optimization is interesting. It contributes to reduce the routing overhead induced at the bandwidth level, the processing level, the memory level and the energy level.

6.5. Applicability statement of EOLSR

In conclusion, EOLSR can operate in two modes:
- ∞ A generic mode where each node maintains a route to any other node in the network. This mode has been detailed in section 4.
- ∞ A strategic mode where any non-strategic node maintains only a route to each strategic node. This mode has been presented in this section. It is made possible by cross-layering between the application and the routing layers.

Both modes share the same neighborhood discovery using *Hello* messages. With regard to topology dissemination, both modes use TC messages. However, in the generic mode all EMPR nodes generate TC messages, whereas in the strategic mode only strategic nodes do.

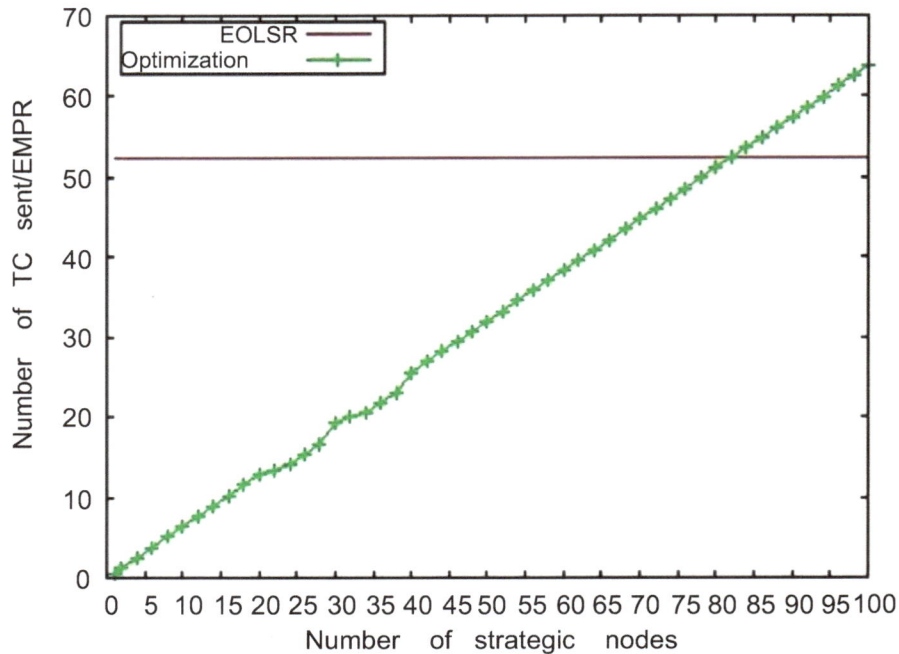

Fig. (13). Number of TCs sent per EMPR node per TC period.

This optimization can be applied to any data gathering application with either a periodic or on-event report, as well as a general on-demand report (i.e. the strategic nodes requests all nodes to send their data). In case of selective query, an additional *Join* message is used. Its goal is to allow the strategic node to establish a route to a node that can be queried individually. In order to reduce the overhead, a node aggregates in a single *Join* message all nodes that can be queried via itself (i.e. all its descendants in the data gathering tree).

The *Join* message could also be used to determine whether some member of a multicast group can be reached via the sender node.

6.6. Benefits of cross-layering

Cross layering is a powerful approach that enables to conciliate generic design approach and protocol optimization targeting both the desired application and the operational environment.

In this section, we have shown how to optimize the EOLSR routing protocol by:
- ∞ reducing the induced overhead by using information provided by the application. EOLSR can adapt its timers to the application phases, and maintain only routes to strategic nodes determined by the application.
- ∞ increasing OLSR reactivity by using information provided by the MAC layer: (e.g. received signal power, knowledge of heard nodes).

- ∞ improving energy efficiency by (i) avoiding nodes with low residual energy, (ii) selecting routes minimizing the consumed energy and (iii) scheduling node activity.

7. CONCLUSION AND PERSPECTIVES

Energy aware routing is a hot topic for wireless sensor networks where it is difficult, expensive or even impossible to renew the energy of battery-operated devices. In this chapter we have positioned energy aware routing among the four classes of energy efficient techniques which aim at maximizing network lifetime: topology control by tuning the transmission power, reducing information transfers, node activity scheduling and energy aware routing. All these techniques should be used to achieve to goal of maximizing network lifetime.

These protocols have to cope with radio interferences, network resources of reduced capacity (e.g. bandwidth, processing power, memory) and limited energy. Hence, they should induce a low overhead, have minimal memory and computation requirements and support sleeping nodes. Different techniques have been introduced for that purpose. We have identified six techniques used by existing energy efficient routing protocols: data centric, hierarchical, geographical, multipath routing and support of sleeping nodes. These techniques can be combined to provide better results. We have briefly presented all these techniques.

Depending on the considered application, the most appropriate routing protocol will be chosen. In any case, cross layering between both the MAC layer and the application layer considerably improves the performance of the routing protocol. First, the routing protocol can react more promptly to (1) variations of the received signal power, and (2) topology changes detected by the MAC layer. Second, the routing protocol can meet the exact set of application requirements and not a superset. Hence, the overhead induced by the routing protocol is calibrated by the application requirements. For instance, only useful routes are maintained and not a route to any other node in the network.

We have then focused on EOLSR, the energy efficient extension of OLSR. EOLSR operates in two modes depending on the application requirements. In the strategic mode, nodes only maintain routes to the strategic nodes, whereas in generic mode any node maintains a route to any other network node. This adaptation of EOLSR is made possible by means of cross-layering.

We have seen that to allow nodes that have nothing to transmit and receive to sleep, considerably increase network lifetime. We have proposed SERENA, a three-hop coloring algorithm, that contributes to a more efficient use of energy by reducing the energy lost in *Interferences* and in the *Idle* state. SERENA can be used in TDMA networks as well as in CSMA/CA networks where network synchronization is provided.

Wireless multimedia sensor networks [60], very large and dense wireless sensor networks, as well as very mobile sensor networks represent new challenges for energy efficient routing protocols.

Energy efficient routing in low power and lossy wireless sensor networks is an active topic in the working groups of standardization bodies, like for instance the ROLL [61] and 6loWPAN [62] working groups at IETF.

ACKNOWLEDGEMENTS

I would like to thank Saoucene Mahfoudh for the simulations results she allowed me to use in this book chapter.

REFERENCES

[1]   IEEE, *IEEE 802.11-2007 IEEE Standard for Information technology-Telecommunications and information exchange between systems-Local and metropolitan area networks-Specific requirements - Part 11: Wireless LAN Medium Access Control (MAC) and Physical Layer (PHY) Specifications*, IEEE, 2007.

[2]   IEEE, *IEEE 802.15.4: Wireless Medium Access Control MAC) and Physical layer (PHY) specifications for Low-Rate Wireless Personal Area Networks (LR-WPANs)*, IEEE Computer Society, LAN/MAN standards committee, October 2003.

[3]   E. Kim, D. Kaspar, C. Gomez, C. Borman, *Problem statement and requirements for 6LoWPAN routing*, draft-ietf-6lowpan-routing-requirements-00, work in progress, 6LoWPAN working group, IETF, November 2008.

[4]   C. Adjih, T. Clausen, P. Jacquet, A. Laouiti, P. Minet, P. Muhlethaler, A. Qayyum, L. Viennot: *Optimized Link State Routing Protocol*, RFC 3626, IETF, 2003.

[5]   S. Mahfoudh, P. Minet, *EOLSR: an energy efficient routing protocol in wireless ad hoc and sensor networks*, Journal of Interconnection Networks, JOIN, AINA 2008 Conference Special Issue in Routing, Scheduling & Load balancing in Networking Systems, December 2008

[6]   S. Mahfoudh, P. Minet, *Maximization of energy efficiency in wireless ad hoc and sensor networks with SERENA*, Journal on Mobile Information Systems, IOS Press, to appear in 2009.

[7]   S. Mahfoudh, P. Minet, *Survey of energy efficient strategies in wireless ad hoc and sensor networks*, ICN 2008, IEEE International Conference on Networking, Cancun, Mexico, April 2008.

[8]   G. Toussaint, The relative neighborhood graph of a finite planar set, Pattern Recognition, Vol 12, 1980.

[9]   J. Wieselthier, G. Nguyen, A. Ephremides, On the construction of energy-efficient broadcast and multicast trees in wireless networks, Infocom 2000, Tel Aviv, Israel, March 2000.

[10]   N. Li, J. Hou, L. Sha, design and analysis of an MST-based topology control algorithm, Infocom 2003, San Francisco, CA, April 2003.

[11]   F. Ingelrest, D. Simplot-Ryl, I. Stojmenovic, Optimal Transmission Radius for Energy Efficient Broadcasting Protocols in Ad Hoc Networks, IEEE Transactions on Parallel and Distributed Systems, June 2006.

[12]   M. Cardei, J. Wu, S. Yang, Topology Control in Ad hoc Wireless Networks with Hitch-hiking, First IEEE SECON04, October 2004.

[13]   S. Lin, J. Zhang, G. Zhou, L. Gu, T. He, J. A. Stankovic, ATPC: Adaptive Transmission Power Control for Wireless Sensor Networks, SenSys'06, Colorado, November 2006.

[14]   W. Heinzelman, A. Chandrakasan, H. Balakrishnan, *Energy-efficient communication protocol for wireless microsensor networks*, HICSS'00, Maui, Hawaii, USA, vol. 2, pp. 3005ˆa3014, January 2000.

[15]   D. Xia, N. Vlajic, *Near-optimal node clustering in wireless sensor networks for environment monitoring*, AINA 2007, Niagara Falls, Ontario, Canada, May 2007.

[16]   K. Kalpakis, K. Dasgupta, P. Namjoshi, *Maximum Lifetime Data Gathering and Aggregation in Wireless Sensor Networks*, IEEE Networks'02, Munich, Germany, August 2002.

[17]   X. Tang, J. Xu, *Extending network lifetime for precision-constrained data aggregation in wireless sensor networks*, IEEE INFOCOM 2006, Barcelona, Spain, April 2006.

[18]   J. Kulik, W. Rabiner, H. Balakrishnan, *Adaptive protocols for information dissemination in wireless sensor networks*, 5th ACM/IEEE Mobicom Conference, Seattle, WA, August 1999.

[19]   G. Pei, M. Gerla, T.-W. Chen, *Fisheye state routing: a routing scheme for ad hoc wireless networks*, IEEE ICC'00, New Orleans, LA June 2000.

[20]   D.Q. Nguyen, P. Minet, *Scalabilty of the OLSR protocol with the Fish Eye extension*, ICN 2007, Sainte Luce, Martinique, April 2007.

[21]   P. Jacquet, A. Laouiti, P. Minet, L. Viennot, *Performance analysis of OLSR multipoint relay flooding in two ad hoc wireless network models*, INRIA Research Report, RR 4260, http://www.inria.fr/rrrt/rr-4260, September 2001.

[22]   J. Wu, H. Li, *On calculating connected dominating set for efficient routing in ad hoc wireless networks*, ACM DIAL M, Seattle, Washington, August 1999.

[23]   F. Dai, J.Wu, *An extended localized algorithm for connected dominating set formation in ad hoc wireless networks* IEEE Trans. on Parallel and Distributed systems, 15(10), 2004.

[24]   F. Ingelrest, D. Simplot-Ryl, I. Stojmenovic, *Smaller connected dominating sets in ad hoc and sensor networks based on coverage by two-hop neighbors*, Proc. 2nd

International Conference on Communication System Software and Middleware, Bangalore, India, to appear, 2007.

[25]   P. Jacquet, *Analytical results on connected dominating sets in mobile ad hoc networks*, INRIA Research Report, RR 5173, http://www.inria.fr/rrrt/rr-5173, April 2004.

[26]   K. Alzoubi, P.J. Wan, O. Fieder, *Distributed heuristics for connected dominating sets in wireless ad hoc networks*, Journal of Communications and Networks, 4(1), March 2002.

[27]   B. Han, H.H. Fu, L. Li, W. Jia, *Efficient construction of connected dominating set in wireless ad hoc networks*, IEEE MASS 2004, Fort Lauderdale, Florida, October 2004.

[28]   M. Cardei, M. Thai, Y. Li, W. Wu, *Energy-efficient target coverage in wireless sensor networks*, IEEE INFOCOM 2005, Miami, Florida, March 2005.

[29]   J. Carle, D. Simplot-Ryl, *Energy-efficient area monitoring for sensor networks*, Computer, vol. 37, no. 2, pp. 40-46, Febuary, 2004.

[30]   M. Cardei, D. Du, *Improving wireless sensor network lifetime through power aware organization*, ACM Journal of Wireless Networks, May 2005.

[31]   V. Rajendran, K. Obraczka, J.J. Garcia-Luna-Aceves, *Energy-efficient, collision-free medium access control for wireless sensor networks*, Sensys'03, Los Angeles, California November 2003.

[32]   V. Rajendran, J.J. Garcia-Luna-Aceves, K. Obraczka, *Energy-efficient, application-aware medium access for sensor networks*, IEEE MASS 2005, Washington, November 2005.

[33]   R.C. Shah, J.M. Rabaey, Energy aware routing for low energy ad hoc sensor networks, IEEE WCNC, Volume 1, pp. 17-21, March 2002.

[34]   D. Ganesan, R. Govindan, S. Shenker, D. Estrin, Highly-resilient, energy-efficient multipath routing in wireless sensor networks, ACM SIGMOBILE MC2R, volume 1, no 2, 2001.

[35]   A. Srinivas, E. Modiano, Minimum energy disjoint path routing in wireless ad hoc networks, MOBICOM'2003 September 2003.

[36]   A. Nasipuri, S. Das, On-demand multipath routing for mobile ad hoc networks, Int. Conf. on Computer Communications and Networks, Boston, MA, October 1999.

[37]   S.M. Senouci, G. Pujolle, Energy efficient routing in wireless ad hoc networks, ICC 2004, IEEE International Conference on Communications volume 7, pp. 4057-4061, June 2004.

[38]   S. Kwon, Ness B. Shroff, Energy-Efficient Interference-Based Routing for Multi-hop Wireless Networks, IEEE INFOCOM'2006, Barcelona, Spain, April 2006.

[39]   H. Hassanein, Jing Luo, Reliable Energy Aware Routing In Wireless Sensor networks, IEEE Workshop DSSNS, April 2006.

[40]   B. Mans, *On the complexity of reducing the energy drain in multihop ad hoc networks*, INRIA Research report, RR-5152, INRIA Rocquencourt, France, March 2004.

[41]   N.Shresta, Reception Awarness for Energy Conservation in Ad Hoc Networks, PhD Thesis, Macquarie University Sydney, Australia, November 2006.

[42]   G. Allard, P. Minet, D.Q. Nguyen, N. Shresta, *Evaluation of the energy consumption in MANET* Adhoc-Now 2006, Ottawa, Canada, August 2006.

[43]   K. Akkaya, M. Younis, *A survey on routing protocols for wireless sensor networks*, Ad Hoc Networks Journal, Vol3, 2005.

[44]   C. Intanagonwiwat, R. Govindan, D. Estrin, *Directed Diffusion: a scalable and robust communication paradigm for sensor networks*, MobiCom 2000, Boston, MA, August 2000.

[46]   A. Manjeshwar, D.P. Agrawal, *TEEN: a protocol for enhanced efficiency in wireless sensor networks*, Workshop on Parallel and distributed Computing Issues in Wireless Networks and Mobile Computing, San Francisco, CA, April 2001.

[47]   A. Manjeshwar, D.P. Agrawal, AP*TEEN: a hybrid protocol for efficient routing and comprehensive information retrieval in wireless sensor networks*, Workshop on Parallel and distributed Computing Issues in Wireless Networks and Mobile Computing, Fort Lauderdale, FL, April 2002.

[48]   Y. Xu, J. Heidemann, D. Estrin, *Geography-informed energy conservation for ad hoc routing*, MobiCom 2001, Rome, Italy, July 2001.

[49]   Y. Yu, R. Govindan, D. Estrin, *Geographical and energy-aware routing: a recursive data dissemination protocol for wireless sensor networks*, UCLA Computer Science Department UCLA-CSD TR-01-0023, May 2001.

[50]   B. Chen, K. Jamieson, H. Balakrishnan, R. Morris, *SPAN: an energy-efficient coordination algorithm for topology maintenance in ad hoc wireless networks*, MobiCom 2001, Rome, Italy, July 2001.

[51]   G. Girling, J. Li, K. Wa, P. Osborn, *The design and implementation of a low power ad hoc protocol stack*, IEEE Personal Communications, 2000.

[52]   M. Liu, J. Cao, G. Chen, X. Wang, *An energy-aware routing protocol in wireless sensor networks*, Sensors Vol.9, 2009.

[53]   W. Kunvilaisah, Y. Hou, Q. Zhang, W. Zhu, C. Jay Kuo, Y. Zhang, *A cross layer quality of service mapping architecture for video delivery in wireless networks*, IEEE Journal on Selectead areas in Communications, Vol21, N10, December 2003.

[54]   V. Kawadia, P. Kumar, *A cautionary perspective in cross layer design*, IEEE Wireless Communication, Vol12, February 2005.

[55]   M. Schaar, S. Shankar, *Cross layer wireless multimedia transmission: challenges, principles and new paradigms*, IEEE Wireless Communication, Vol12, N4, August 2005.

[56]   R. Winter, J. Schiller, N. Nikaeim, C. Bonnet, *Crosstalk: cross layer decision support based on global knowledge*, IEEE Communication Magazine, Vol44, January 2006.

[57]   V. Raisinghani, S. Iyer, *ECLAIR: an efficient cross layer architecture for wireless protocol stacks*, 5th World Wireless Congress, San Francisco, USA May 2004.

[58]   P. Minet, S. Mahfoudh, *Cross layering in wireless sensor networks*, International Wireless Communications and mobile Computing Conference, IWCMC 2009, Leipzig, Germany, June 2009.

[59]   M-H. Bertin, A. van den Bossche, G. Chalhoub, T. Dang, S. Mahfoudh, J. Rahme and J-B. Viollet, *OCARI for industrial wireless sensor networks*, invited paper to IFIP Wireless Days Conference, Dubai, United Arab Emirates, November 2008.

[60]   I.F. Akyildiz, T. Melodia, K.R. Chowdhury, *A survey on wireless multimedia sensor networks*, Computer Networks, 2006.

[61]   http://www.ietf.org/html.charters/roll-charter.html
[62]   http://www.ietf.org/html.charters/6lowpan-charter.html

CHAPTER 5

Theory and Practice of Geographic Routing

Stefan Rührup

Department of Computer Science, University of Freiburg, Germany

Geographic routing algorithms use position information for making packet forwarding decisions. Unlike topological routing algorithms, they do not need to exchange and maintain routing information and work nearly stateless. This makes geographic routing attractive for wireless ad hoc and sensor networks. Most geographic routing algorithms use a greedy strategy that tries to approach the destination in each step, e.g. by selecting the neighbor closest to the destination as a next hop. However, greedy forwarding fails in local minimum situations, i.e. when reaching a node that is closer to the destination than all its neighbors. A widely adopted approach to recover from such situations is planar graph routing, which guides the packet around the local minimum and guarantees delivery, required that a planar subgraph of the network graph can be constructed. A combination of greedy forwarding with a recovery mechanism is still the state-of-the-art in geographic routing, and many algorithms have been developed that follow this scheme. This chapter gives an overview of the fundamentals of geographic routing as well as theoretical results and new developments towards practical applicability.

1   Introduction

Geographic routing (also known as position-based routing or geometric routing) is a technique to deliver a message to a node in a network over multiple hops by means of position information. Routing decisions are not based on network addresses and routing tables; instead, messages are routed towards a destination location. With knowledge of the neighbors' location, each node can select the next hop neighbor that is closer to the destination, and thus advance towards the destination in each step. The fact that neither routing tables nor route discovery activities are necessary makes geographic routing attractive for dynamic networks such as wireless ad hoc and sensor networks. In such networks, acquiring and maintaining routing information is costly as it involves additional message transmissions that require energy and bandwidth and frequent updates in mobile and dynamic scenarios. In contrast, there are geographic routing algorithms that work nearly stateless and can provide high message delivery rates under mobility. All this applies under the following assumptions:

1. A node can determine its own position.

2. A node is aware of its neighbors' positions.

3. The position of the destination is known.

With GPS or other satellite based navigation systems, position information can be made available to even small mobile devices. Further location systems for indoor applications are described in [36]. The second assumption requires broadcasting the position information locally to other participants in the network. With

this information a node is able to determine the next hop that is closer to the destination. In Section 4 we will see that there are even algorithms that do not need neighborhood information in advance. The third assumption can be met by means of a location service that maps network addresses to geographic locations. Section 7 reviews some of these approaches. In some cases, the destination is inherently known to the nodes, e.g. in some sensor network applications where a single sink node collects all the data measurement information.

The main prerequisite to meet the three assumptions is a positioning system. If this is available, geographic routing provides an efficient and scalable solution for routing in wireless and mobile networks. However, forwarding a message greedily by simply minimizing the distance to the destination location in each step cannot guarantee message delivery. Nodes usually have a limited transmission range and thus there are situations where no neighbor is closer to the destination than the *forwarder*, i.e. the node currently holding the message. Greedy algorithms cannot resolve such dead-end or local minimum situation. Therefore, *recovery* methods have been developed, the most prominent of which are based on planar graph routing, where the message is guided around the local minimum by traversing the edges of a planar subgraph of the network communication graph. Altogether, greedy forwarding in combination with a recovery strategy can be considered as state-of-the-art technique in geographic routing.

Planar graph routing techniques can provide delivery guarantees under the assumption of an ideal network model, which is called the *unit disk graph* model. The

Hai Liu / Xiaowen Chu / Yiu-Wing Leung (Eds.)

unit disk graph model is an often-used basic model to describe wireless networks. Formally, a unit disk graph (UDG) of a node set contains an edge $e = (u, v)$ between two nodes u and v, if $|uv| \leq 1$. In other words, assuming a restricted transmission range normalized to 1, the links between the nodes of a given node set form a unit disk graph. Unit disk graphs rely on the assumption that transmission ranges are uniform and imply that all links are bidirectional. This assumption can be weakened and we will see in Section 5 how recovery can be realized under more realistic network models.

This chapter gives an overview of geographic routing starting with greedy algorithms and recovery strategies in Section 2 and Section 3, covering also theoretical results on their efficiency. Section 4 describes contention-based routing, a fully reactive variant of geographic routing, which does not require the neighborhood to be known in advance. In Section 5 algorithms and methods for geographic routing under realistic network models are reviewed. Further variants for multicasting and geocasting are described in Section 6. Section 7 outlines methods for providing a location service that allows to look up the destination location. Section 8 gives examples for the application of geographic routing. Finally, Section 9 concludes the chapter.

2 Geographic Greedy Forwarding

The first approaches for geographic routing were developed in the 1980s for packet radio networks [86, 37] and wired networks [18]. These approaches describe local rules used by the forwarder to select a neighbor as a next hop. As routing decisions are locally optimal, these approaches are termed *greedy forwarding*.

2.1 Greedy and Compass Routing

The first approaches for geographic routing were developed in the 1980s for packet radio networks [86, 37] and wired networks [18]. They are all greedy strategies, where the forwarding node makes locally optimal decisions to select next-hop neighbors based on the distance to the destination or on the so-called progress. In general, the next hop selection in greedy forwarding can be based on the following criteria (cf. Figure 1).

- Progress, i.e. the projection of the location of neighbor x on the s-t-line, which connects source and target node ($|x't| = \vec{st} \cdot \frac{\vec{st}}{|st|}$).

- Distance to the destination ($|xt|$) or advance, i.e. the distance gain towards the destination ($|yt| = |st| - |xt|$).

- Angular distance / angular separation ($\angle xst$).

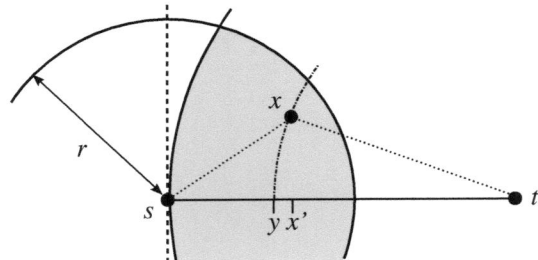

Figure 1: Progress and advance.

The notion of progress was used to define the MFR rule [86], which chooses the neighbor with the most forwarding progress within the transmission radius (see Figure 2). Similar to this rule, the *greedy method* in [18] selects the neighbor that minimizes the distance to the destination, which is equivalent to maximizing the advance. The angular criterion is used in Compass routing (CR)[47], where the neighbor is selected that minimizes the angular separation with respect to the destination.

Usually, the next hop in greedy forwarding is chosen among the neighbors with a positive progress (right of the dashed line in Figure 1) or with a positive advance (shaded area in Figure 1, also called *greedy area*). Selecting the next hop by the minimum distance or the maximum progress (MFR, greedy) gives an inherently loop-free forwarding rule independent of the unit disk graph assumption. Compass routing, which is based on the direction, is not loop-free [84].

Motivated by the observation that energy consumption can be reduced when using short links, required that the transmission range can be adjusted, the NFP (nearest with forwarding progress [37]) and NC (nearest closer [85]) criteria have been proposed. They select a neighbor which is closest to the forwarding node among all neighbors, but closer to the destination than the forwarding node itself, w.r.t. distance or progress.

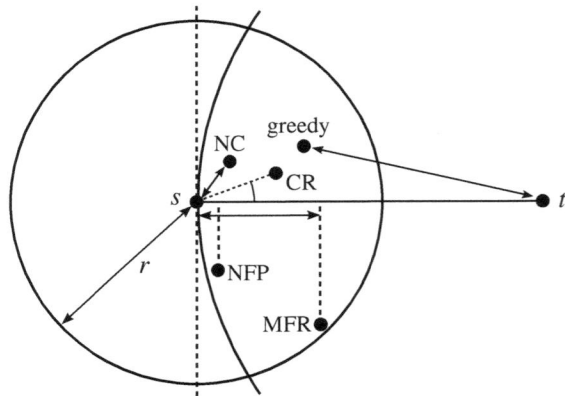

Figure 2: Variants of greedy forwarding.

2.2 Advanced Strategies

Greedy forwarding has one major drawback: it fails in local minimum situations, where the forwarding node has no other neighbors closer to the destination. In some cases, a simple backward step is sufficient to be able to resume the greedy strategy successfully; in other cases, a more sophisticated strategy is necessary to recover from this situation.

The GEDIR [84] method is a greedy strategy that uses backward steps. Whenever a message has reached a local minimum, the packet is sent back to the previous hop, which applies the greedy rule again while excluding previously visited dead end nodes from the selection. This strategy is also loop-free.

Further improvements of the basic strategies Greedy, MFR and CR can be achieved if 2-hop information is available [84]. In this case, the forwarder selects a suitable node out of the 2-hop neighborhood and forwards the packet to the direct neighbor that is connected to the selected node. Note, that 2-hop information has to be distributed, which requires a higher communication overhead.

A greedy-based algorithm that goes beyond using 2-hop information is SPEED [33], which is designed to increase the relay speed. It uses an additional "backpressure" heuristic to avoid congested areas and void regions. The protocol relies on beaconing, extended by on-demand beacons for delay estimation and backpressure information. The forwarding works as follows: Nodes from the greedy area, whose relay speed is above a certain threshold, are selected probabilistically. The higher the relay speed the higher the probability to be selected. If no neighbor meets the relay speed requirement, the node drops the packet with a certain probability that depends on the failure ratio of packet forwarding to the neighbors. The necessary information to derive the failure ratio is gained from the neighbors by backpressure beacons, which are sent in case of congestion or in a local minimum situation. This method can alleviate local minima problems in case of small void regions, but it cannot guarantee delivery in general.

3 Planar Graph Routing and Recovery Strategies

Planar graph routing is a geographic routing strategy that is able to overcome the local minimum problem of greedy forwarding. Local minima exist at the border of *void regions*, where a node cannot find a neighbor closer to the destination than itself. Such nodes are also called *dead-end* nodes or *concave* nodes. Planar graph routing is a key concept for recovery from a local minimum situation. It is based on the idea that the network links form a communication graph, and a message can be routed along a sequence of faces in this graph. Routing along a face means that the nodes of a face pass the message along the incident edges by locally applying the *left-hand* or *right-hand* rule (see Figure 3). This rule is well-known from maze problems: One can find a way out of every simply connected maze when keeping the right-hand always in touch of the wall while walking. Applying the right-hand or left-hand rule to network graphs means to find a successor node in (counter-)clockwise order after the predecessor. This results in a *traversal* of a face of the communication graph. For a successful application of this rule, the underlying graph has to be planar.

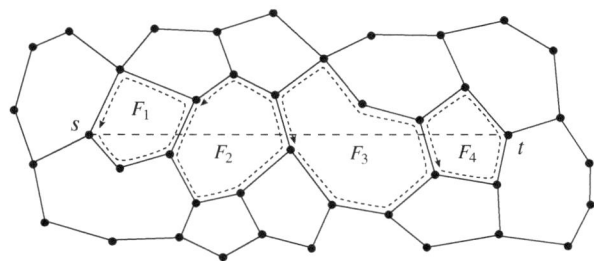

Figure 3: Planar graph routing: A path from s to t is found by sequential traversals of adjacent faces $F_1, ..., F_4$.

3.1 Face Routing

The first face routing strategies were proposed in 1999 by Kranakis et al. [47] and Bose et al. [10] under the names "Compass Routing II" and "Face-2", respectively. Compass Routing II traverses a sequence of adjacent faces until reaching the destination as shown in Figure 3. Each face is traversed completely in order to determine the edge that intersects the s-t-line and is closest to the target. Then the message is passed to an endpoint of this edge, where the face is changed and the traversal of the next face continues. Face-2 [10] also visits a sequence of faces, but it avoids the complete traversals and performs the face change before crossing the s-t-line, as depicted in Figure 4. On each face traversal, a node u checks whether the edge to the next node (u, u') intersects the s-t-line. If this is the case, then u changes the face and continues traversing the next face. A detailed description of face change rules can be found in [21]. Face routing has the advantage that it guarantees delivery on planar graphs while the nodes use only local position-based rules and do not need to keep state information.

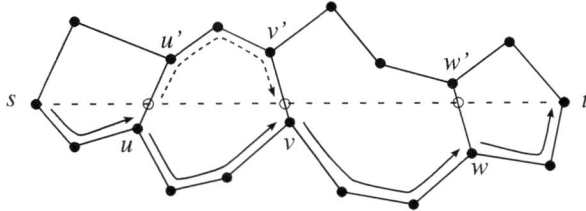

Figure 4: Face routing by FACE-2. A face change takes place at nodes u, v, and w

The planarity of the underlying network graph is required for assuring delivery guarantees, because crossing links as shown in Figures 5 and 6 can cause detours or routing loops. Therefore, an arbitrary unit disk graph has to be transformed into a planar graph first. This can be done locally by removing crossing edges using geometric criteria. The removal of edges however can increase the hop count, which makes face routing steps less efficient than greedy routing. Therefore, Bose et al. proposed the Greedy-Face-Greedy algorithm (GFG) [10], a combination of the efficient greedy forwarding and face routing on a planar subgraph to recover from local minima. A variant of this algorithm is known as GPSR [42].

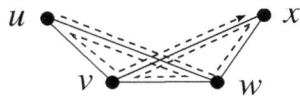

Figure 5: Crossing links causing a detour (starting from node u)

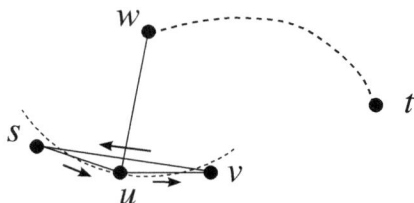

Figure 6: Crossing links causing a face routing failure (starting from node s)

GFG and GPSR use greedy forwarding as long as possible. If greedy routing fails, a face traversal starts until the greedy strategy can be resumed. When starting recovery, the distance of the first node to the target d_r and the first edge e_r have to be stored in the packet header. If the first edge e_r is visited again for the second time, then the destination is not reachable and the packet is dropped. The distance d_r is used to check whether the next hop on the face traversal is closer to the destination than the node entering recovery mode. If such a node

is found, greedy forwarding can be resumed instead of continuing the traversal until crossing the s-t-line (this is known as *sooner-back procedure* [14]). Pseudo-code for such a combined greedy and face routing algorithm is presented in the following. An example is shown in Figure 7.

When using combined greedy/face routing algorithms, the greedy part can be performed using all links of the unit disk graph, while face routing needs a local planar subgraph. We will see in the next section how a planar subgraph can be constructed.

A Combined Greedy/Face-Routing Algorithm
(GFG with sooner-back procedure [14])
Variables: previous hop p, current node u, target t, first edge in recovery mode e_r and distance successor e_n

---

if packet in greedy mode
    select next hop v according to the greedy rule
    if no such neighbor exists
        select next hop v in ccw. direction from (u, t)
        switch packet to recovery mode
        store current distance to the destination d_r
            and $e_r \leftarrow (u, v)$ in the packet header
    endif
else (packet is in recovery mode)
    if there is a neighbor v with $\|v - t\| < d_r$
        switch packet to greedy mode
    else
        select next hop v in ccw. direction from (u, p)
        (using only nodes of a GG or RNG subgraph)
        if (u, v) equals the 1st edge e in recovery mode
            drop packet; return
        endif
    endif
endif
forward packet to v

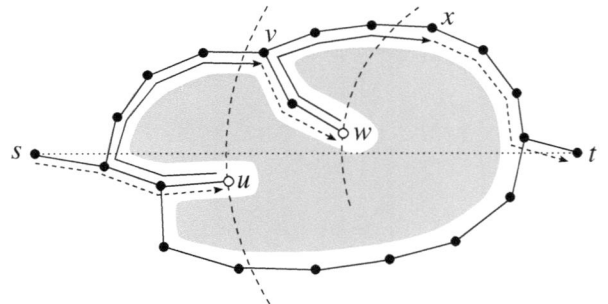

Figure 7: Combined greedy/face routing: After reaching local minimum u in greedy mode (dashed arrow), a face traversal is started (solid arrow) until a node v is found that is closer to the target than u.

3.2 Planarization

In their paper on face routing, Bose et al. [10] proposed a local planar subgraph construction based on the so-called Gabriel graph (GG) [26]. The Gabriel graph of a given point set contains an edge uv if Thales' circle on uv, i.e. the circle having uv as diameter, is empty. This circle is also called *Gabriel circle* over uv within this context. The Gabriel graph is known to be planar and connected.

This construction rule can be applied locally to a node's 1-hop neighborhood in order to extract a planar subgraph. The Gabriel graph construction and the so-called relative neighborhood graph (RNG) [87, 38] are the two most prominent local planarization schemes. Planarization using the GG criterion removes an edge uv if Thales' circle on uv contains another node w. Following the RNG criterion, an edge uv is eliminated, if the intersection of two circles with radius $|uv|$ centered at u and v contains another node w (see Figure 8). Applying the GG or RNG criterion to a unit disk graph yields a planar and connected graph, if the unit disk graph is connected.

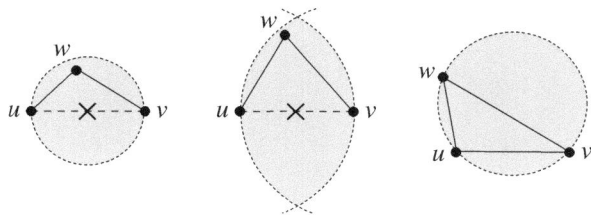

Figure 8: GG (left), RNG (middle) and Delaunay triangulation (right)

As planarization removes crossing edges it may induce detours due to missing edges. Therefore, planar subgraph constructions should approximate the original graph as closely as possible. This property can be formally described by the so-called *spanning ratio* or *stretch factor*, which is defined by the maximum ratio of the shortest path length between two nodes u and v in the subgraph over the shortest path length between u and v in the original graph. A desired property is a constant stretch factor, as it guarantees a constant overhead for any path in the subgraph.

For Gabriel graph and RNG, however, the spanning ratio is unbound. Bose et al. [7] have proven length stretch factors of $\Theta(\sqrt{n})$ for the Gabriel graph and $\Theta(n)$ for the RNG, i.e. the detours induced by these subgraph constructions are not bounded by a constant. In terms of hop count, both GG and RNG have unbounded stretch factors as well.

To alleviate this problem, local construction schemes for the Delaunay triangulation were considered, which is known to have a constant spanning ra-

tio. The Delaunay triangulation of a given point set contains all triangles whose circumcircle is empty (see Figure 8). In contrast to the GG or RNG, this criterion cannot be checked locally by using only 1-hop information. Therefore, variants of the Delaunay triangulation were considered, which can be constructed locally [28, 58, 59]. They are described in the following.

The Restricted Delaunay Graph (RDG) [28] is obtained by locally constructing Delaunay triangles, exchanging the local triangulations, and finally removing all edges uv if there is another node connected to u or v without having uv in its local triangulation. This scheme requires communication to obtain the desired subgraph, but provides a subgraph with constant stretch factor.

The Partial Delaunay Triangulation (PDT) [59] has been proposed in two variants, using either only 1-hop or 2-hop information. Both variants keep the Gabriel graph edges. A non-GG edge uv has at least one node in Gabriel circle over uv, and if there are two or more of such nodes left and right of uv within the circle, the edge is removed. If these nodes are located either only left or only right of uv within the circle, the maximum Delaunay circle among u, v and those 1-hop neighbors is considered. With 1-hop information, u keeps the edge uv if its transmission range covers the Delaunay circle (i.e. it would be able to reach every other node within this circle) and the circle is empty. With 2-hop information u and v communicate and keep the edge if both cover the Delaunay circle and there is no other node within this circle. The PDT scheme reduces the communication cost compared to the RDG, but it is unknown whether it can provide a constant factor spanner.

A localized reactive approach to planar subgraph construction has been presented in [20], which is called *Direct Planarization*. Direct planarization checks edges explicitly for possible edge intersections before they are used by the routing algorithm and decides in case of an intersection, which edge has to be removed. Two criteria were proposed, based on angle and Delaunay circles. Using the angle-based direct planarization (ADP), an edge uv is preferred over an intersecting edge wx, if either $\angle xuw$ or $\angle wvx$ is the maximum angle in the quadrilateral $uwvx$ (see Figure 9). The Delaunay-based direct planarization (DDP) favors an edge uv over wx, if x is not contained in the circumcircle of uvw.

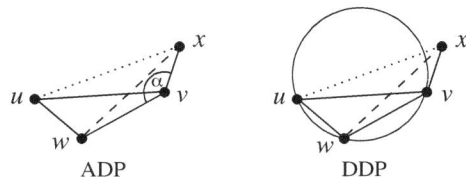

Figure 9: Angle-based and Delaunay-based direct planarization

Note that all the planarization criteria presented in this section rely on the unit disk graph assumption and bidirectional links. Problems of planar graph routing in non-unit disk graphs and possible solutions are described in Section 5.3.

3.3 Improved Planar Graph Routing

Though planar graph routing works stateless and uses local information only, it has two disadvantages: first, the construction of a planar subgraph removes edges and may increase the hop count. Second, a wrong choice of the traversal direction can lead to a long detour in the network.

The first problem is due to the planar subgraph construction. Planarization schemes such as the Gabriel subgraph construction remove long edges in favor of short ones, which results in an increased hop count when traversing a face of the resulting subgraph. This problem can be alleviated, if more information of the neighborhood is available. With 2-hop information, the forwarder can determine the local planar subgraph of its neighbors. Thus, instead of following the face traversal hop by hop, one can determine more next hops in advance and use a *shortcut* to the most advanced hop [14].

The Greedy Path Vector Face Routing (GPVFR) [56] is also based on the idea to exploit multi-hop information in order to broaden the horizon for forwarding decisions. GPVFR distributes information among the nodes of the same face. If greedy forwarding fails, a node might know another node on the same face being closer to the destination. Then this node is chosen as an intermediate target, which can be reached by face routing, even if the complete information about the current face is not given.

Another technique to reduce the detour on a planar subgraph is to use the nodes of a connected dominating set [14, 1]. In a dominating set, each node is either part of the set, or adjacent to such node. A connected dominating set can be constructed locally using only position information of the 1-hop neighborhood. Then, the planar subgraph construction and the face traversal is performed on the internal nodes of the dominating set only, which usually leads to a better subgraph than obtained by planarization of the original network graph. It was shown by Datta et al. [14] that using shortcuts and internal nodes of the dominating set can effectively reduce the hop count of face routing or GFG. Especially the use of internal nodes contributes significantly to a hop count reduction while requiring only 1-hop information for determining the internal node status.

Geographic clustering can also reduce the complexity of the underlying topology. Nodes can be grouped into clusters that are defined by geographic areas. In [71] the nodes are mapped onto a grid of quadratic cluster areas. This grid structure provides the planarity property implicitly and can be used for a virtual routing along grid cells. In [19] the unit disk graph is first planarized using the Gabriel graph criterion. Afterwards a clustering into hexagonal areas is applied. These clusters are the basis for a cluster graph, which contains an edge between two clusters, if nodes within the respective hexagonal cells are connected. The cluster graph is planar and provides the basis for face routing. The advantage of geographic clustering is that a face routing algorithm has the freedom of choice among the nodes within a cluster. It is also more robust in mobile scenarios, because the resulting graph does not change until a cluster cell changes is entered by a first node or left by the last node, i.e. it changes its status.

The second problem of planar graph routing is to find the right traversal direction when starting a face traversal. As an example, if node u in Figure 10 chooses v as next hop, the traversal of F_3 during face routing leads through w along the complete outer boundary until reaching the s-t-line again. A traversal of F_3 in the opposite direction is here the better choice as it crosses the s-t-line after 5 hops. Choosing the optimal direction is not possible with only local information, but the detour can be bounded by restricting the search area. Adaptive Face Routing (AFR) proposed by Kuhn et al. [49] is a face routing variant that restricts the search area by a bounding ellipse during face traversals (see Figure 10): Whenever the message reaches the ellipse on the traversal path, it is sent back into the opposite direction. The face traversal is finished when the ellipse is reached for the second time, or if the traversal has reached the start point. After the traversal, the message is sent to the node closest to the destination on the current face (white nodes in Figure 10). This node changes the face and continues the traversal of the next face. The original face routing, by contrast, performs the face change when crossing the s-t-line.

The bounding ellipse has s and t as foci and the initial size of the major axis depends on the implementation. In [51] Kuhn et al. recommend to use an initial size of the major axis of $1.2\,|st|$ and an enlargement factor of $\sqrt{2}$. If there is no path to the target within the bounding ellipse, the size of the ellipse is doubled and the source starts face routing again.

AFR can be used on its own or as as a recovery strategy in combination with greedy forwarding. This combination is called Greedy Other Adaptive Face Routing (GOAFR) [51]. A further improvement of this algorithm, called GOAFR+ is presented in [48]. It employs method other than the bounding ellipse to restrict the search area, namely a circle centered at the destination, which initially contains the source node and is gradually reduced when the packet approaches the target. Furthermore, GOAFR+ uses an early fallback strategy to leave the recovery mode sooner to resume greedy forwarding. In contrast to the sooner back procedure, which leaves greedy mode as soon as the distance to the destination is decreased since entering face routing mode, GOAFR+ uses the following criterion: It maintains two counters for the nodes on the traversal that are closer and for those that are not closer to the destination than the start node of the traversal. If the number of nodes closer to the destination exceeds the rest of the nodes on the traversal by a certain factor, the traversal is stopped and the message is passed to the node that is closest to the destination among the visited nodes and greedy forwarding is resumed. The use of the two counters avoids multiple traversals of nodes that were already participating in a traversal before. Through this strategy the algorithm retains its asymptotic efficiency. An overview of AFR and its variants is given in [51].

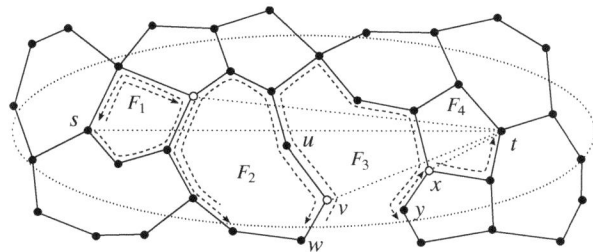

Figure 10: Adaptive Face Routing (AFR) [51]. Faces are traversed completely while the search area is restricted by a bounding ellipse.

3.4 Recovery beyond Planarization

Recovery from local minima does not necessarily require creating a planar subgraph prior to routing. One approach is to identify possible local minima beforehand, such that a path around a void region is already established when a packet in greedy mode arrives at a dead-end node. For this purpose Fang et al. [15] propose the BoundHole algorithm, that identifies so-called stuck nodes by applying geometric rules locally. Stuck nodes are located on the border of a void region. They are not dead-end nodes in general, but for some specific target locations they are local minima. The void region can be identified then by communication among the stuck nodes. The BoundHole algorithm can be used in conjunction with a combined greedy and face routing algorithm. When reaching a local minimum, the face routing part can use the pre-computed information about the border of a void region and immediately select the shorter path around this region. This yields shorter paths at the expense of an additional communication overhead for the communication among stuck nodes.

A similar idea led to the NEAR algorithm [2] that assigns virtual coordinates to nodes in a dead-end region. These coordinates are called elevation values and

based on the angle between a node and its neighbors. Elevated nodes are avoided by the routing algorithm. A typical situation where high elevation values are assigned is a "peninsula" of nodes which extends into a void region. The nodes in this dead-end region are elevated successively such that the dead-end region is predictable before entering it. This mechanism is complemented by a void identification algorithm that is started by the nodes at the border of a void region. Thus the perimeter information is available beforehand and can be used to find shorter routes around void regions.

Another approach for identifying the boundary of void regions is presented in [63] as part of the Greedy Anti-void Routing (GAR) routing algorithm. Here, the idea for the boundary traversal is to roll a ball whose diameter is the transmission range along the nodes on the boundary of a void region. The next node v that is hit by the ball satisfies that the edge from the previous node u is not intersected by another edge having one endpoint neither connected to u nor v. Thus, it is ensured that no important edge on the traversal is missed. The algorithm establishes pointers along the traversal direction which are used to circumvent void regions.

The described techniques are based on geometric criteria and assume a unit disk graph. There are further recovery techniques that do not rely on this assumption. One of the underlying concepts is an identification of crossing links or paths around void regions by graph traversals. These approaches are described in Section 5.3 on recovery in non-unit disk graphs.

3.5 Delivery Guarantees and Asymptotic Efficiency

The prominent geographic routing algorithms GFG, GPSR and GOAFR+ have been subject to simulative studies as well as to theoretical considerations. All three algorithms guarantee delivery on GG or RNG subgraphs, which can be constructed locally under the unit disk graph assumption. GFG provides this delivery guarantee even on any planar graph. Frey and Stojmenovic showed that the delivery guarantees on GG and RNG are due to a structural graph property of these graphs [21]: In GG and RNG there is always an edge intersecting the s-t-line having one endpoint closer to the target t than the source s, and this implies that a face traversal always finds a node closer to the target.

The performance of the aforementioned geographic routing algorithms depends mainly on the face routing part. Like in all combined greedy/face routing algorithms, the face routing part is needed to find paths around void regions and the resulting detours significantly influence the performance. Consider a face traversal starting at node u in Figure 10 as an example: Turning left at this point is obviously the shorter path to the target, while turning right leads along the boundary of the network which can result in an arbitrarily long detour. An efficient algorithm finds a path whose length is close to the optimal path length. Therefore, the efficiency is described with respect to the shortest path length or, more generally, to the optimal cost. This is also termed a *competitive* measure.

In situations as shown in Figure 10, where a traversal can lead along the network boundary, GFG and GPSR produce worst-case paths that cannot be bounded by a function of the shortest path length. A bounded detour can be achieved by the bounding ellipse technique, which was introduced in Adaptive Face Routing [49] and used for GOAFR and its variants. Kuhn et al. showed that AFR finds a path of cost $O(c^2)$ in the worst case, where c is the cost of the optimal path. The quadratic bound is obtained because the detour is limited by the area of the bounding ellipse and doubling the ellipse does not affect the asymptotic complexity. For this cost bound it is required that the minimum distance between any two nodes is bounded by a constant, which is called $\Omega(1)$-model. The GOAFR+ algorithm, which in addition performs greedy routing, has the same asymptotic efficiency. Kuhn et al. also prove that there is a quadratic lower bound on the cost. Therefore, AFR and GOAFR+ are asymptotically optimal.

The lower bound construction from [49] is depicted in Figure 11. It consists of $2k$ nodes on a ring that are just able to reach each other. Every second node on this ring is attached to a chain of $\Theta(k)$ nodes pointing towards the center. Only one of these chains leads to the target. In this graph any deterministic or randomized geographic routing algorithm needs to explore at least half of the dead-end chains in the (expected) worst case, before finding the target. This results in a path cost of $O(k^2)$ while the shortest path cost is $O(k)$.

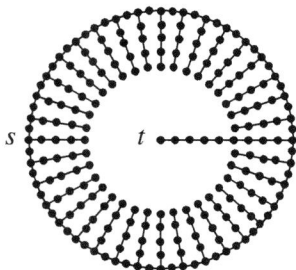

Figure 11: Lower bound construction for geographic routing algorithms [49]

This lower bound holds for any randomized or deterministic geographic routing algorithm. A similar lower bound holds for greedy algorithms only. Greedy algorithms cannot guarantee delivery in the worst case, but if there is a greedy path, it is not even close to the optimal path in the worst case. Considering the graph in

Figure 12, a greedy choice based on distance minimization leads from s to node v that is closer to the target. The path from v to t brings the message closer to the target in each step, but its length is quadratic in the length of the optimal path, which leads from s through u to t. Thus, for distance-based greedy forwarding, there is a quadratic lower bound with respect to the shortest path length [28].

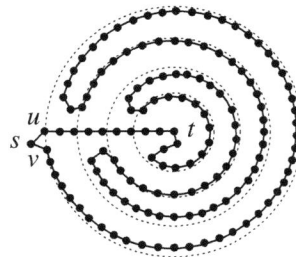

Figure 12: Lower bound for greedy forwarding [28]

Considering the hop count metric, the quadratic lower bound for geographic routing implies that a quadratic number of messages is needed. This bound on the message complexity can be reached by a flooding algorithm as well. Actually, flooding visits all nodes in the network, but it can be limited by a doubling technique that repeats restricted flooding while doubling the hop limit. This technique is also known as expanding ring search [40] and has a quadratic message complexity. The quadratic lower bound, which is defined in terms of the shortest path, suggests that geographic routing strategies have the same worst case message complexity than flooding algorithms, while flooding algorithms are obviously faster.

In fact, geographic routing is not as inefficient in the worst case as it seems. We have seen that the difficulty of the geographic routing problem depends on the void regions which are local minima to a greedy strategy and require a traversal. Following the rationale in [5], one can show that in the worst case the traversal of void regions is unavoidable. Thus, there is a lower bound on hop count and message complexity of $\Omega(d+p)$ for geographic single-path strategies, where d is the shortest path length and p the perimeter of void regions. This analysis uses an abstraction from the geometric issues connected with the problem of void identification and graph planarization: By a geographic clustering technique [71], a unit disk graph can be represented by a grid with usable and defective regions. This way the geographic routing problem on unit disk graphs can be transformed to the problem of routing on a defective grid with only local information. It inherently provides a minimum distance property as defined in the $\Omega(1)$-model.

The lower bound graph in Figure 11 states a special case of the generalized lower bound of $\Omega(d + p)$ with $p = \Theta(d^2)$, i.e. having a total perimeter length that is quadratic in the shortest path length. The fact that any single-message strategy has to examine the complete perimeter in the worst case leads to the quadratic bound for hop count and message complexity in this case. The question whether geographic single-path strategies are as inefficient as flooding in terms of messages can also be answered by considering the perimeter length. While geographic single-path strategies can find paths of length $O(d + p)$ using the same number of messages, expanding ring search (as a flooding or multi-path strategy) can route a packet in $O(d)$ steps, but uses always $O(d^2)$ messages, regardless of the perimeter length. As a result, geographic routing is efficient, if void regions are small in comparison to the shortest path length. It also raises the question whether there is an algorithm that is as fast as flooding, but uses less messages. This is answered in [72] by a multi-path strategy that approaches the lower bound of $\Omega(d + p)$ on the message complexity up to a poly-logarithmic factor, while preserving the asymptotic optimal time bound of $O(d)$.

Other competitive algorithms in this context have been presented by Bose and Morin [9, 8] for routing in triangulations and planar graphs with certain properties. However, the considered graphs have no local minima, which does not comply with the unit disk graph model.

4 Contention-based Routing

The geographic routing algorithms described so far require the locations of 1-hop neighbors to be known as stated by the second assumption for geographic routing in the Introduction. This knowledge can be acquired by a regular exchange of beacon messages containing the own position information. However, the knowledge of the neighbors' positions is not required for forwarding a message greedily. Indeed, without knowing the neighborhood, the forwarding node cannot select the next hop explicitly, but the next hop can select itself in a contention with other neighbors. This kind of routing is called *contention-based* or *beaconless* routing, because a beacon exchange is not required.

4.1 Contention-based Greedy Forwarding

The first contention-based georouting algorithms were proposed in 2003 by independent groups under the names Beacon-less Routing (BLR) [34], Contention-based Forwarding (CBF) [25], and Implicit Geographic Forwarding (IGF) [6]. They all follow the same principle: First, the forwarder broadcasts the message to its (unknown) neighbors. The neighbors that are located in the *forwarding area*, an area closer to the destination

and where all nodes can overhear each other, are the *candidates* for the next hop and contend for the message (see Figure 13). They set a set a timer in accordance to their distance to the destination. More specifically, the timer is determined by a *delay function* depending on the advance, such that the candidate closest to the destination has the shortest timeout. Such a delay function is defined as follows, based on the advance a of the candidate, the transmission range r, and the maximum timeout $t_{\max}$, which defines the length of the contention period.

$$t(a) = \frac{a}{r} \cdot t_{\max}$$

Once the first timer expires, the respective candidate re-transmits the message. The other candidates overhear the re-transmission and cancel their scheduled transmissions. The re-transmission also serves as a passive acknowledgement to the forwarder.

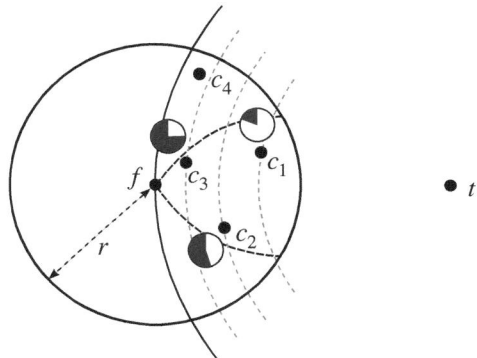

Figure 13: Contention-based routing. Only the candidates in the forwarding area (shaded) participate in the contention. Candidate c_1 has the shortest timeout and takes over the message.

The choice of the forwarding area is implementation-dependent, and there are a few possibilities (see [34, 89] such as a 60°-sector directed towards the target, a circular region, or the Reuleaux triangle, which is shown in Figure 13. The only prerequisite is that all nodes within this area have to be able to overhear each other. Otherwise, two candidates could re-transmit the packet without knowing each other, which leads to an undesired packet duplication. Another problem pointed out in [89] occurs, if two candidates c_1 and c_2 start their re-transmission almost simultaneously. Then, these two nodes initiate two contention-rounds in parallel. The new candidates in the intersection of the transmission range of c_1 and c_2 receive the first transmission by c_1 and also overhear the second transmission by c_2, which leads to the misinterpretation that c_2 won the contention and became the next hop. If in this situation there is no other candidate that could hear only one transmission, the forwarding stops and the packet is dropped. This can be solved by storing a hop counter in each packet, so that a candidate cancels its scheduled transmission only if another node re-transmitted the packet before and the hop counters are different.

The timer-based or contention-based selection of the candidate enables a completely reactive greedy forwarding without any message overhead. However, the contention costs a certain delay and the candidates are selected from a rather restricted area. It is possible to use the complete greedy area, i.e. all neighbors closer to the destination than the forwarder participate in the contention process. This has a positive effect on the performance [12], but it requires that the forwarder actively selects the candidate, which needs additional control messages. This scheme works as follows: The forwarder broadcasts a *request to send* (RTS) to its neighbors. The neighbors being closer to the destination set a timer in accordance to their distance to the destination. The first candidate whose timer expires replies with a *clear to send* (CTS). Then the forwarder sends the data packet immediately. The other candidates overhear the CTS by the candidate or the data transmission by the forwarder and cancel their scheduled replies. Finally, the forwarder sends the packet to the selected candidate by unicast.

The previously described scheme implicitly assumes a continuous time model. Practically, one cannot require a fine-grained time resolution such that no nodes answer simultaneously and cause a packet collision. Geographic Random Forwarding (GeRaF) [91] is an approach that solves the problem of colliding control packets. GeRaF uses the RTS/CTS scheme and a forwarding area that includes all neighbors closer to the destination than the forwarder. The forwarding area is divided into zones and the candidates within these zones contend for being the forwarder in the next round. If two candidates from the same zone cause a collision while sending their CTS, they will retransmit it with probability $1/2$ in the next round. This probabilistic drop out reduces the probability of collisions step by step because colliding nodes from the last round survive with probability $1/2$.

In networks where the nodes can adjust their their transmission power, energy can be saved by adapting the transmission range to a suitable relay node. In beaconless protocols, however, the problem is that the relay nodes are not known in advance and suitable candidates have to be found by broadcasting requests at increasing transmission ranges. As this probing itself consumes energy, the question is how the transmission range should be increased. Moreover, if a candidate is found, is it worth to increase the transmission range in order to search for a better candidate? Galluccio et al. [27] address this problem and propose a beacon-less routing protocol that discovers candidates by such probing strategy. In the first round of the proposed algorithm, candidates are discovered by sending an RTS at an initial transmission range, and the best neighbor replies. Then the transmission range is increased, but re-transmitting an RTS at a higher transmission power is connected with some cost. The optimal point for stopping a further range increase is found when the benefit of finding a better neighbor is smaller than the cost of the range increase. The benefit here is a progress factor which is essentially the same as the ratio of the transmission cost over the progress achieved. The concept of cost-over-progress will be explained in Section 5.1 in the context of realistic transmission models.

4.2 Reactive Recovery Strategies

Contention-based greedy forwarding suffers from the same local minimum problem as described for conventional greedy forwarding. In a contention-based or beaconless routing algorithm, the recovery cannot rely on known neighborhood information. A straightforward solution to reactive recovery is the request-response approach of BLR [35]. Whenever the forwarder finds no candidate, it request all neighbors to send their position. With this 1-hop knowledge, a local planar subgraph construction and face routing as described in Section 3 is applied. This strategy can be seen as reactive beaconing as it involves the complete neighborhood in exchanging position information.

A reactive scheme for face routing, which guarantees delivery and does not require communication with all neighboring nodes, is described in [41]. The main problem is that face routing requires an underlying planar subgraph and planarization requires some knowledge of the neighborhood. According to the two tasks of planarization and selecting the next hop edge, two strategies have been proposed: Beaconless Forwarder Planarization (BFP) performs the reactive planarization first, such that face routing can continue; Angular Relaying selects the next edge on a face traversal first and checks then, whether the selected node is part of a planar subgraph.

BFP is a generalization of the earlier proposed GDBF protocol [11] and can be used with the Gabriel graph and the relative neighborhood criterion. BFP is proposed together with a modified subgraph construction which is similar to the Gabriel graph but allows to bound the number of messages, which is not possible when using the Gabriel graph criterion. In contrast, the request-response approach of BLR cannot provide this bound on the number of messages as it involves communication with all neighbors. BFP uses a delay function of the distance to the forwarder, i.e. the neighbor closest to the forwarder may reply first:

$$t(d) = \frac{d}{r} \cdot t_{\max}$$

If a neighbor v overhears an earlier reply by another neighbor w, it checks whether w is located within the Gabriel circle over fv. If this is the case, the edge fv is not part of a Gabriel subgraph and thus v becomes a *hidden node* and cancels its reply. Now the problem is that v itself could violate the Gabriel graph condition for a neighbor that responds later. Thus, the hidden nodes are given the opportunity to protest against replies in a second phase. An example is shown in Figure 14. Finally, the forwarder obtains the neighborhood of a local planar subgraph and can apply any planar graph routing algorithm.

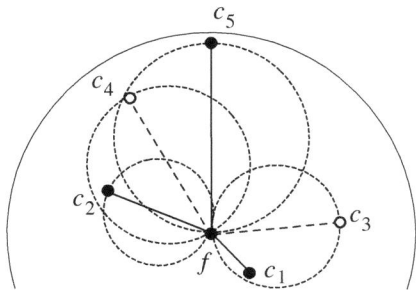

Figure 14: Beaconless Forwarder Planarization (BFP) using the Gabriel graph criterion. The candidates reply in the order c_1, c_2, c_5; c_3 and c_4 are hidden nodes. In a second phase c_4 protests against c_5.

Angular Relaying finds the next neighbor in counter-clockwise order and checks then if the connecting edge fulfills the Gabriel graph condition. It follows a *select-and-protest* principle: If the first candidate in counter-clockwise order is selected, then another candidate with a larger delay, which has not replied at this point, may lie within the Gabriel circle over the selected edge. This candidate has to be given the chance to correct the initial decision. Thus, this candidate sends a protest message, that is received by the forwarder and the previously selected candidate as well. Now the protesting node becomes implicitly selected. If there is no other node violating the Gabriel condition for the new edge, the contention ends and the currently selected candidate will receive the data packet.

Angular Relaying as depicted in Figure 15 uses a delay function that depends on the angle θ between the previous hop, the forwarder and the candidate:

$$t(d, \theta) = \frac{\theta}{2\pi} \cdot t_{\max}$$

With this delay function, the area of possibly protesting nodes is half of the Gabriel circle over the currently

selected edge. In this area, the nodes have a longer time-out than the currently selected node and may not reply before this selection. When using other delay functions, the area of possible protests can be reduced. Further details can be found in [41].

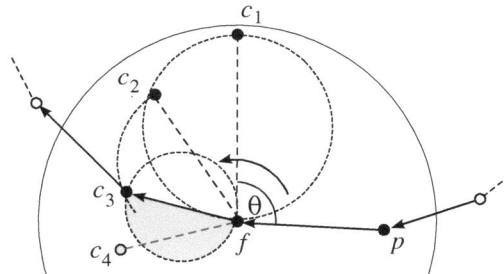

Figure 15: Angular Relaying: The candidates reply according to angle θ: After c_1's reply, c_2 and c_3 protest. c_3 finally becomes the next hop neighbor.

5 Georouting under Realistic Network Models

In practice the transmission radius is not uniform as assumed in the unit disk graph model. Usually one can observe stable links near to the transmitter and no connection beyond a certain distance to the transmitter. In between there is a transitional region with volatile connections [92]. In order to transform this observation into an abstract model, the following two approaches have been proposed:

From a more graph-theoretic perspective, weakening the unit disk graph assumption has led to the definition of *Quasi Unit Disk Graphs* (QUDG) [3, 50]. A Quasi Unit Disk Graph contains all edges shorter than r and no edges longer than a cutoff distance R (see Figure 16). Nodes in between, i.e. at a distance between r and R, may or may not communicate directly, which corresponds to the transitional region between stable short-range connections and the cutoff distance.

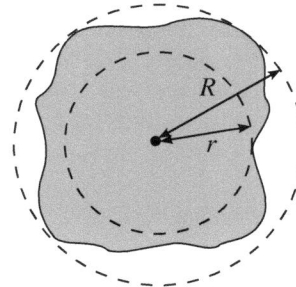

Figure 16: Quasi Unit Disk Graph

From a physical-layer perspective, the stability of communication links decreases as the distance to the transmitter increases. Based on the lognormal shadowing or log-distance path loss model, this can be modeled by a function that returns the reception probability for a given distance [69, 53] (see Figure 17).

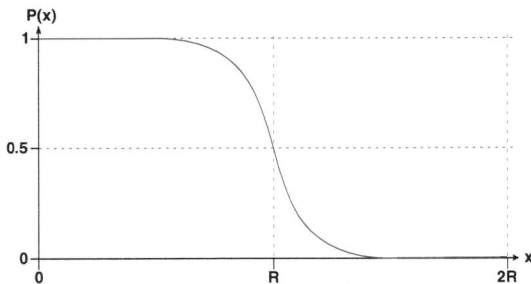

Figure 17: Reception probability versus distance

Both models were used to investigate geographic routing strategies under more realistic assumptions. We will see in the remainder of this section that in greedy forwarding the consideration of reception probability has led to new local forwarding rules, while in planar graph routing and recovery the Quasi Unit Disk Graph model has been studied.

5.1 Greedy Forwarding with Realistic Physical Layer

Under realistic physical layer considerations, the pure greedy forwarding, which selects the neighbor with the maximum advance in each step, does not yield optimal results, because it is designed with respect to the hop count metric and does not take lossy links into account. If a node in the transitional region with low link quality is selected as a next hop, it might take a few transmission attempts to successfully forward a packet, whereas another node with a smaller advance could be reached on the first try. Hence, the metric for doing such forwarding decisions should include the cost for re-transmissions [76]. The cost for re-transmissions can be estimated by the number of transmissions needed to send a data packet over a specific link. By comparing this to the progress a link can provide, one can find a balance between costly retransmissions over long distance links and the increased hop count when using short links.

The expected number of re-transmissions can be derived from the packet reception rate (PRR). The packet reception rate is the ratio of successfully received packets over the total number of transmitted packets over a specific time period. If this data is recorded by a node,

it can serve as a reception probability p for future transmissions. The reciprocal $1/p$ describes the expected number of transmissions needed for a successful reception, if acknowledgements are not taken into account.

Seada et al. [74] propose to use the product of the packet reception rate and the advance towards the destination as a metric for forwarding decisions. As a low PRR causes a high number of re-transmission attempts, this metric penalizes lossy links. Assumed that the packet reception rate for communicating with the neighbors is known, the forwarder chooses a neighbor based on this metric. In addition the authors propose different blacklisting strategies to filter out the farthest neighbors or the neighbors with the worst reception rate.

A general metric for dealing with a realistic physical layer model is the cost-over-progress ratio presented by Kuruvila et al. [53, 54]. Minimizing the cost-over-progress ratio means to find a next hop neighbor that requires the minimal cost for transmission per progress towards the destination. The PRR × distance metric in [74] also follows this concept, as it is essentially a ratio of the advance over the expected number of transmissions, and maximizing this ratio is equivalent to minimizing the cost over progress. Note, that cost can be an arbitrary measure and include the number of re-transmission attempts or energy-related metrics. Likewise, progress can be defined in terms of distance, by which the packet advances, or by the projected distance as in the MFR rule for greedy routing.

Kuruvila et al. use the cost-over-progress concept in their expected progress routing (EPR) [53] algorithm. Progress is here defined as the advance towards the destination and an expected hop count (EHC) serves as a cost metric. The EHC is defined as the expected number of transmissions including data and acknowledgements and based on the reception probability p. It is calculated by $1/p^2 + 1/p$, which includes the retransmissions due to lost acknowledgements. EPR selects the neighbor that minimizes EHC over advance.

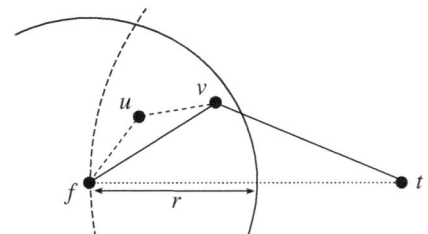

Figure 18: Iterative expected progress routing.

Sometimes it can be more efficient if the selected neighbor is not reached directly, but through an additional intermediate hop. Therefore, an iterative version of this algorithm has been proposed, which works as follows: The forwarder f first selects a neighbor v that minimizes the EHC over advance. Afterwards it tries to find an intermediate node u for which $\text{EHC}(f, u) + \text{EHC}(u, v)$ is the minimum of all neighbors and smaller than $\text{EHC}(f, v)$. If such neighbor exists, it will be selected as a next hop (see Figure 18). An overview of the cost-over-progress framework can be found in [83].

5.2 Localization errors and mobility

Geographic routing relies on precise position information, which is in practice not always available. Inaccurate positioning devices or node mobility can lead to wrong or out-dated position information. Especially in mobile scenarios the approaches that rely on beaconing to announce position information bear the problem of out-dated information. Contention-based strategies are advantageous in those scenarios as position information is acquired on demand. But also reactive methods are confronted with problems in highly mobile scenarios. A node moving out of range during a transmission can cause a short-term asymmetric link. This can lead to packet loss (in the unacknowledged case) or to packet duplication as the sender is not aware that the packet was received and is already being forwarded. This problem is not specific to geographic routing. However, if the localization method or the positioning device is unreliable, one has to deal with localization errors even in static scenarios.

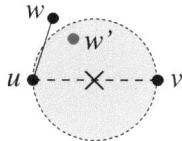

Figure 19: Localization error causing disconnection after planarization

While greedy forwarding is almost not affected by moderate localization errors (<25%) [32], recovery strategies such as face routing rely on geometric criteria, which require precise position information about the neighborhood. The effect of such errors on planarization and face routing has been studied by Seada et al. [73]. Localization errors cause two main problems: First, an incorrect position information broadcasted to the neighbors can lead to a network disconnection during planarization when using local criteria such as the Gabriel graph condition (see Figure 19). A network disconnection after applying the GG or RNG planarization can be prevented by requiring a mutual witness: An edge is only removed, if both endpoints are connected to the node violating the GG or RNG condition. The second problem occurs, if a crossing edge is not

removed during planarization, because of a wrong estimated position. As a result, face routing will operate on a non-planar graph.

The effect of mobility on geographic routing is investigated by Son et al. in [75]. They identify two problems: lost links and loop problems. Lost links occur mainly in greedy forwarding if nodes close to the border of the transmission range are used. This is specific to the plain greedy method, other strategies based on cost-over-progress usually select candidates closer to the forwarder, which alleviates this problem. For mobility-related problems, Son et al. propose a mobility prediction strategy. The nodes extrapolate the new position of a neighbor from previous beacon information, such that they can estimate future locations of their neighbors.

5.3 Recovery in Non-Unit-Disk-Graphs

In networks that do not obey the unit disk graph assumption the planarization schemes described in Section 3.2 do not work correctly and can cause a network disconnection as shown in Figure 20.

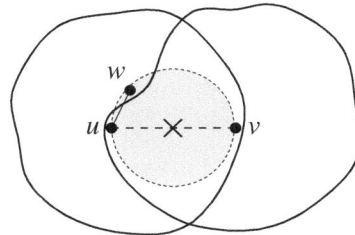

Figure 20: Disconnection after planarization due to irregular transmission ranges

Under a weaker condition than the unit disk connectivity the planarization and a subsequent face routing is possible. Such condition was introduced by Barrière et al. [3] and later generalized to the *Quasi Unit Disk Graph* (QUDG) by Kuhn et al. [50]. In a Quasi Unit Disk Graph with minimum and maximum transmission ranges r and R, links of length smaller than r are guaranteed and no links longer than R exist. Links with length between r and R may or may not exist. If all links are bidirectional and the ratio R/r is at most $\sqrt{2}$, a planar graph can be constructed by using only local information [3]. This is possible because any node within the Gabriel circle over a link uv is either connected to u or v under this condition. Therefore, nodes u and v can agree by communication on whether the Gabriel condition for the edge uv is fulfilled or the edge has to be removed. If the edge uv is removed because of a node w inside the Gabriel circle over uv, a *virtual edge* between u and w is introduced, if w is connected to v, but not to u. Analogously, a virtual edge vw is created, if vw does not exist in the original graph. The

Gabriel graph condition is applied to virtual edges as well, such that the removal of a virtual edge requires the introduction of a new virtual edge. The resulting subgraph extended by virtual edges is planar and connected, such that face routing can be applied. Routing over virtual edges is then performed by communication of the endpoints, which are always connected by a path in the original graph. The drawback of this method is that using a virtual edge might require routing between the endpoints over multiple hops in the original graph. The length of this routing path can be bounded if there is a minimum distance between any two nodes; otherwise, it is unbounded (see the discussion in [3]). The route length bound can be preserved without the minimum distance assumption by using a backbone construction based on clustering as described in [52].

Instead of introducing virtual edges, one can define virtual nodes for edge intersections [51]. In QUDGs with $R/r \leq \sqrt{2}$ at least two endpoints of an intersecting edge are connected so that these intersections can be detected locally. Hence, routing over a virtual node can be performed by direct communication of the endpoints of the intersecting edge [60]. Nesterenko et al. [68] propose a routing strategy based on a concept that is equivalent to the virtual nodes. It performs face traversals without prior planarization and does not avoid crossing edges. Whenever the face traversal reaches a crossing edge, the next edge is determined after communication by the endpoints (Figure 21). For this algorithm, a geometric property such as the QUDG with $R/r \leq \sqrt{2}$ is not required. However, as the endpoints need to communicate, the authors require the network to satisfy a topological property called intersection semi-closure, which states that the endpoints of intersecting edges are connected by paths of restricted length. VOID routing can be combined with greedy forwarding and guarantees delivery in networks that obey the semi-closure property.

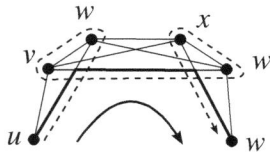

Figure 21: The VOID routing principle [68]

Irregular transmission ranges in general result in Quasi Unit Disk Graphs where the ratio R/r exceeds $\sqrt{2}$. The main problems in such graphs are planarization errors as described in the previous section, and incorrect face changes [44]. The correctness of various face routing algorithms in those graphs depends on when the face change takes place and the choice of the traversal direction. A detailed analysis on this issue

can be found in [21]. The bottom line is that GFG can guarantee delivery on any planar graph, and the remaining problem in networks under irregular transmission ranges is to remove crossing links.

Kim et al. [43] propose the Cross Link Detection Protocol (CLDP) that detects and removes crossing links through repeated face traversals. This is achieved through probing messages that contain the information about the end points of a link. While this message is sent along a face, each node checks whether the next link on the traversal intersects the edge specified in the message. This link is marked non-routable unless the probing message has traversed this link twice in opposite directions – in this case a removal would cause a network partition. After this preprocessing the planar graph routing continues on the resulting network graph. As this method incurs a significant message overhead, the same authors propose a strategy that does not start the cross link detection pro-actively, but on-demand whenever the routing protocol selects a link [45].

Similar in spirit to the cross link detection protocol is the face tracing method by Zhang et al. [90]. The preprocessing comprises the following steps: In a first step, clusters of nodes are built with the clusterhead being adjacent to all cluster members. Then a cluster graph is set up that represents the interconnection of the clusters. In the cluster graph the longest edge of each triangle is removed. Then the faces of the cluster graph are identified by sending inquiry messages along the incident edges. Each face is given an ID, which the incident nodes remember. Routing on this graph is done by traversing the faces of the cluster graph (*face tracing*). The IDs of traversed faces are stored in the message, and the order of the traversed faces is selected by a depth-first search. This guarantees that all parts of the network can be reached.

Apart from detecting crossing links, the location-based depth-first search routing in [77] is one of the earliest approaches to guaranteed-delivery georouting in arbitrary connected networks. The idea is to route the packet according to a depth first search algorithm, where a node of the search tree selects the children in the order of their distance to the destination. Once a message is returned from a dead-end node, the current node proceeds with the next unvisited neighbor or, if no unvisited neighbor exists, it returns the message to its parent node. This strategy requires the nodes to memorize the state of the depth-first search. An improved version with reduced communication overhead by using information from overheard messages and reduction of the network to a dominating set is presented in [88].

A further strategy for routing in non-unit disk graphs is GDSTR [55], a protocol that is based on a distributed spanning tree construction. This spanning tree contains in each node the information about the area that is covered by the subtree. More precisely, a node stores the convex hull of all node locations in the subtree and also the convex hull information of its descendants. For a recovery from a local minimum, a message is routed upwards in the tree until a node is found, whose convex hull contains the destination. From this point, the message is routed downwards in the tree until the destination is found.

Recovery strategies for arbitrary non-unit disk graphs such as CLDP and GDSTR need multi-hop communication to identify crossing links or to gather the necessary information for successful recovery, i.e. these protocols are not localized. On the other hand, localized protocols such as GFG, GPSR and GOAFR cannot guarantee delivery in arbitrary non-unit disk graphs.

6 Geocast and Multipath Routing

Multi-path strategies send duplicates of a message along different paths to the destination in order to increase the delivery rate and the resilience to routing errors. These strategies can overcome routing problems that are due to mobility and out-dated position information. Especially out-dated location information about the destination node can lead to delivery failures under mobility. DREAM [4] tries to overcome this problem by letting each node forward a message to all neighbors that are lying within a cone including the expected target area (see Figure 22 left). The target area is a circle around the last known position of the target having a radius that represents the maximum possible movement since the last position update. This strategy is also termed *restricted directional flooding*. In a similar way, LAR [46] restricts the flooded area to a rectangle including the expected target area (see Figure 22 right).

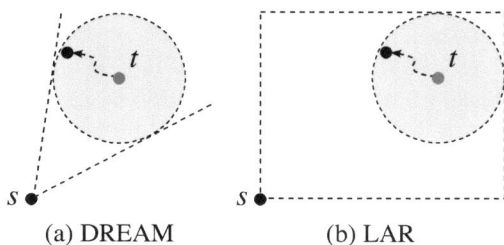

| (a) DREAM | (b) LAR |

Figure 22: Multi-path routing by DREAM and LAR

Apart from the flooding algorithms of DREAM and LAR, multi-path algorithms can be based directly on greedy forwarding or planar graph routing. Greedy forwarding can be generalized by selecting the c best neighbors according to the forwarding criterion in each step, instead of considering only one candidate [61]. A

multi-path strategy based on face traversals is the concurrent face routing (CFR) [13] algorithm. CFR follows the idea of face routing and duplicates a message whenever a face is encountered that is closer to the destination. Then the duplicate traverses the new face, while the original continues the traversal of the old face.

While multi-path strategies try to increase the chance of reaching a single target, geocasting algorithms deliver a message to multiple targets within a specific geographic area. Flooding-based strategies such as LAR allow to perform geocasting. However, sending a message by unicast into the target area and subsequent flooding with geographic restrictions is not sufficient to guarantee delivery to all target nodes. If the target area is intersected by a void region, i.e. there are two nodes within the target area that are only connected by a path that leaves the target area, then the restricted flooding reaches the first node, but stops at the border of the target area and does not reach the second node. In this case, additional messages have to be sent around the target area to reach the second node. Here, face routing can serve as strategy to traverse the void region and find further nodes within the target area. [81].

A comprehensive overview on geocasting techniqes can be found in the surveys by Jiang and Camp [39], Maihöfer [65] and Stojmenovic [82].

7 Location Service

The third assumption for position-based routing is that the position of the destination node is known. Providing each requesting node with this information is the task of a *location services*.

There are similarities between the problem of locating the destination node and the route discovery problem in ad hoc routing protocols. *Proactive* schemes disseminate routing information before it is needed, whereas *reactive* schemes start the route discovery on demand. Similarly, in the case of a location service the question can be asked, whether location information should be spread proactively or whether a requesting node should look up this information on demand.

Location services can be roughly divided into the following categories:

- Flooding-based location dissemination
- Quorum-based and home-zone-based strategies
- Movement-based location dissemination

Flooding-based location dissemination is the fastest way to spread information in the network. It is used in DREAM [4] and LAR [46]. In DREAM each node maintains a location database and distributes its own position proactively throughout the network at regular intervals. In contrast, LAR works reactively: If the destination's position is unknown, the network is flooded with a route request, while the flooded area is restricted to a geographic region where the destination is expected. Flooding-based approaches distribute location information effectively, but at the expense of a high communication overhead.

Quorum-based and *home-zone-based* strategies try to reduce the high communication overhead of flooding. In quorum-based approaches, the location information is held by a group of nodes, which have to be contacted to obtain the target location, whereas in home-zone-based approaches the location is stored by a single node, which is determined by a geographic location. Early approaches for this kind of strategies were proposed by Stojmenovic in [78, 79]. A good example for a quorum-based location service, which uses a geographic criterion for selecting the quorum, is described in [62]. In this scheme the position information is stored along "rows and columns", i.e. a row of nodes having almost the same latitude and a column of nodes with similar longitude store the location information for a specific node. In order to distribute the information, messages are sent along longitudes and latitudes in the network, using geographic routing. A location query can be sent simply in longitudinal or in latitudinal direction in order to find a node of the quorum. For a location service, the nodes of a quorum do not have to be geographically co-located. In the Grid Location Service (GLS) by Li et al. [57] the location servers are distributed according to a hierarchical subdivision of the plane, which is used to assign location information to specific nodes.

In home-zone-based approaches each node has a home-zone with another node that can answer location queries. This is similar to the concept of the home agent in Mobile IP. In order to determine a home zone in a distributed way, a hash function can be used that maps addresses to geographic locations. This is the idea of Geographic Hash Tables (GHT) [70]. Given a node and its location as a key-value pair, a hash function maps the key to a geographic location. The node closest to this location then stores the key-value pair. Location queries are routed to the hash location using geographic routing. As the hash location usually does not match exactly a node's location, a face traversal along the nodes surrounding the hash location finally returns the closest node that answers the query.

A *movement-based* dissemination strategy is presented in [29]. Here, the nodes do not spread information over multiple hops. Location information is exchanged only locally, but by the nodes' movement the information is disseminated in the network. Node exchange location information whenever they encounter other nodes. Thus, the information dissemination is provided by mobility. Each node holds a table of locations and timestamps of the last encounter with other

nodes. Required that the mobility pattern allows an encounter of all nodes, this information is sufficient to route messages by following the newest information about the target node.

An overview of location services can be found in [80] and [22].

8 Applications

Due to its stateless nature, geographic routing is considered to be superior to topological routing in dynamic and mobile wireless networks. However, without topological information, the routing success depends on the likelihood of encountering local minima and the robustness of the recovery strategy. Many known recovery strategies have limitations from a practical point of view because they rely on unrealistic assumptions or they are inefficient because of a high communication overhead caused by traversals or local flooding.

Greedy forwarding, especially the contention-based variants, can provide efficient and reactive routing, also in mobile networks. Consequently, these strategies are attractive for vehicular networks and have been used in projects on car-to-car communication. Vehicular networks aim at providing a fast and secure exchange of safety information such as obstacle warnings or lane change warnings, or the communication with road side units for the purpose of traffic information and infotainment applications. As cars can easily be equipped with positioning capabilities and wireless transceivers, they provide a suitable platform for geographic routing protocols.

A real-world implementation of a geographic routing protocol was used for inter-vehicle communication in the FleetNet project [30]: Cars were equipped with GPS, a WLAN transceiver and a Linux router. GPSR was used as a routing protocol and target locations were obtained reactively by flooding a request. Experimental results with a small number of cars in a static and mobile setting are described in [31] and [67]. At the same time, the idea of contention-based forwarding [24] was developed within the same project and adopted for vehicular networks [23]. As contention-based forwarding is a pure greedy strategy, which is prone to the local minimum problem, a specific recovery strategy for street scenarios was proposed [64]: The Greedy Perimeter Coordinator Routing (GPCR) is based on the idea that the streets, where network nodes reside, form a natural planar graph. Nodes on junctions can serve as coordinators and decide to which junction a packet will be forwarded, while between the junctions a plain greedy scheme can be used. Based on the assumption that street and junctions form a planar graph, a recovery strategy using the right-hand rule can be applied. Whether nodes are on junctions and obtain the role of a coordinator can be determined by using beaconing with 2-hop information or from a evaluating the linear relationship between the neighbors positions statistically.

The work on communication in vehicular networks has been continued in the Network-on-Wheels (NOW) project [17], which targets at developing reliable and secure protocols for car-to-car and car-to-infrastructure communication. Within this project, various protocols were developed, e.g. a position-based greedy forwarding protocol with transmit power control [16] that aims at reducing interference on the wireless channel. Ongoing projects such as GeoNet [66] aim at establishing a reference implementation for georouting in vehicular networks.

9 Conclusion

Geographic routing is an elegant alternative to topology-based routing. Since the early approaches of greedy routing in the 1980s and the emergence of face routing in 1999, various techniques have been developed to improve forwarding efficiency and success rate. A combination of greedy forwarding combined with a recovery strategy is still considered the state-of-the-art technique in geographic routing. The most prominent protocols belong to this type and guarantee delivery on certain network structures. Table 1 gives an overview of the delivery guarantees of some selected protocols.

Many of the described geographic routing protocols rely on geometric properties and assumptions regarding the communication graph. These assumptions enable a theoretical analysis of the efficiency, but they are often violated under practical considerations, e.g. if localization is not precise or if transmission ranges are irregular. This does not imply that geographic routing does not work at all under these conditions, but the basic greedy/face routing protocols loose their delivery guarantees. However, there are techniques to overcome the unit disk graph assumption and to solve problems due to mobility and localization errors.

Greedy forwarding is still an efficient and robust method for geographic routing in dense networks. The development of new greedy strategies has led to cost-efficient methods under realistic physical layer assumptions and for reactive message-efficient routing. Greedy strategies have been evolved towards practical applicability. However, they are prone to the local minimum problem and need to be assisted by a recovery strategy. The development of robust and localized recovery strategies is still subject of ongoing research.

Acknowledgements

The author would like to thank Hannes Frey for many helpful suggestions and discussions.

References

[1] K. Alzoubi, X.-Y. Li, Y. Wang, P.-J. Wan, and O. Frieder, "Geometric spanners for wireless ad hoc networks," *IEEE Trans. on Parallel and Distributed Systems*, vol. 14 (4), pp. 408–421, 2003.

[2] N. Arad and Y. Shavitt, "Minimizing recovery state in geographic ad-hoc routing," in *7th ACM Int. Symposium on Mobile Ad hoc Networking and Computing (Mobi-Hoc)*, 2006, pp. 13–24.

[3] L. Barrière, P. Fraigniaud, L. Narayanan, and J. Opatrny, "Robust position-based routing in wireless ad hoc networks with irregular transmission ranges," *Wireless Communications and Mobile Computing*, vol. 3 (1), pp. 141–153, Mar. 2003.

[4] S. Basagni, I. Chlamtac, V. R. Syrotiuk, and B. A. Woodward, "A distance routing effect algorithm for mobility (DREAM)," in *4th Annual Int. Conf. on Mobile Computing and Networking (MobiCom)*, 1998, pp. 76–84.

[5] A. Blum, P. Raghavan, and B. Schieber, "Navigating in unfamiliar geometric terrain," *SIAM Journal on Computing*, vol. 26 (1), pp. 110–137, Feb. 1997.

[6] B. Blum, T. He, S. Son, and J. Stankovic, "IGF: A state-free robust communication protocol for wireless sensor networks," University of Virginia, USA, Tech. Rep. CS-2003-11, Apr. 2003.

[7] P. Bose, L. Devroye, W. Evans, and D. Kirkpatrick, "On the spanning ratio of gabriel graphs and beta-skeletons," *SIAM Journal on Discrete Mathematics*, vol. 20 (2), pp. 412–427, 2006.

[8] P. Bose and P. Morin, "Competitive online routing in geometric graphs," *Theoretical Computer Science*, vol. 324 (2-3), pp. 273–288, Sep. 2004.

[9] ——, "Online routing in triangulations," *SIAM Journal on Computing*, vol. 33 (4), pp. 937–951, May 2004.

[10] P. Bose, P. Morin, I. Stojmenovic, and J. Urrutia, "Routing with guaranteed delivery in ad hoc wireless networks," in *3rd Int. Workshop on Discrete Algorithms and Methods for Mobile Computing and Communications (DIAL-M '99)*, 1999, pp. 48–55.

[11] M. Chawla, N. Goel, K. Kalaichelvan, A. Nayak, and I. Stojmenovic, "Beaconless position-based routing with guaranteed delivery for wireless ad hoc and sensor networks," *ACTA AUTOMATICA SINICA*, vol. 32 (6), pp. 846–855, Nov. 2006.

[12] D. Chen, J. Deng, and P. K. Varshney, "Selection of a forwarding area for contention-based geographic forwarding in wireless multi-hop networks," *IEEE Trans. on Vehicular Technology*, vol. 56 (5), pp. 3111–3122, Sep. 2007.

[13] T. Clouser, M. Miyashita, and M. Nesterenko, "Fast geometric routing with concurrent face traversal," in *12th Int. Conference on Principles of Distributed Systems (OPODIS'08)*, 2008, pp. 346–362.

[14] S. Datta, I. Stojmenovic, and J. Wu, "Internal node and shortcut based routing with guaranteed delivery in wireless networks," *Cluster Computing*, vol. 5 (2), pp. 169–178, 2002.

Protocol	Guaranteed delivery on ...			Localized	Other properties
	GG, RNG	any planar graph	any connected graph		
GFG [10]	•	•	–	•	
GOAFR+ [51] **	•	•	–	•	asympt. optimal
GPSR [42] *	•	–	–	•	
GPVFR [56]	•	–	–	–	
GVG [68]	•	•	semi-closures	–	
DFS [77]	•	•	•	–	
CLDP [43]	•	•	•	–	
Face Tracing [90]	•	•	•	–	
GDSTR [55]	•	•	•	–	

*) perimeter routing on its own cannot guarantee delivery, cf. [21]   **) this holds for the closest-point variant, cf. [21]

Table 1: Selected geographic routing protocols with guaranteed delivery

[15] Q. Fang, J. Gao, and L. J. Guibas, "Locating and bypassing routing holes in sensor networks," in *23rd Conference of the IEEE Communications Society (INFOCOM)*, Mar. 2004.

[16] A. Festag, R. Baldessari, and H. Wang, "On power-aware greedy forwarding in highway scenarios," in *4th Int. Workshop on Intelligent Transportation (WIT)*, 2007.

[17] A. Festag, G. Noecker, M. Strassberger, A. Lübke, B. Bochow, M. Torrent-Moreno, S. Schnaufer, R. Eigner, C. Catrinescu, and J. Kunisch, "NoW - network on wheels: Project objectives, technology and achievements," in *6th Int. Workshop on Intelligent Transportation (WIT)*, Mar. 2008.

[18] G. G. Finn, "Routing and addressing problems in large metropolitan-scale internetworks," University of Southern California, Tech. Rep. ISI/RR-87-180, Mar. 1987.

[19] H. Frey, "Geographical cluster based routing with guaranteed delivery," in *2nd IEEE Int. Conference on Mobile Ad-hoc and Sensor Systems (MASS 2005)*, 2005.

[20] H. Frey and S. Rührup, "Paving the way towards reactive planar spanner construction in wireless networks," in *GI/ITG Fachtagung Kommunikation in Verteilten Systemen (KiVS 2009)*, Mar. 2009.

[21] H. Frey and I. Stojmenovic, "On delivery guarantees of face and combined greedy-face routing in ad hoc and sensor networks," in *12th Annual Int. Conference on Mobile Computing and Networking (MobiCom)*, 2006, pp. 390–401.

[22] R. Friedman and G. Kliot, "Location services in wireless ad hoc and hybrid networks: A survey," Israel Institute of Technology, Haifa, Israel, Tech. Rep. CS-2006-10, 2006.

[23] H. Füßler, H. Hartenstein, J. Widmer, M. Mauve, and W. Effelsberg, "Contention-based forwarding for street scenarios," in *1st Int. Workshop in Intelligent Transportation (WIT 2004)*, Mar. 2004, pp. 155–160.

[24] H. Füßler, J. Widmer, M. Käsemann, M. Mauve, and H. Hartenstein, "Beaconless Position-Based Routing for Mobile Ad-Hoc Networks," Department of Computer Science, University of Mannheim, Germany, Tech. Rep. TR-03-001, Feb. 2003.

[25] H. Füßler, J. Widmer, M. Mauve, and H. Hartenstein, "A novel forwarding paradigm for position-based routing (with implicit addressing)," in *IEEE 18th Annual Workshop on Computer Communications (CCW 2003)*, Oct. 2003, pp. 194–200.

[26] K. R. Gabriel and R. R. Sokal, "A new statistical approach to geographic variation analysis," *Systematic Zoology*, vol. 18 (3), pp. 259–278, 1969.

[27] L. Galluccio, A. Leonardi, G. Morabito, and S. Palazzo, "A mac/routing cross-layer approach to geographic forwarding in wireless sensor networks," *Ad Hoc Networks*, vol. 5 (6), pp. 872–884, Aug. 2007.

[28] J. Gao, L. J. Guibas, J. E. Hershberger, L. Zhang, and A. Zhu, "Geometric spanner for routing in mobile networks," in *2nd ACM Int. Symposium on Mobile Ad Hoc Networking & Computing (MobiHoc)*, 2001, pp. 45–55.

[29] M. Grossglauser and M. Vetterli, "Locating mobile nodes with ease: learning efficient routes from encounter histories alone," *IEEE/ACM Trans. on Networking*, vol. 14 (3), pp. 457–469, 2006.

[30] H. Hartenstein, B. Bochow, A. Ebner, M. Lott, M. Radimirsch, and D. Vollmer, "Position-aware ad hoc wireless networks for inter-vehicle communications: the fleetnet project," in *2nd ACM Int. Symposium on Mobile Ad Hoc Networking & Computing (MobiHoc)*, 2001, pp. 259–262.

[31] H. Hartenstein, H. Füßler, M. Mauve, and W. J. Franz, "Simulation results and a proof-of-concept implementation of the fleetnet position-based router," in *8th International Conference on Personal Wireless Communications (PWC)*, 2003, pp. 192–197.

[32] T. He, C. Huang, B. M. Blum, J. A. Stankovic, and T. F. Abdelzaher, "Range-free localization and its impact on large scale sensor networks," *Trans. on Embedded Computing Sys.*, vol. 4 (4), pp. 877–906, 2005.

[33] T. He, J. A. Stankovic, C. Lu, and T. Abdelzaher, "Speed: A stateless protocol for real-time communication in sensor networks," in *International Conference on Distributed Computing Systems (ICDCS)*, 2003, p. 46.

[34] M. Heissenbüttel and T. Braun, "A novel position-based and beacon-less routing algorithm for mobile ad-hoc networks," in *3rd IEEE Workshop on Applications and Services in Wireless Networks*, 2003, pp. 197–209.

[35] M. Heissenbüttel, T. Braun, T. Bernoulli, and M. Wälchli, "BLR: Beacon-less routing algorithm for mobile ad-hoc networks," *Computer Communications*, vol. 27 (11), pp. 1076–1086, Jul. 2004.

[36] J. Hightower and G. Borriello, "Location systems for ubiquitous computing," *IEEE Computer*, vol. 34 (8), pp. 57–66, Aug. 2001.

[37] T.-C. Hou and V. Li, "Transmission range control in multihop packet radio networks," *IEEE Trans. on Communications*, vol. 34 (1), pp. 38–44, Jan. 1986.

[38] J. W. Jaromczyk and G. T. Toussaint, "Relative neighborhood graphs and their relatives," *Proc. of the IEEE*, vol. 80 (9), pp. 1502–1517, 1992.

[39] X. Jiang and T. Camp, "Review of geocasting protocols for a mobile ad hoc network," in *Proceedings of the Grace Hopper Celebration (GHC)*, 2002.

[40] D. B. Johnson and D. A. Maltz, "Dynamic Source Routing in Ad Hoc Wireless Networks," in *Mobile Computing*, T. Imielinski and H. Korth, Eds. Kluwer Academic Publishers, 1996, pp. 152–181.

[41] H. Kalosha, A. Nayak, S. Rührup, and I. Stojmenovic, "Select-and-protest-based beaconless georouting with guaranteed delivery in wireless sensor networks," in *27th Annual IEEE Conference on Computer Communications (INFOCOM)*, Apr. 2008, pp. 346–350.

[42] B. Karp and H. T. Kung, "GPSR: greedy perimeter stateless routing for wireless networks," in *6th Annual ACM/IEEE Int. Conference on Mobile Computing and Networking (MobiCom)*, 2000, pp. 243–254.

[43] Y.-J. Kim, R. Govindan, B. Karp, and S. Shenker, "Geographic routing made practical," in *2nd USENIX/ACM Symposium on Networked System Design and Implementation (NSDI'05)*, May 2005, pp. 217–230.

[44] ——, "On the pitfalls of geographic routing," in *3rd Int. Workshop on Discrete Algorithms and Methods for Mobile Computing and Communications – Principles of Mobile Computing (DIALM-POMC)*, 2005, pp. 34–43.

[45] ——, "Lazy cross-link removal for geographic routing," in *4th Int. Conference on Embedded Networked Sensor Systems (SenSys'06)*, 2006, pp. 112–124.

[46] Y.-B. Ko and N. H. Vaidya, "Location-aided routing (LAR) in mobile ad hoc networks," in *4th Annual ACM/IEEE Int. Conference on Mobile Computing and Networking (MobiCom)*, Oct. 1998, pp. 66–75.

[47] E. Kranakis, H. Singh, and J. Urrutia, "Compass routing on geometric networks," in *11th Canadian Conference on Computational Geometry (CCCG'99)*, Aug. 1999, pp. 51–54.

[48] F. Kuhn, R. Wattenhofer, Y. Zhang, and A. Zollinger, "Geometric ad-hoc routing: Of theory and practice," in *22th ACM Symposium on Principles of Distributed Computing (PODC'03)*, 2003, pp. 63–72.

[49] F. Kuhn, R. Wattenhofer, and A. Zollinger, "Asymptotically optimal geometric mobile ad-hoc routing," in *6th Int. Workshop on Discrete Algorithms and Methods for Mobile Computing and Communications (DIALM)*. ACM Press, 2002, pp. 24–33.

[50] ——, "Ad-hoc networks beyond unit disk graphs," in *2003 Joint Workshop on Foundations of Mobile Computing (DIALM-POMC)*, 2003, pp. 69–78.

[51] ——, "Worst-case optimal and average-case efficient geometric ad-hoc routing," in *4th ACM Int. Symposium on Mobile Ad Hoc Networking and Computing (MobiHoc)*, 2003, pp. 267–278.

[52] ——, "Ad hoc networks beyond unit disk graphs," *Wireless Networks*, vol. 14 (5), pp. 715–729, 2008.

[53] J. Kuruvila, A. Nayak, and I. Stojmenovic, "Hop count optimal position-based packet routing algorithms for ad hoc wireless networks with a realistic physical layer," *IEEE Journal on Selected Areas in Communications*, vol. 23 (6), pp. 1267–1275, 2005.

[54] ——, "Greedy localized routing for maximizing probability of delivery in wireless ad hoc networks with a realistic physical layer," *J. Parallel Distrib. Comput.*, vol. 66 (4), pp. 499–506, 2006.

[55] B. Leong, B. Liskov, and R. Morris, "Geographic routing without planarization," in *3rd USENIX/ACM Symposium on Networked Systems Design and Implementation (NSDI '06)*, 2006, pp. 339–352.

[56] B. Leong, S. Mitra, and B. Liskov, "Path vector face routing: Geographic routing with local face information," in *13th IEEE Int. Conference on Network Protocols (ICNP'05)*, 2005, pp. 147–158.

[57] J. Li, J. Jannotti, D. S. J. De Couto, D. R. Karger, and R. Morris, "A scalable location service for geographic ad hoc routing," in *6th Annual Int. Conference on Mobile Computing and Networking (MobiCom)*, 2000, pp. 120–130.

[58] X.-Y. Li, G. Calinescu, and P.-J. Wan, "Distributed construction of planar spanner and routing for ad hoc wireless networks," in *21st Annual IEEE Conference on Computer Communications (INFOCOM)*, 2002, pp. 1268–1277.

[59] X.-Y. Li, I. Stojmenovic, and Y. Wang, "Partial delaunay triangulation and degree limited localized bluetooth scatternet formation," *IEEE Trans. on Parallel and Distributed Systems*, vol. 15 (4), pp. 350–361, 2004.

[60] K. M. Lillis, S. V. Pemmaraju, and I. A. Pirwani, "Topology control and geographic routing in realistic wireless networks," *Ad Hoc & Sensor Wireless Networks*, vol. 6, pp. 265–297, 2008.

[61] X. Lin, M. Lakshdisi, and I. Stojmenovic, "Location based localized alternate, disjoint, multi-path and component routing schemes for wireless networks," in *2nd ACM Int. Symposium on Mobile Ad Hoc Networking & Computing (MobiHoc)*, Oct. 2001, pp. 287–290.

[62] D. Liu, X. Jia, and I. Stojmenovic, "Quorum and connected dominating sets based location service in wireless ad hoc, sensor and actuator networks," *Computer Communications*, vol. 30 (18), pp. 3627–3643, 2007.

[63] W.-J. Liu and K.-T. Feng, "Greedy anti-void routing protocol for wireless sensor networks," *IEEE Communications Letters*, vol. 11 (7), pp. 562–564, Jul. 2007.

[64] C. Lochert, M. Mauve, H. Füßler, and H. Hartenstein, "Geographic routing in city scenarios," *SIGMOBILE Mobile Computing and Communication Reviews*, vol. 9 (1), pp. 69–72, 2005.

[65] C. Maihöfer, "A survey of geocast routing protocols," *IEEE Communications Surveys and Tutorials*, vol. 6 (2), pp. 32–42, 2004.

[66] M. Mariyasagayam, H. Menouar, and M. Lenardi, "Geonet: A project enabling active safety and ipv6 vehicular applications," in *IEEE Int. Conference on Vehicular Electronics and Safety*, Sep. 2008, pp. 312–316.

[67] M. Möske, H. Füßler, H. Hartenstein, and W. Franz, "Performance measurements of a vehicular ad hoc network," in *59th IEEE Vehicular Technology Conference (VTC 2004-Spring)*, May 2004, pp. 2116–2120.

[68] M. Nesterenko and A. Vora, "Void traversal for guaranteed delivery in geometric routing," in *IEEE Int. Conference on Mobile Adhoc and Sensor Systems (MASS'05)*, Nov. 2005, pp. 6 pp.–715.

[69] L. Qin and T. Kunz, "On-demand routing in manets: The impact of a realistic physical layer model," in *2nd Int. Conference on Ad-hoc, Mobile, and Wireless Networks (ADHOC-NOW)*, 2003, pp. 37–48.

[70] S. Ratnasamy, B. Karp, L. Yin, F. Yu, D. Estrin, R. Govindan, and S. Shenker, "Ght: A geographic hash table for data-centric storage in sensornets," in *1st ACM Int. Workshop on Wireless Sensor Networks and Applications (WSNA'02)*, Sep. 2002.

[71] S. Rührup and C. Schindelhauer, "Competitive time and traffic analysis of position-based routing using a cell structure," in *5th IEEE Int. Workshop on Algorithms for Wireless, Mobile, Ad Hoc and Sensor Networks (WMAN'05)*, 2005, p. 248.

[72] ——, "Online multi-path routing in a maze," in *17th Int. Symposium on Algorithms and Computation (ISAAC), LNCS 4288*. Springer-Verlag, Dec. 2006, pp. 650–659.

[73] K. Seada, A. Helmy, and R. Govindan, "Modeling and analyzing the correctness of geographic face routing under realistic conditions," *Ad Hoc Networks*, vol. 5 (6), pp. 855–871, 2007.

[74] K. Seada, M. Zuniga, A. Helmy, and B. Krishnamachari, "Energy-efficient forwarding strategies for geographic routing in lossy wireless sensor networks," in *2nd Int. Conference on Embedded Networked Sensor Systems (SenSys'04)*, 2004, pp. 108–121.

[75] D. Son, A. Helmy, and B. Krishnamachari, "The effect of mobility-induced location errors on geographic routing in mobile ad hoc and sensor networks: Analysis and improvement using mobility prediction," *IEEE Trans. on Mobile Computing*, vol. 3 (3), pp. 233–245, 2004.

[76] I. Stojmenovic, A. Nayak, and J. Kuruvila, "Design guidelines for routing protocols in ad hoc and sensor networks with a realistic physical layer," *IEEE Communications Magazine*, vol. 43 (3), pp. 101–106, Mar. 2005.

[77] I. Stojmenovic, M. Russell, and B. Vukojevic, "Depth first search and location based localized routing and qos routing in wireless networks," in *Int. Conference on Parallel Processing (ICPP)*, 2000, pp. 173–180.

[78] I. Stojmenovic, "Home agent based location update and destination search schemes in ad hoc wireless networks," University of Ottawa, Tech. Rep. TR-99-10, Sep. 1999.

[79] ——, "A routing strategy and quorum based location update scheme for ad hoc wireless networks," University of Ottawa, Tech. Rep. TR-99-09, Sep. 1999.

[80] ——, "Location updates for efficient routing in ad hoc networks," in *Handbook of Wireless Networks and Mobile Computing*. Wiley, 2002.

[81] ——, "Geocasting with guaranteed delivery in sensor networks," *Wireless Communications*, vol. 11 (6), pp. 29–37, Dec. 2004.

[82] ——, "Geocasting in ad hoc and sensor networks," in *Theoretical and Algorithmic Aspects of Sensor, Ad Hoc Wireless and Peer-to-Peer Networks*, J. Wu, Ed. Auerbach Publications, 2006, pp. 79–97.

[83] ——, "Localized network layer protocols in wireless sensor networks based on optimizing cost over progress ratio," *IEEE Network*, vol. 20 (1), pp. 21–27, 2006.

[84] I. Stojmenovic and X. Lin, "Loop-free hybrid single-path/flooding routing algorithms with guaranteed delivery for wireless networks," *IEEE Trans. on Parallel and Distributed Systems*, vol. 12 (10), pp. 1023–1032, 2001.

[85] ——, "Power-aware localized routing in wireless networks," *IEEE Trans. on Parallel and Distributed Systems*, vol. 12 (11), pp. 1122–1133, 2001.

[86] H. Takagi and L. Kleinrock, "Optimal transmission ranges for randomly distributed packet radio terminals," *IEEE Trans. on Communications*, vol. 32 (3), pp. 246–257, Mar. 1984.

[87] G. T. Toussaint, "The relative neighborhood graph of a finite planar set," *Pattern recognition*, vol. 12 (4), pp. 261–268, 1980.

[88] B. Vukojevic, N. Goel, K. Kalaichevlan, A. Nayak, and I. Stojmenovic, "Depth first search-based and power-aware geo-routing in ad hoc and sensor wireless networks," *Autonomous and Adaptive Communications Systems*, vol. 1 (1), pp. 41–54, 2008.

[89] M. Witt and V. Turau, "BGR: Blind geographic routing for sensor networks," in *3rd Workshop on Intelligent Solutions in Embedded Systems (WISES)*, 2005, pp. 51–61.

[90] F. Zhang, H. Li, A. Jiang, J. Chen, and P. Luo, "Face tracing based geographic routing in nonplanar wireless networks," in *26th IEEE Int. Conference on Computer Communications (INFOCOM)*, 2007, pp. 2243–2251.

[91] M. Zorzi, "A new contention-based mac protocol for geographic forwarding in ad hoc and sensor networks," in *IEEE Int. Conference on Communications (ICC)*, 2004, pp. 3481–3485.

[92] M. Zuniga and B. Krishnamachari, "Analyzing the transitional region in low power wireless links," in *1st IEEE Conference on Sensor and Ad Hoc Communications and Networks (SECON'04)*, Oct. 2004, pp. 517–526.

Ad Hoc and Sensor Wireless Networks: Architectures, Algorithms and Protocols, 2009, 89-107

CHAPTER 6

Distributed Localization in Wireless Sensor Networks

Winston K.G. Seah*[1], Eddie B.S. Tan[1], Sau-Yee Wong[1] and Jeffrey Tay[2]

[1]*Networking Protocols Department, Institute for Infocomm Research, Singapore*
[2]*Tapper School of Business, Carnegie Mellon University, Pittsburgh, USA*

Abstract: Wireless sensor networks (WSNs) continue to be an active research area as the deployment of low cost wireless sensors is a promising technique for various applications such as early warning and alert systems, ecosystem monitoring, warehousing, logistics and surveillance. Sensor data is typically interpreted with reference to a sensor's location, e.g. reporting the occurrence of an event, tracking of a moving object or monitoring the physical conditions of a region. The process of determining the location of a sensor node in a wireless sensor network, commonly known as localization, is a challenging problem as reliance on infrastructure-based technology like GPS is infeasible due to constraints arising from limited on-board computation power and energy supply, as well as, physical deployment conditions (e.g. indoors or underwater). In this chapter, we focus on range-free distributed localization schemes, in particular, schemes based on hop count that can function under realistic conditions.

INTRODUCTION

A wireless sensor network (WSN) is an ad hoc wireless network comprising tiny nodes with sensing capabilities. These low-cost sensor nodes are characterized by their limited battery lives and computational power, and zero or low mobility. Hundreds or thousands of such sensors form a wireless network to perform coordinated tasks [1]. Many sensor network applications have been proposed, such as disaster early warning, habitat and environmental monitoring, inventory control, and surveillance. Localization is the ability of a sensor to determine its physical coordinates and this is a critical aspect of WSN applications because location information is crucial in understanding the application context, e.g. event reporting, moving object tracking or monitoring the physical conditions of a region. Localization in WSNs is a challenging problem as reliance on technology like GPS [2] is infeasible due to cost and energy constraints, and also physical constraints like indoor environments.

In very large and dense wireless sensor networks, it may not be feasible to accurately measure the exact location of every sensor and furthermore, a coarse estimate of the sensor's location may suffice for most applications. In this chapter, we focus on distributed range-free localization that utilizes hop count to estimate the location of sensors within the network. First, we discuss related work on localization in wireless sensor networks, emphasizing on range-free schemes. We then present the Density-Aware Hop count Localization scheme [18][19] and Selective Multilateration [20] for improving the localization accuracy. Next, a method to dynamically compute the

hop count distance [21] is presented, followed by the practical issues in deploying WSNs [22], and future work, before concluding the chapter.

RELATED WORK

Generally, localization schemes orientate sensor nodes with respect to a global coordinate system defined by anchors whose positions are known priori [3]. The positions of anchors are determined either through the use of positioning systems like GPS [2] or using manual calibration. Nodes either estimate their distances to anchors, or estimate node-to-node angles. A computation methodology, such as triangulation [4], is then used to compute position estimates. Localization can be categorized into range-based (or fine-grained) and range-free (or coarse-grained) schemes. In range-based localization, specialized and often expensive hardware is used to obtain absolute point-to-point distance estimates or angle estimates to compute location. On the other hand, range-free localization does not rely on such hardware and instead, uses mere connectivity information making it very suitable for WSN usage. In the following subsections, we will first briefly discuss range-based localization schemes, followed by range-free localization. We will then focus on hop count based localization schemes.

Range-based Localization

Range-based localization protocols use a variety of techniques, including Time of Arrival (ToA), Time Difference of Arrival (TDoA), Angle of Arrival (AoA) and Received Signal Strength Indicator (RSSI). In ToA and TDoA technologies, signal propagation time is used

Hai Liu / Xiaowen Chu / Yiu-Wing Leung (Eds.)

to extract range information. An example of a scheme that employs TDoA is Ad Hoc Localization System (AHLos) [5]. Systems using such technologies require expensive and energy-consuming electronics that may not be suitable for low-power sensor network devices. AoA techniques require nodes to estimate relative angles between neighbors for location computation, e.g. [6]. Like TDoA, AoA demands additional hardware and computation capability that may not be cost effective for large scale sensor networks. The RSSI-based approach has been proposed in schemes such as RADAR [7] and DV-Distance [8], where either theoretical or empirical models are used to translate signal strength into distance estimates. Such models are often impeded by physical-layer problems inherent in RF systems, such as erratic signal propagation, background interference and multi-path fading [9]. These problems make RSSI unreliable for use in WSN localization. A more extensive review of range-based localization can be found in [10].

Range-free Localization

The impracticality, particularly in terms of energy and implementation costs, associated with range-based localization schemes in WSNs, has made range-free schemes a much more viable alternative. This is especially so because many WSN applications do not demand very high degree of precision in their localization requirement. Range-free localization schemes rely only on connectivity information among nodes to estimate positions and such information can be obtained either explicitly or implicitly from packets exchanged among nodes. Range-free localization schemes can be further divided into the following subcategories.

Proximity-based

In proximity-based protocols like Centroid [11] and Approximate Point In Triangulation (APIT) [12], each sensor node is within the transmission range of enough anchors such that a reasonable location estimate can be inferred. A key disadvantage of such approaches is that many anchors are required in the network, which is usually not feasible.

Geometric Constraint-based

Another approach to range-free localization is based on solving geometric constraints. For instance, MDS-MAP [13] is a complex mathematical analysis technique which considers every bit of connectivity information, i.e. which node is connected to which other nodes, while another scheme uses convex optimization to solve a set of geometric constraints [14]. Such techniques require highly intensive

computation which usually can only be performed by a powerful sink node in a WSN. Not only is this usually infeasible for large WSNs, it also violates the distributed nature of WSN localization.

Hop count-based

The drawbacks of the above-mentioned approaches in sensor network localization have prompted a need for localization techniques suitable for WSNs. The multi-hop nature and the vast quantity of low-mobility sensors in a typical sensor network pave the way for the hop count-based approach to localization. In such an approach, localization is carried out by keeping track of the minimum number of hops to anchors. Thus, a node need not be in direct transmission range of the anchors. Hop count-based schemes are generally range-free, distributed in nature, simple to implement on a real WSN, and typically do not require many anchors. Early examples of hop count-based schemes are: DV-Hop [15] and Amorphous [16]. However, these assume the network to be isotropic, that is, when the properties of the graph are the same in all directions, i.e. the nodes are randomly placed in the network with a uniform distribution. Hence, the distance covered by a hop (henceforth known as the hop size) is generally assumed to be constant. However, this assumption does not usually hold true in actual sensor networks because of deployment constraints, e.g. air dropped sensors tend to accumulate at the bottom of a slope or hilly terrain, thus, causing node density to be higher at the bottom than at the peak of a slope; sensors can be swept away by strong current, corroded by harsh chemical solution, moved away or damaged by animals/hostile elements; and, node density changes due to network dynamism arising from sleep/wake scheduling or nodes running out of power. Thus, network density and sensor distribution can be easily altered. Therefore, DV-Hop and Amorphous provide poor localization accuracy, especially in non-uniform networks where the hop sizes can vary greatly [17].

Density-aware Hop count Localization (DHL) [18][19], which is the focus of this chapter, addresses the problem of non-uniformly distributed nodes by estimating the size of each hop based on the local connectivity (i.e. the number of neighbours of a node) at each hop. DHL extensions improve the localization accuracy through selective iterative multi-lateration [20] and dynamically compute the distance estimation with respect to changing network conditions [21]. More recently, similar schemes, e.g. [23], have been proposed to improve the localization accuracy of range-free schemes in networks with non-uniformly deployed nodes and/or regions with no nodes (i.e. holes.) However, they rely on complex geometric methods which make them impractical to implement in typical low-cost sensors.

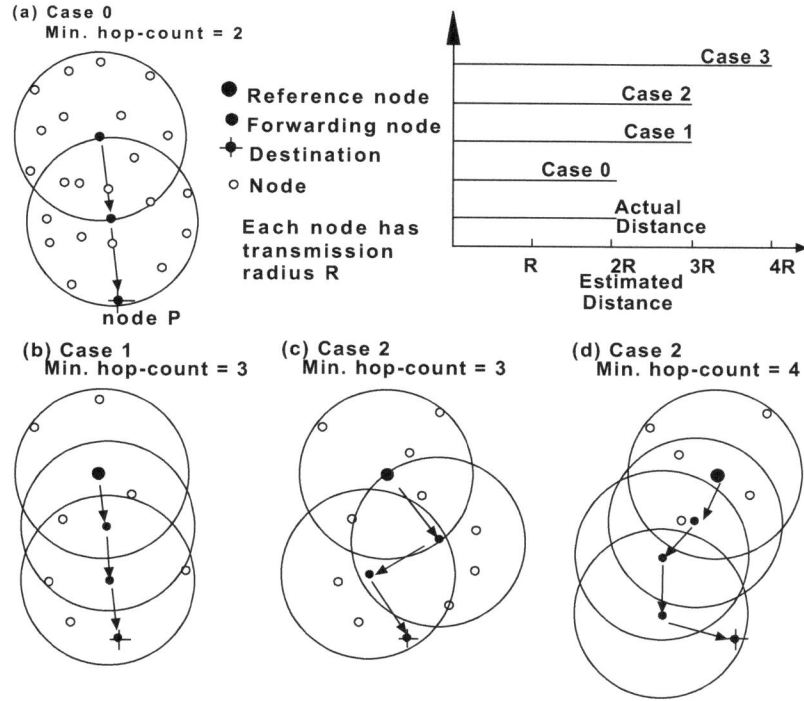

Fig. (1). Node density and euclidean distance.

DENSITY-AWARE HOP COUNT LOCALIZATION

We first discuss two issues that affect the accuracy of hop count localization before presenting the main algorithm, viz. node density and path length.

Node Density and Euclidean Distance

In a 2D (or 3D) WSN topology, we assume that there are at least three (or four) nodes that have a priori location information to serve as Reference Nodes (RNs) from which other nodes in the network can determine their location. In a highly dense, uniformly distributed network, there exists (with high probability) a direct multihop path between an RN and any arbitrary node in the network, and the distance between them estimated by the product of hop count and transmission, i.e. $D=HC \times R$ where D is the estimated Euclidean distance, HC is the hop count from RN and R is the transmission range. This is shown in (a) Case 0 of Fig. (1 where $D=2R$. On the other hand, if the nodes are sparse, the product of hop count and transmission range is very likely to overestimate the distance from RN, as shown in Cases 1, 2 and 3. In Case 1, the forwarding node is not sufficiently close to the boundary of the transmission range, while in Case 2, the end-to-end

path between RN and the destination node is not straight. Case 3 shows a combination of the previous two cases, resulting in even greater overestimation.

Thus, it can be summarized that in a sparse network, the actual distance for each hop is less than R since the probability of finding a point close to the boundary in the direction of travel diminishes.

Path Length

A downside of distance summation using hop count localization is that estimation error accumulates as the hop count increments over multiple hops, and this cumulative error becomes increasingly significant. This is especially true for large networks with few reference nodes where long propagation paths tend to prevail. For each hop, the difference between actual progressed distance and transmission radius is accumulated as the hop counts increase. In reality, an estimated hop-distance (the incremented distance by travelling a hop), L, is imprecise and the uncertainty should be reflected in the expression, i.e., $L \pm \varepsilon$, where ε is the maximum error. If a sensor is m hops from a reference node its estimated distance is $m(L \pm \varepsilon)$, which is $mR[\lambda \pm \varepsilon/R]$ for uniform networks, where λ is the average range ratio and λR is the average hop-distance (i.e., distance per hop), or $R\Sigma_{i=1..m} [\mu_i \pm \varepsilon_i/R]$ for non-uniform networks. From the two equations, when R is infinitely large and sensors are within hearing range from one another, the error is negligible, but this is infeasible since the transmission power of sensors is limited. It is therefore desirable to choose paths with few hops to minimize the cumulative error.

Main DHL Algorithm

We consider a typical WSN which is assumed to be fully connected and nodes are quasi-static with little or low mobility. Due to broadcast nature of wireless channel, each node is assumed to know the number of its neighbours after a network is deployed. An omni-directional radio propagation model (transmission range R) and a 2D network model that is extendable to 3D are assumed. In our network model, there exists a total of N sensors, of which only K sensors (where $0<K<N$), known as reference nodes/sensors, are equipped with position information while the rest of the nodes seek to discover their positions through multi-hop communication. Two nodes can communicate if their distance is less than R, where R is the transmission range (which varies with the transmission power and technology used). Local density is defined as the number of neighbouring nodes per unit transmission area. For simplicity, the number of neighbouring nodes or local connectivity, c, is used to estimate the density surrounding a node which can be easily determined due to the broadcast nature of the wireless link. Depending on local connectivity, we classify the node density into a few categories and each category has a corresponding range ratio. Range ratio, μ, represents the ratio of expected hop-distance to the transmission range for a particular local density. The algorithm strives to integrate density-awareness when propagating hop counts throughout the network. Range ratio is a function of local density, i.e., a sensor node's connectivity per unit transmission coverage.

Let an arbitrary reference node, P_i ($i=1,...,K$) be deployed at a point (X_i, Y_i). For an arbitrary sensor S_j at (u_j, v_j), $j=1,...,N-K$, is assumed to know its local density by listening to the broadcasts of its neighbouring nodes. For the basic design of the DHL algorithm, a predefined set of density categories is assumed, e.g. low, medium and high, and a sensor deduces the category it falls into based on its local density. Each category is mapped to a corresponding range ratio μ that reflects the ratio of transmission range a packet most probably advances if forwarded to the next hop. The number of density categories used is a tradeoff between accuracy and overhead. Increasing the number of categories can increase the accuracy of expected hop-distance, but at the expense of more messages exchanged. The steps to be executed are as follows:

Step A: P_i broadcasts a set of tuples: ID(P_i), Position(P_i), Total Hops to P_i, and Total Range Ratio to P_i, i.e. {ID, (X_i, Y_i), $\sum k_i = 0$, $\sum \mu_i = 0$}.

Step B: S_j stores {ID, (X_i, Y_i), $(\sum k_i)+1$, $(\sum \mu_i)+\mu$} and forwards the information.

Step C: S_j estimates distance to P_i by $L_i = (\sum \mu_i) \times R$.

Step D: If S_j subsequently receives packet with smaller $\sum k_i$ or $\sum \mu_i$, it repeats **Step B** to C.

Step E: S_j associates L_i with a low / high confidence rating depending on the Path Length (as discussed in the previous section.) When an adequate number (i.e. ≥ 3) of distances from reference nodes have been received, S_j will perform triangulation using only L_i values associated with high confidence rating.

The algorithm is basically divided into two phases. The purpose of the first phase, *Density-aware Phase (Step A to D)*, is to enable individual nodes to share hop count information collaboratively in order to determine their distances from individual reference nodes. The hop count distance incorporates density information so that it provides more accurate distance estimation. In the second phase, *Path-Length aware Phase (Step E)*, a node determines the confidence level for each estimated distance and decides if the distance should be used in position computation using triangulation. The first phase uses a node's local density information to address the *density issue*, whereas the second phase assigns confidence level to address the *path length issue*.

Range Ratio and Confidence Level

Range ratio as a function of local connectivity, c, has been derived in [27]. Using a continuous function to determine the range ratio can result in unlimited density categories and immense transmission overhead. If densities are divided into n categories, a node at m hops from a reference node can potentially receive $n+(n-1)(m-2)$ different accumulated range ratios, triggering more packet forwarding. A more heuristic approach using empirical techniques is used to determine the range ratio by investigating its relationship with the local connectivity. To create a network of connectivity c, a total of $cA/(\pi R^2)$ nodes are created randomly within network area of size A. The range ratio is derived according to the percentage of nodes with estimated locations that are within one transmission range from their actual locations; optimal range ratio values for three categories are shown in **Table 1**.

Next, assuming the network diameter is x, a distance computed from more than x/R hops is unlikely to approximate a Euclidean path and thus can be

Table 1. Range ratio for different density categories.

Categories	Local Density	Range Ratio
Low Density	1-6	$\mu_l = 0.6$
Medium Density	7-12	$\mu_m = 0.7$
High Density	>12	$\mu_h = 0.8$

associated with low confidence level. Since a node requires at least three (four) reference nodes to perform triangulation for 2D (3D) networks, it assigns hop counts from the three (four) nearest reference nodes with high confidence. A confidence threshold can be determined within the range of y and x/R to select hop counts with high reliability, where y is the largest hop counts from among the three (four) nearest reference nodes. For simplicity, a node can assign hop counts from other reference nodes with high confidence if they are less than $\frac{1}{2}(x/R+y)$. Only hop counts from reference nodes with high confidence levels will be used in the triangulation.

Communications Overhead

The volume of traffic generated by protocols in a WSN has a strong effect on the performance and the aim is to minimize such communications overhead. Generally, conventional hop count localization requires two separate flooding stages, viz. Hop count Accumulation, and Correction. In the Hop count Accumulation stage, hop count information is disseminated (flooded) from each reference node to, ideally, all the nodes in the network so that each node has a coarse estimation of its position. In the Correction stage, the flooding can be used to spread information that enhances the estimation accuracy. For example, DV-Hop [15] broadcast average hop-distance to every node in the network through controlled flooding, and Amorphous [16] broadcasts each node's coarse position for local averaging. However, network-wide flooding is an expensive process as a lot of energy is consumed for computation and communication, and thus causes scaling problems. The overhead increases linearly with the number of nodes and reference nodes ratio in the network. While increasing reference nodes ratio in the network aids in increasing the localization accuracy, it also tends to increase communication overheads between nodes.

Some algorithms propose using Time-to-Live (TTL) to limit hop count propagation [8]. This is only useful if the reference nodes ratio in the network is high. Otherwise, majority of nodes in the network may not be able to receive sufficient information to compute their positions. Another approach is for a node to stop forwarding once it has received hop count

information from a number of reference nodes defined by a *flood limit* [17]. However, if reference nodes initiate hop count broadcasting at different times, a node may receive information from reference nodes that are further away and stop forwarding once the "flood limit" number of reference nodes has been reached. Thus, the node is unable to take advantage of hop count information from nearer reference nodes that initiate the flooding later.

In comparison, DHL combines the correction process in the hop count accumulation stage to account for the localization errors caused by density variation. When hop count is accumulated in the flooding process, the correction by range ratio is applied simultaneously to all the nodes in the network. Therefore, we do not require a separate flooding stage for correction. This approach effectively helps to reduce the number of transmitted messages, conserve energy, and reduce the time consumed in computing a node's position. Although DHL has slightly more packet transmissions in the first flooding stage due to more hop count adjustment, the second flooding stage is eliminated and thus the total number of packets transmitted is less than that required by other hop count localization schemes.

Performance Evaluation

DHL is validated using simulations and compared against DV-Hop for a non-uniform 500-node network scenario as shown in Fig. (2. There are 8 reference nodes (along the perimeter), R=5m and A=50m×50m. Both Regions I and III have three times more nodes than Regions II and IV. Based on the local density, nodes use range ratio values as shown in **Table 1**. A distance associated with less than 10 hops is assigned a high confidence rating and used in triangulation.

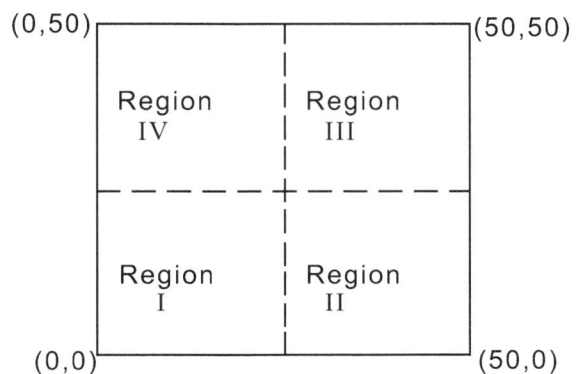

Fig. (2). Simulation topology.

With density-awareness, approximately 78% of the nodes managed to estimate their locations within the transmission range from their actual locations in contrast to 63% using DV-Hop (Fig. 3). With the average density of Regions I and Region III at 23 (i.e. having 23 neighbours) and that of Regions II and IV is at 7, the ratio of density is about 3.3. Based on the

Cumulative Error Distribution

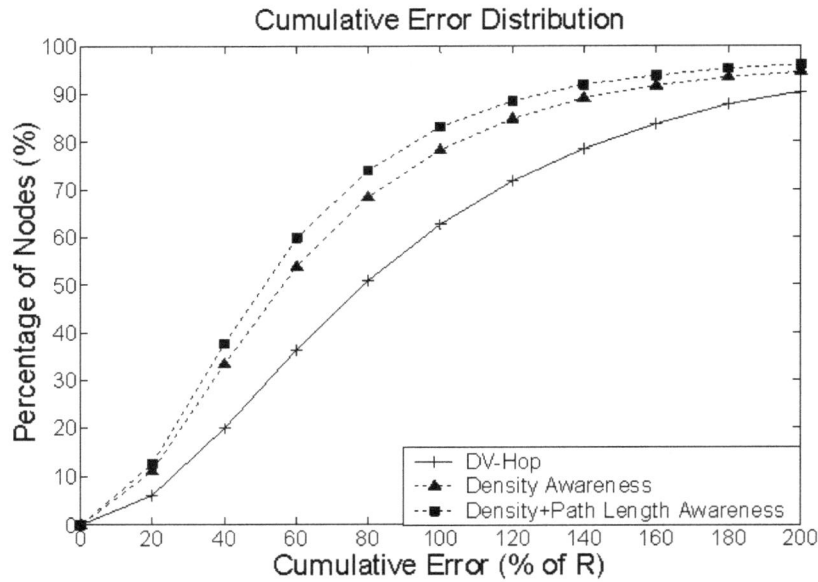

Fig. (3). Cumulative error distribution.

findings on the relationship between range ratio and local density, the distance covered per hop tends to be further with higher node density. Thus, it is clear that by assigning appropriate range ratios, better position estimation is achieved. It is also shown that with both density and path-length awareness, the percentage of nodes with estimation errors within their transmission range rises to 83%.

Fig. (4, comparing the relationship between estimated distance errors and hop counts, shows that localization error increases rapidly with hop counts and the rate of increment is higher for DV-Hop.

Nodes further from the reference nodes tend to miscalculate their distances with greater probability and by applying path-length awareness and filtering distances with large hop counts before triangulation, DHL achieves higher localization accuracy. Other results can be found in [18] and [19].

SELECTIVE ITERATIVE MULTI-LATERATON (SIM)

The initial estimates in hop count-based localization can be fine-tuned using an additional refinement technique known as *iterative multilateration* [24], in which nodes that have successfully estimated their

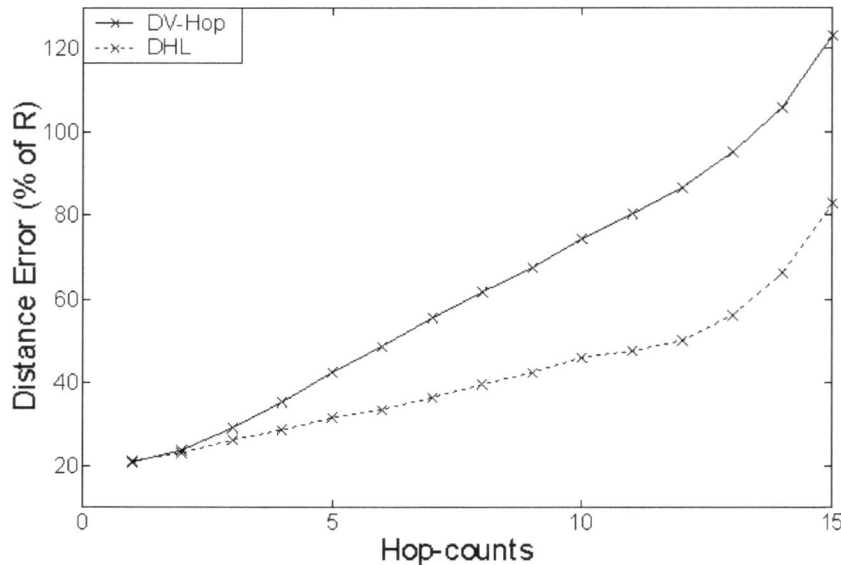

Fig. (4). Distance error vs Hop counts.

positions can act as new anchors. These nodes then propagate their own estimated locations with the aim of refining the initial estimates to achieve higher accuracy, albeit with additional communication costs. In the Ad Hoc Localization System (AHLoS) [25], each node calculates an initial estimate of its location based on geometric constraints, and nodes within direct transmission range of three or more anchors become new anchors and initial estimates are iteratively improved. This iterative technique can be used only when the percentage of anchors is high, which may not be practical. Moreover, large errors introduced by nodes can easily propagate throughout the network. In Recursive Position Estimation [26] where RSSI measurement capability is assumed, localized nodes are selected to be new anchors, subjected to constraints imposed using measured

ranges. Too many iterations lead to excessive energy usage which is not good in WSNs. Furthermore, assuming the presence of RSSI capability makes it unsuitable for WSNs. Other common problems that exist in traditional iterative multilateration techniques include propagation of large errors, excessive overhead, and the lack of scalability.

In view of the abovementioned shortcomings and that careful selection of new anchors is critical, a novel Selective Iterative Multilateration (SIM) [20] is proposed to improve the accuracy of location estimation in hop count-based localization schemes without incurring unnecessary overhead costs. New anchors are selected judiciously such that their initial position estimates are sufficiently accurate. For both DV-Hop [15] and DHL [18][19], results have shown

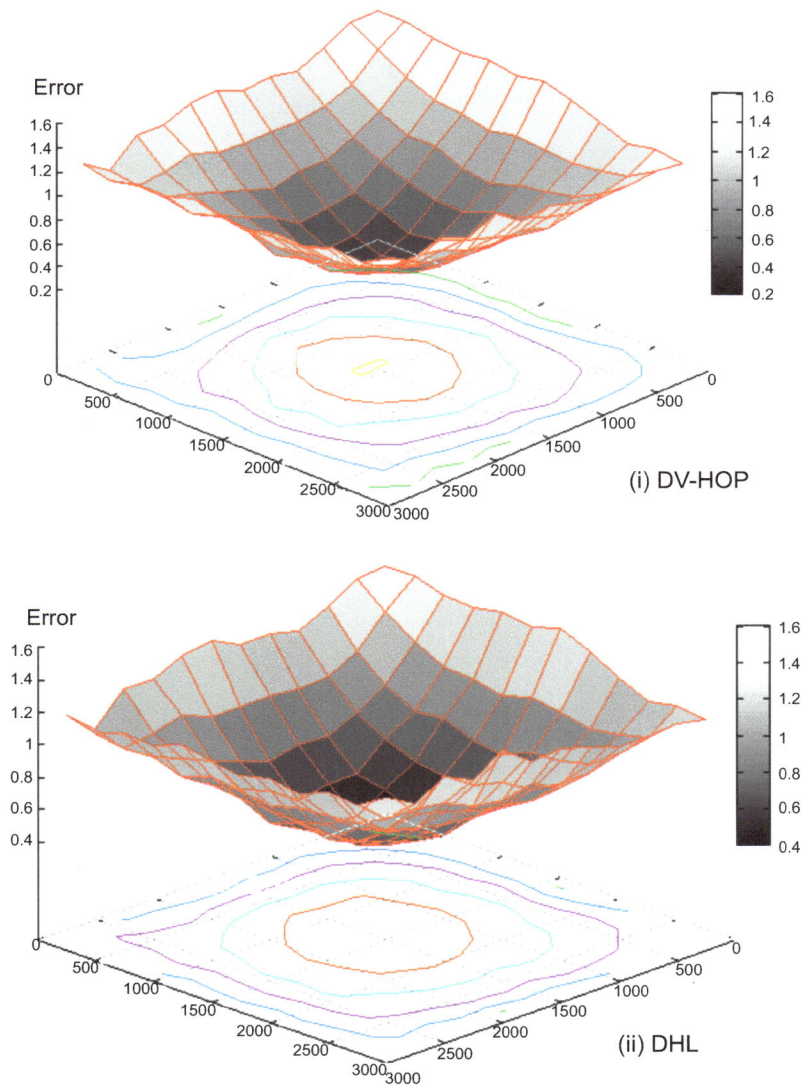

Fig. (5). Geographical error distribution (y-axis measured in % of R) for (i) DV-Hop and (ii) DHL.

that large errors often gather around the edges of the network (see Fig. (5) when anchors are placed at the perimeters of the terrain, which has been shown to be ideal locations for anchors [16].

SIM Algorithm

After the initial execution of the hop count localization algorithm (i.e. DHL), every node would have obtained an initial location estimate. SIM is then executed, as follows [20]. First, nodes that "think" they are near the network center broadcast a message to surrounding nodes. A candidate node is defined as a node that finds its location estimate within one hop from the centroid of the anchors. The centroid position of N anchors is given by the following formula:

$$(X_{Centroid}, Y_{Centroid}) = \left(\frac{X_1 + ... + X_N}{N}, \frac{Y_1 + ... + Y_N}{N} \right) \quad (1)$$

Hence, a node with an initial estimate (X_{est}, Y_{est}) is a candidate node if and only if the following condition is satisfied:

$$\sqrt{(X_{est} - X_{Centroid})^2 + (Y_{est} - Y_{Centroid})^2} \leq R \quad (2)$$

where R is the transmission range of each node.

During refinement, each candidate node starts to broadcast a CENTER message to its immediate neighbors, indicating that its estimate lies within one hop from the centroid of the anchors. At the same time, each candidate node keeps count of the number of CENTER messages, $CENTER_{rcvd}$, it receives from its neighbors. As each node knows its number of neighbors, it computes the proportion P of neighbors whose estimates also lie within one hop from the centroid of the anchors (e.g. in Fig. (6, P values for the nodes in the "centre" regions are $P_1=3/5$, $P_2=2/6$, $P_3=3/4$, $P_4=2/4$ and $P_c=4/4$.)

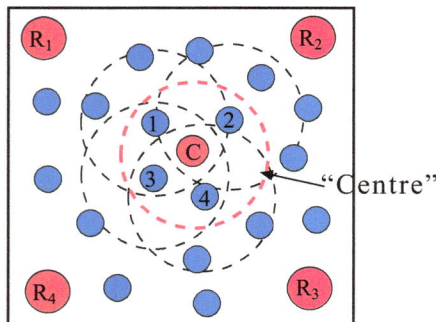

Fig. (6). Computation of P values in the "centre".

However, to minimize the occurrence of more than one node having the same value of P, we append a small random number r to the value of P.

$$P = \frac{CENTER_{rcvd}}{N_{ngbr}} + r \quad (3)$$

In other words, if there is more than one candidate node with the highest P value, in almost all instances, only one of them is chosen randomly as the new anchor. Finally, we propagate a node's P value around the network center, in order to establish a single node as the new anchor. Each candidate node S_j broadcasts a tuple $\{ID(S_j),\ P_j\}$. Every node stores and broadcasts the highest known P value and its corresponding candidate node and this propagation is restricted to a certain hop limit so that unnecessary communications overhead is minimized. After a stipulated time of inactivity, if a candidate node realizes that no other node has a higher P value, it declares itself as the new anchor, and begins to disseminate its estimated position to the network. Sensor nodes then adjust their location estimates with this new anchor's information.

Performance Analysis

Three different network scenarios were studied. Scenario A depicts a network topology where the node density is skewed towards the centre, and scenario B depicts a topology where the node density is sparse in the centre, as shown in Fig. (7, while Scenario C depicts a network where the nodes are randomly deployed with a uniform distribution. The network area is 3000m×3000m with four reference (or anchor) nodes located at the corners. Scenarios A and B used 1000 nodes with an average density (i.e. connectivity or average number of neighbors per node) of 23 and 21 respectively. For Scenario C, a range of density is used, from 8 through 20 (steps of 2), corresponding to 400 through 1000 nodes. SIM is applied to both DV-Hop and DHL to achieve better accuracy.

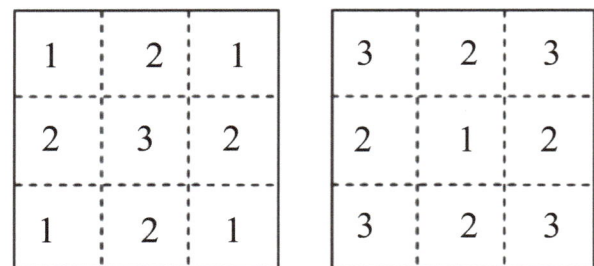

Fig. (7). Ratio of node densities for non-uniform networks.

In Scenario A, where node density is higher in the center, SIM improves both DV-Hop and DHL only slightly, as shown in Fig. (8(i). However, for Scenario B, where the nodes are sparser in the center, SIM provides a much better improvement for both DV-Hop and DHL. This is because there is a higher concentration of nodes at the corners of the network in this scenario than in Scenario A. Hence, there is a greater number of nodes in Scenario B with higher error

Scenario A

(i)

Scenario B

(ii)

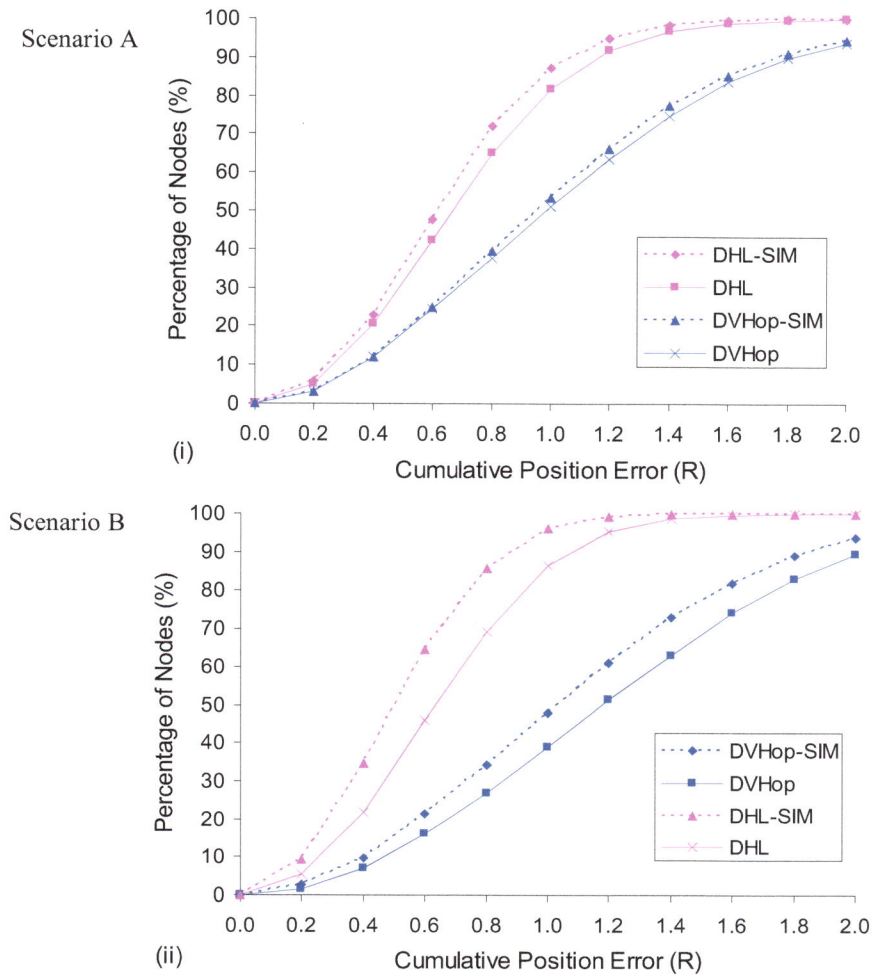

Fig. (8). Cumulative position error for (i) Scenario A, and (ii) Scenario B.

(see Fig. (5) and could benefit more from SIM. SIM improves the localization accuracy of DV-Hop and DHL in Scenario A by an average of 3.1% and 7.8% respectively. For Scenario B, SIM improves the accuracy of DV-Hop and DHL by an average of 11.4% and 20.1% respectively.

When SIM is applied to Scenario C (uniform network) and the network density varied, SIM improves the accuracy of DV-Hop by 7.4% and DHL by 13.0% on average, as shown in Fig. (9. Hence, SIM performs consistently well in improving the localization accuracy in both uniform and non-uniform networks.

In other iterative multilateration, no consideration is given to the fact that too many new anchors in a particular region may not result in justifiable gains in accuracy. In the scenarios studied, only one new anchor is elected within the region bounded by the anchors. This reduces unnecessary communications overhead, averaging about 27% over the original hop count-based localization schemes (25% from

dissemination of new anchor's location and 2% from the election process.)

DYNAMIC HOP SIZE COMPUTATION

DV-Hop [15], Amorphous [16] and DHL [18][19] operate in similar ways, except in the way hop size is computed. DV-Hop and Amorphous assumes that the hop size along a path is constant for that path. This assumption does not hold, especially in a non-uniform network where hop sizes vary greatly from one hop to another. Although DHL varies the size of each hop, DHL's location estimation performance is still not always better than DV-Hop and Amorphous, especially in uniformly dense networks. To address these issues, the size of every single hop should be dynamically and more accurately computed. The accuracy of the estimated hop count distance depends on various factors including the local density as well as the distance of the estimating (intermediate) node from the destination. In the following subsections, the various factors are discussed before the dynamic hop size computation (DHC) algorithm [21] is presented.

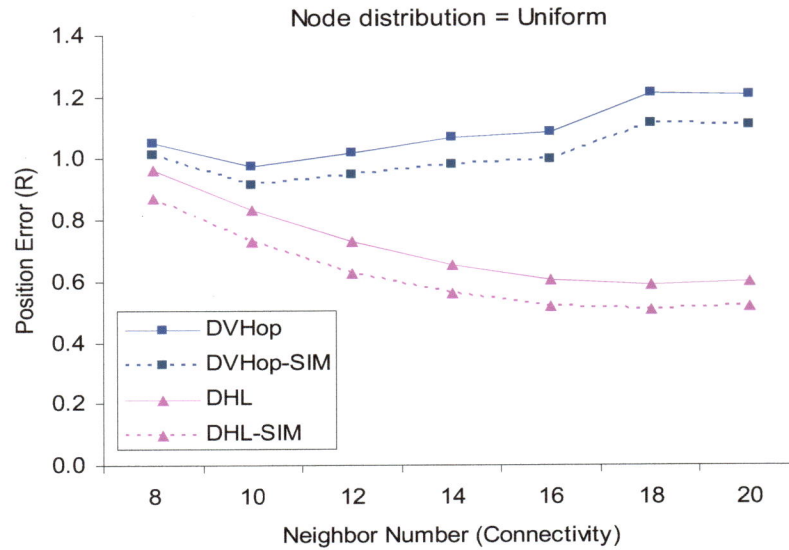

Fig. (9). Estimation error with varying density for a uniform network.

Factors Affecting Expected Hop Size

The expected hop size depends not only on node density, but also on the Euclidean (i.e. straight-line) distance between the source node (i.e. the node at the beginning of the path whose hop size is being computed) and the destination node (i.e. the node to be localized). Fig. (10 illustrates how the expected hop size h depends on the node density. A larger hop size is expected when the node density is higher (Fig. (10(i)) because the probability of finding a node closer to the boundary in the direction of travel increases. Conversely, when node density is low, the probability of finding a node closer to the boundary in the direction we wish to travel diminishes (Fig. (10(ii)) [27]. Thus, the expected hop size h is smaller.

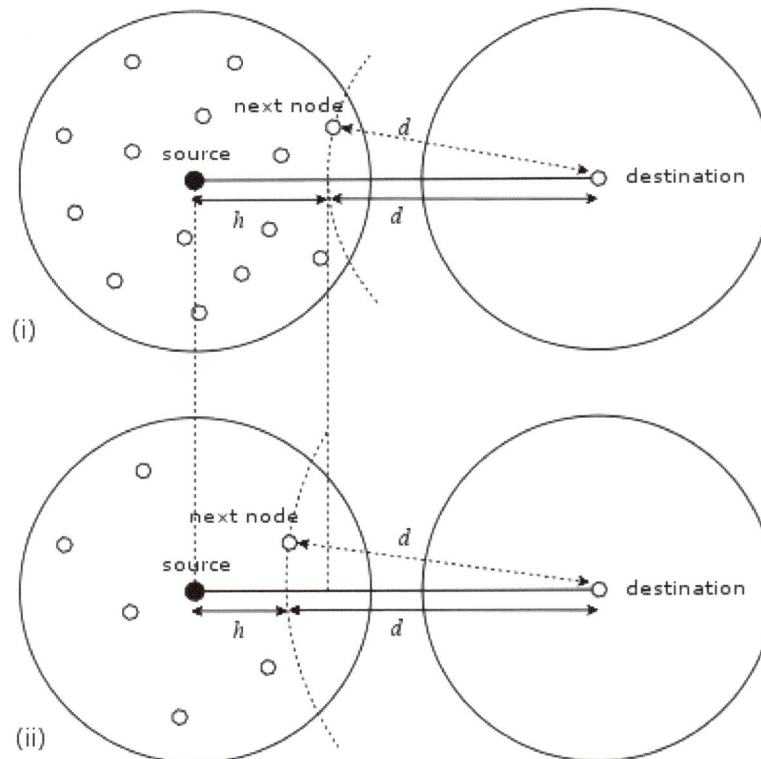

Fig. (10). Hop size differs because of (i) high local density, (ii) low local density.

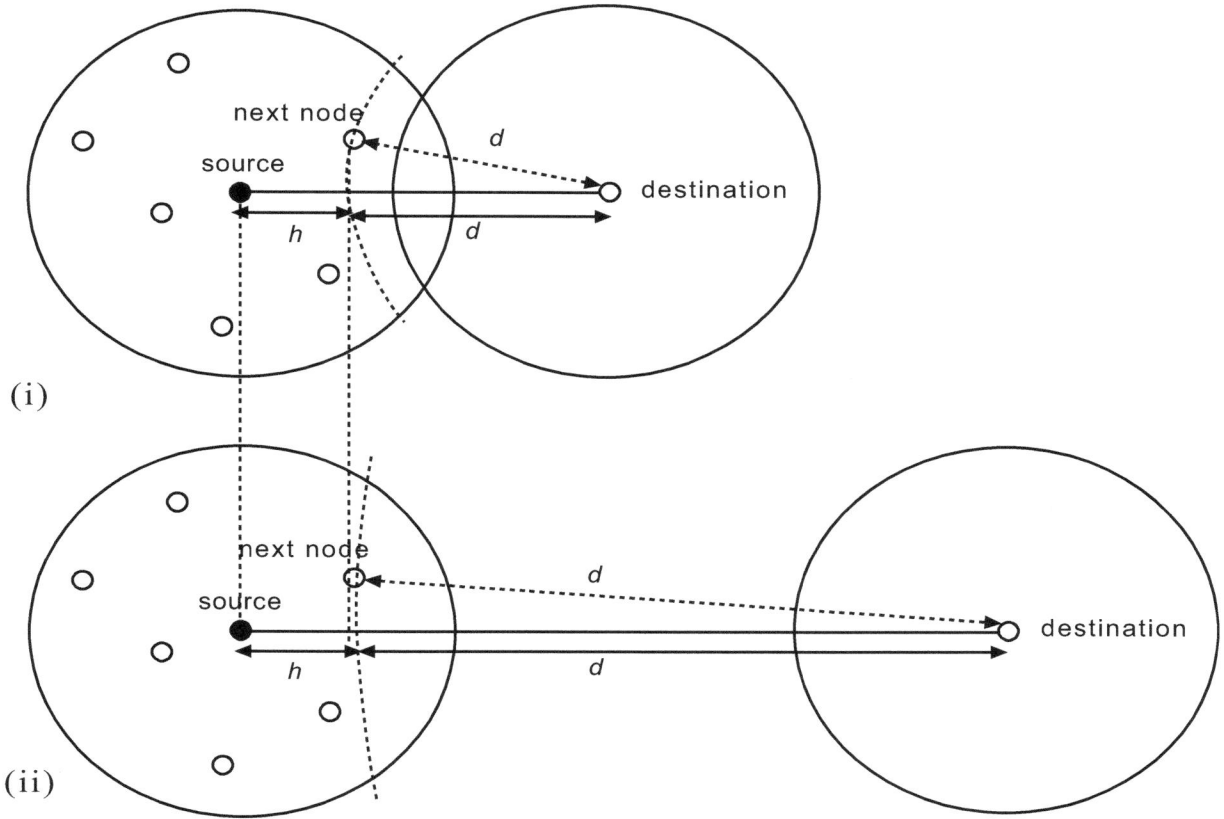

Fig. (11). Hop size difference when destination is (i) closer, or (ii) further away.

Fig. (11 shows the expected hop size being slightly larger when the destination node is further away from the source node (i.e. node at which hop size is being computed.) This is because the curvature of the arc centered at the destination node is flatter when the node is further away.

Expected Hop Size and Euclidean Distance

The expected hop size $h(D,N)$ of the first hop in the shortest (in terms of hop count) path from a node a to any other node b in the network is given by [21]:

$$h(D,N) =$$

$$
\begin{cases}
R\left(1+e^{-N} - \int_{-1}^{1} e^{\frac{-N}{\pi}\left(\arccos t + (1+D^2-2Dt)\arctan\left(\frac{\sqrt{1-t^2}}{D-t}\right) - D\sqrt{1-t^2}\right)} dt\right) & D > 1 \\
\frac{2}{3}R & 0 < D \leq 1
\end{cases}
\tag{4}
$$

where R is the transmission radius of each sensor node (assumed to be constant), D is the Euclidean distance (in terms of R) between node a and node b, and N is the average number of nodes within R.

To estimate the Euclidean distance between two nodes, $node_0$ and $node_{n_{hops}}$, each hop $h(D_i,N_i)$

$0 \leq i < n_{hops}$ along the path from $node_0$ to $node_{n_{hops}}$ is summed up, giving the estimated distance D_{est} over n_{hops} hops as:

$$D_{est} = \sum_{i=0}^{n_{hops}-1} h(D_i, N_i) \tag{5}$$

where D_i is the Euclidean distance (in terms of R) from $node_i$ to $node_{n_{hops}}$, and N_i is the average number of nodes in a transmission radius. Since the values of both D_i and N_i are unknown, suitable approximations will have to be made. We approximate the value of D_i by summing the hop sizes along the path using Eqn. (6) [27] while N_i is approximated using the number of nodes in the transmission radius of $node_i$, henceforth known as the *local density*.

$$\text{Hop Size} = R\left(1+e^{-N} - \int_{-1}^{1} e^{\frac{-N}{\pi}\left(\arccos t - t\sqrt{1-t^2}\right)} dt\right) \tag{6}$$

Thus, D_i is estimated as follows (see Fig. (12):

$$D_i \approx \sum_{k=i}^{n_{hops}-1} R(1+e^{-N_k} - \int_{-1}^{1} e^{\frac{-N_k}{\pi}\left(\arccos t - t\sqrt{1-t^2}\right)} dt) + \frac{2}{3}R \tag{7}$$

where $n_{hops} > 1$ and $0 \leq i < n_{hops} - 1$. The term $\frac{2}{3}R$ is the expected distance $D_{n_{hops}-1}$ of the last hop towards $node_{n_{hops}}$.

anchor / node $_0$

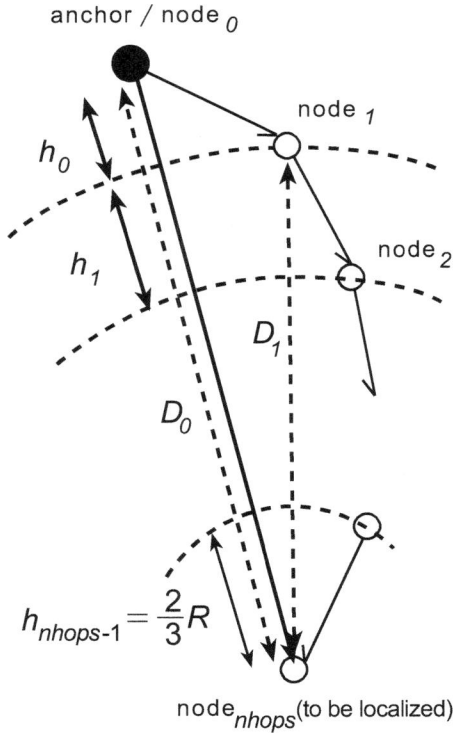

node $_1$

h_0

h_1

node $_2$

D_1

D_0

$h_{nhops-1} = \dfrac{2}{3}R$

node$_{nhops}$(to be localized)

Fig. (12). Calculating the estimated distance D_i.

DHC Algorithm

The DHC algorithm is executed, as follows:

Step A: Each anchor AN_i broadcasts a packet containing {ID(AN_i), Position(AN_i), $n_{hops}-1$, {$N_0, N_1, ..., N_{n_{hops}-1}$}}, i.e. AN_i broadcasts {ID(AN_i), Position(AN_i), 0, {N_0}}, where {$N_0, N_1, ..., N_{n_{hops}-1}$} denotes a list of local densities from node$_0$ to node $_{n_{hops}}$.

Step B: A node S_j that receives the packet stores {ID(AN_i), Position(AN_i), n_{hops}, {$N_0, N_1, ..., N_{n_{hops}}$}} and broadcasts this locally.

Step C: S_j estimates the distance to AN_i using (5).

Step D: When S_j gets distance estimates to at least 3(4) anchors in 2D(3D) terrain, it estimates its location using triangulation.

Step E: If S_j subsequently receives a packet with a smaller n_{hops} or D_{est}, it repeats Steps II through V. This has the effect of having each node keep track of the either the minimum number of hops to anchors, or the minimum estimated distances.

DHC Implementation Issues

In this section, some practical implementation issues of DHC are presented, focusing on ways to reduce communications overheads.

i)   Restricting the Size of the Local Density List
When the number of hops from an anchor is large, it may be sufficient to keep track of only the most recent local densities. If n_{max} denotes the number of most recent densities, then only the last n_{max} are computed using Eqn. (3) while those before are computed using Eqn. (6). Upon receiving a packet, a node will compute the distance estimate as:

$$D_{est} = \sum_{i=n_{hops}-n_{max}}^{n_{hops}-1} h(D_i, N_i) + overflow \qquad (8)$$

Clearly, the higher the value of n_{max}, the more accurate the localization will be. On the other hand, decreasing n_{max} will reduce the packet size.

ii)   Limiting Packet Forwarding
If an incoming packet's estimated distance differs from the stored estimated distance by only a small amount (say, $0.1R$), it can be ignored so as to reduce the amount of packet propagation. A local parameter, ε ($0<\varepsilon<1$), can be defined such that a node may refrain from forwarding a new packet if its estimated distance differs from that of the last packet forwarded by the node by less than εR.

iii)   Smoothing Hop Counts
Although the size of the final hop in a path is always set at $\frac{2}{3}R$ in Eqn.(7), smoothing [16] can be applied on the last hop for higher accuracy.

Performance Analysis

DHC performance is measured using the metric *estimated position accuracy*, which is the most important performance metric in any localization scheme, using the same three representative scenarios used in the SIM study, viz., non-uniform network scenarios A and B (cf: Fig. (7) and scenario C (uniform network.) The same parameter values have also been used in this study.

Fig. (13 shows the percentage of nodes with less than or equal to the cumulative position error, for both non-uniform scenarios A and B. The results show that DHC's dynamic computation can estimate the hop size more accurately compared to the other schemes especially when the hop size fluctuates from hop to hop. Next, Fig. (14 shows the position error of the different schemes when varying the connectivity in a uniform network scenario. For all the schemes, localization accuracy generally improves as the node density increases. DHC consistently outperforms the three other schemes in terms of localization accuracy regardless of connectivity, with improvement of up to 33%. Hence, it can be seen that DHC does well in both low and high density networks. With connectivity of 14 or more, position error is less than $0.4R$, which is required for good performance in location-based

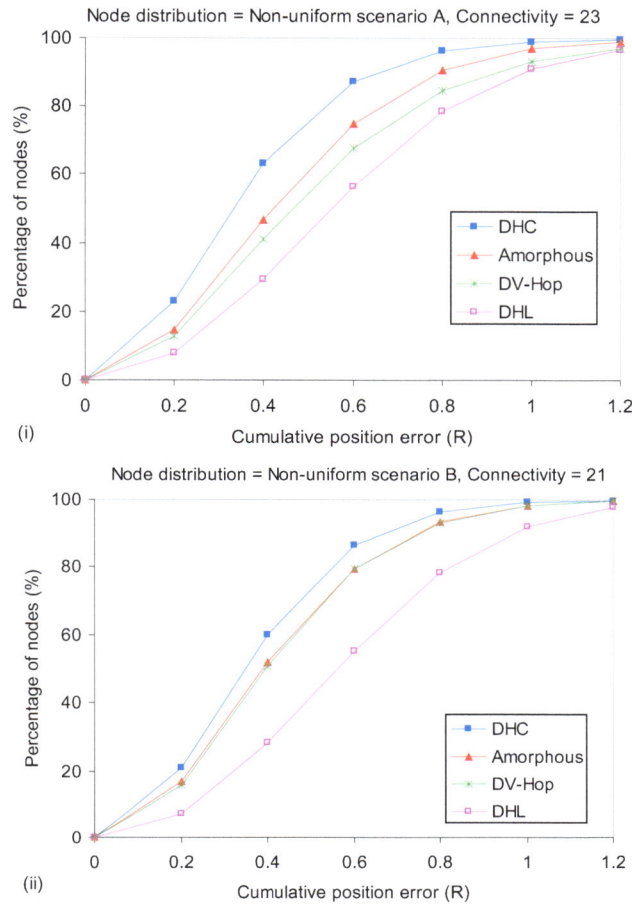

Fig. (13). Cumulative error distribution for non-uniform (i) Scenario A, and (ii) Scenario B.

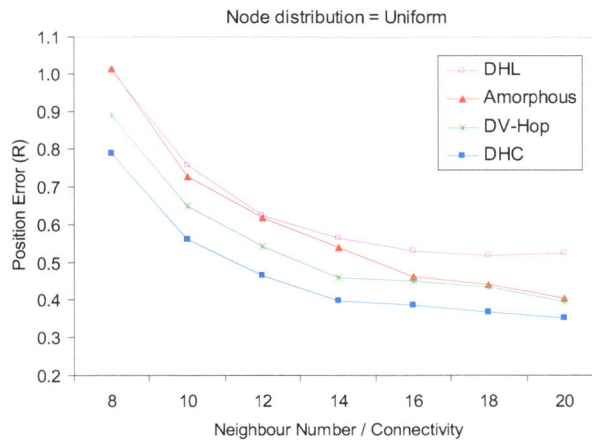

Fig. (14). Position error with varying density/ connectivity in uniform network.

routing [12]. This is especially noteworthy because only four anchors are used.

PRACTICAL ISSUES IN HOP COUNT LOCALIZATION

Several common assumptions are usually made in wireless network system simulation or modelling

tools. It is well known that one of them is the circular radiation pattern of wireless transmission. The analogy in analytical approaches is the use of the Unit Disk Graph to model the transmission coverage of a node. However, this is far from true in reality, due to constructive and destructive multipath fading, background interference, direction of the antenna and even battery power level of the nodes, leading to

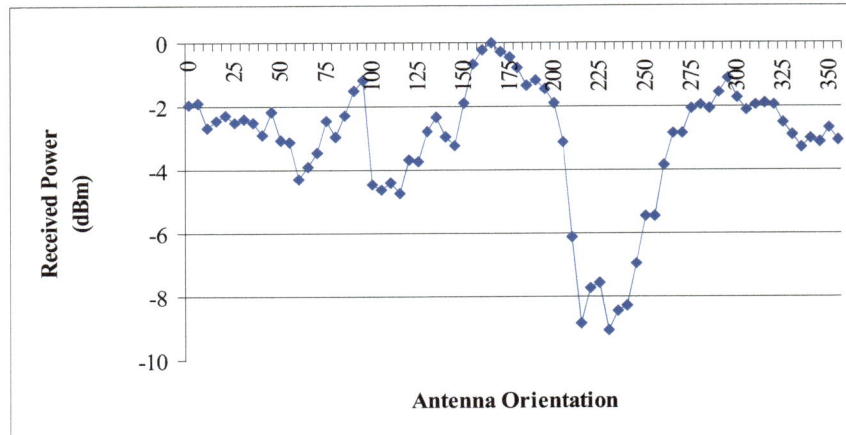

Fig. (15). Radio propagation pattern of MicaZ mote in anechoic chamber.

irregularities of the propagation pattern. A simple measurement of the radio propagation pattern of a Crossbow MicaZ mote was carried out in an anechoic chamber and the results are shown in Fig. (15.

The irregularity of the radio propagation pattern is further aggravated by background interference, walls or objects that reflect the radio signal. It has been shown that the indoor environment has comparatively more grey area than outdoor environment [28] and the reception of data packets in these grey areas is likely to be irregular. Grey areas can occupy more than 30% of the communication region in some environments and this makes the reception of the packets less predictable which the design of various networking protocols must account for. To bridge the discrepancy between circular propagation pattern assumptions and physical reality of radio signals, the Radio Irregularity Model (RIM) [29] has been proposed for use in simulations.

Implementation of Hop Count Localization

An experiment was carried out using a simple WSN testbed with 21 MicaZ motes. Hop count localization based on DV-Hop [15] was implemented and tested in a 7m×5m partitioned area surrounded by 1ft partitions (as shown in Fig. (16.) As shown in Fig. (17, the nodes (from ID 31 to ID 46) are spread out non-uniformly in the area, with four reference nodes, ID 1 to ID 4, placed outside the network and they are set to transmit beacons at one second intervals for

localization. The expected (theoretical) hop count from the four reference nodes are shown in the accompanying table. The MicaZ motes are set to transmit at their lowest possible output power of –25 dBm giving a transmission range of about 1.5m, dividing the testbed into roughly 3 columns and 4 rows. Tiny AODV (Ad hoc On Demand Vector) is used to perform the multihop routing of the hop count information from all the nodes to the Sink node. Tiny AODV is a simplified version of the AODV routing protocol implemented in TinyOS [30]. Hop count data from all the nodes are forwarded to the sink node where triangulation is then performed to obtain the estimated location of the nodes which is displayed graphically.

Fig. (16). Physical WSN testbed.

The indoor environment contains more grey areas due to interference and multipath fading that result in unpredictable signal radiation patterns. The hop count localization algorithm is unable to estimate the hop size and occasionally exceeds the expected range by more than twice, i.e. nodes that are placed at two hops away from the transmitter read as only one hop. Table 2 shows hop count data generated by multiple executions of the localization algorithm, where errors with respect

Node ID	Ref 1	Ref 2	Ref 3	Ref 4
31	1	3	4	4
32	2	2	4	4
33	3	1	4	4
34	3	1	4	4
35	2	3	3	3
36	2	2	3	3
37	3	2	3	2
38	3	2	3	2
39	3	3	3	2
40	3	3	3	2
41	3	3	2	2
42	3	3	2	3
43	4	4	3	1
44	4	4	3	1
45	4	4	2	2
46	4	4	1	3

Expected Hop Count from 4 Reference Nodes

to the expected hop count (Fig. (17) are shown in columns Error 1~Error 4. "Total Error" shows the sum of absolute hop count errors from all 4 reference nodes. In the experiment, there is a total error of 35 hops in the 16-node testbed.

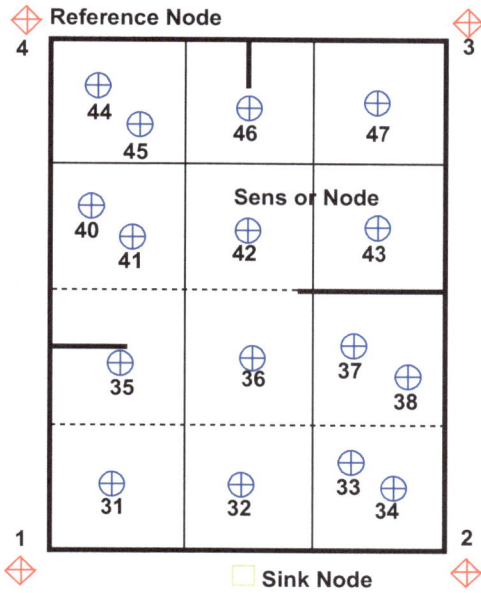

Fig. (17). Physical node placement in testbed.

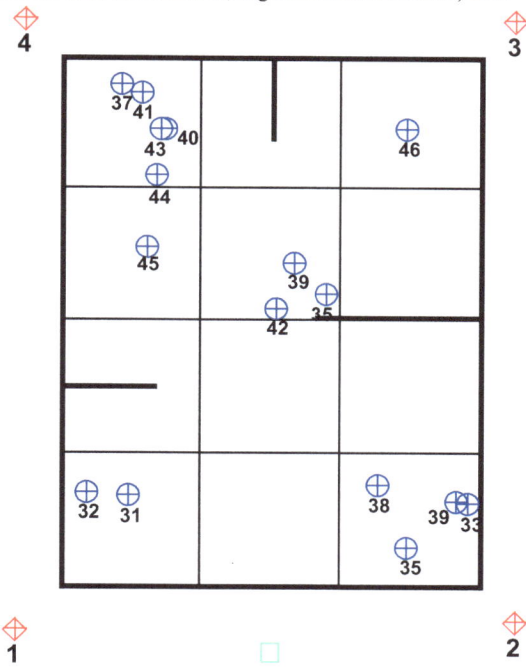

Fig. (18). Sensors' locations estimated by hop count localization algorithm.

The sink node uses the hop count data generated by the localization algorithm (Table 2) to produce a graphical display of the estimated locations of the network nodes, as shown in Fig. (18. From the results, it is clear that

Table 2. Hop count data from experiments.

Node ID	Ref 1	Ref 2	Ref 3	Ref 4	Error R1	Error R2	Error R3	Error R4	Total Error
31	1	3	3	3	0	0	-1	-1	2
32	1	2	3	3	-1	0	-1	-1	3
33	3	1	2	2	0	0	-2	-2	4
34	2	1	3	2	-1	0	-1	-2	4
35	2	1	2	2	0	-2	-1	-1	4
36	2	2	3	2	0	0	0	-1	1
37	2	2	3	1	-1	0	0	-1	2
38	3	1	3	2	0	-1	0	0	1
39	2	2	3	2	-1	-1	0	0	2
40	3	3	3	1	0	0	0	-1	1
41	3	3	2	1	0	0	0	-1	1
42	3	2	2	2	0	-1	0	-1	2
43	3	4	4	1	-1	0	1	0	2
44	3	3	4	1	-1	-1	1	0	3
45	4	3	3	2	0	-1	1	0	2
46	4	3	1	3	0	-1	0	0	1

there is a spatial and temporal fluctuation in the transmission range of the node, in consensus with the measurements shown in Fig. (15. This arises from the interference of the radio signal by components within the node, as well as by objects around the node. The cause of the erroneous hop count readings can be attributed to the occasional "extension" of range during the transmission process when the radio signal goes beyond what was expected at that transmission power. Again, this may be due to the external environment, which may be changing as a function of time. Since the inherent algorithm of hop count localization scheme takes the lowest hop count to be the optimal one, such abnormalities are treated as valid readings. Hence, modifications are proposed address these issues and improve the accuracy of hop count localization algorithms.

RSSI Threshold

The MicaZ mote provides the ability to capture the RSSI of the packet received which then enables the algorithm to define a threshold value for the RSSI of a received packet to be equivalent to one that is received at 1.5m. Therefore, if the RSSI of a received packet is lower than the cut off strength, it is deemed to have come from a node that is too far away even though the mote is able to successfully receive and decode the packet.

Sliding Window for Hop Count Sampling

A sliding sample window is introduced at the receiver to sample hop counts more accurately. In the sliding sample window, only a number of hop count broadcast received that exceeds a pre-determined threshold level (e.g. "4" in this study) is considered as a valid hop count, as described previously. In the testbed, the sliding sample window size is set to 40. This size may vary with the density of the nodes. With the pre-determined non-uniformly distributed nodes, each node will have at most 10 neighbors in its single hop transmission range. If the number of neighbors increases, the sliding sample window is expected to increase as well to have enough samples.

With this implementation, the hop count localization algorithm will not stay at its lowest hop count it receives from its neighbors permanently. It will adapt and converge with respect to the network environment. This modification allows the hop count localization algorithm to work in a mobile network environment as the nodes select a new lowest hop count from the sliding window all the time. The original hop count localization algorithm is not able to achieve that; all the nodes' memory has to be cleared on every re-execution of the localization algorithm.

Variable Broadcast Rate

Despite having the sliding sample window, the chance of the escalating hop count phenomenon occurring remains. When a node in the middle of the network, which is far away from the reference nodes, has more neighbor nodes with higher hop counts to the reference nodes, there is a possibility that the sliding sample window is occupied by these higher hop counts. The lower hop count broadcast from other neighbors may be flushed or pushed out of the sliding window. As a result the node in the middle of the network may register a higher hop count than desired, resulting in the escalating hop count phenomenon.

A variable broadcast rate is introduced in the implementation to favor the lower hop count broadcasting in the network. The node with the smaller hop count, which is supposedly closer to the reference nodes, will broadcast at a faster rate as compared to a node further away from the reference nodes. This helps to ensure that the hop count localization algorithm converge to the lower hop count. In this implementation, the transmission rate has been set with respect to the lowest hop count a node is from the four reference nodes. For example if a node has a hop count of 1,3,4,4 from the four reference nodes respectively, the hop count of '1' is used to determine the broadcast frequency of the hop count information of this node. A reference node which has a hop count of '0' with respect to itself will broadcast at 1-second intervals. A node which has a lowest hop count of one hop from a reference node will broadcast the hop count information at 2-second intervals. A node which has a lowest hop count of two hops from the reference nodes will transmit the beacon at 4-second intervals. We set the maximum transmission rate for the beacon at 8-second intervals, which is when a node has a lowest hop count of more than two hops from the four reference nodes. With the variable broadcast rate, we are able to receive lower hop count broadcast at a faster rate and enhance the convergence to the lowest hop counts in the hop count localization algorithm.

Experimental Results

Table 3 shows the result of the hop count localization algorithm with the above three modifications. With the modifications, we are getting a total error of 20 hops. It is a significant improvement over the original algorithm. In this layout, we know that the maximum hop count from one corner to the other is four, assuming it is a fully connected network, hence we set the cutoff of the maximum hop count at four hops.

Table 3. Hop count data from modified algorithm.

Node ID	Ref 1	Ref 2	Ref 3	Ref 4	Error R1	Error R2	Error R3	Error R4	Total Error
31	1	3	4	4	0	0	0	0	0
32	2	2	4	3	0	0	0	-1	1
33	4	1	4	4	1	0	0	0	1
34	3	1	4	4	0	0	0	0	0
35	2	3	4	3	0	0	1	0	1
36	3	3	4	3	1	1	1	0	3
37	3	2	3	3	0	0	0	1	1
38	4	2	3	4	1	0	0	2	3
39	3	4	3	1	0	1	0	-1	2
40	3	4	3	2	0	1	0	0	1
41	4	3	3	2	1	0	1	0	2
42	4	3	2	4	1	0	0	1	2
43	4	4	4	1	0	0	1	0	1
44	4	4	4	1	0	0	1	0	1
45	4	4	2	3	0	0	0	1	1
46	4	4	1	3	0	0	0	0	0

Fig. (19 shows the results from the same 30-minute experiment after incorporating the above modifications into the hop count localization algorithm. The nodes were randomly placed in the grids and if a node has hop count of {1,3,4,4} it is should be located in the first grid

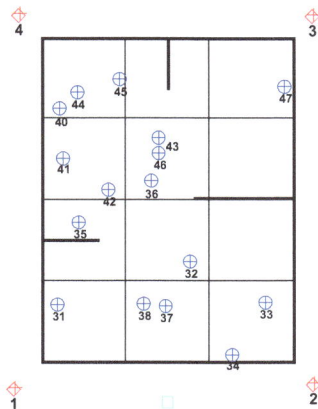

Fig. (19). Sensors' Locations Estimated by Modified Algorithm.

from node #1, and similarly, hop count of {2,3,3,3} indicates that a node is in the second grid from node #1, as shown in Fig. (19. Comparing Figure 17, 18 and 19 it can be seen that the original hop count

localization algorithm only managed to correctly estimate the locations of five nodes in the network whereas the modified algorithm improved the results with eight correctly located nodes. For those nodes whose locations were incorrectly estimated by the modified algorithm, the deviation was at most one hop. In the original hop count algorithm, errors were in the order of multiple hops.

FUTURE WORK AND CONCLUSIONS

Hop count-based schemes have emerged as a viable and practical approach to sensor network localization. The earlier schemes that emerged like DV-Hop [16] perform poorly in terms of localization accuracy in a variety of network topologies because many of them assume nodes to be uniformly and often densely deployed over the entire network. However, such deployment scenarios are rarely true to be realistic. The Density-aware Hop count Localization (DHL) addresses this problem by considering node density when estimating the distance covered across each hop, thus improving the localization accuracy in non-uniformly distributed networks. Further improvement in accuracy can be achieved by picking well localized nodes within the network to serve as new reference points, and repeating the localization process. This is the process of Selective Iterative Multilateration (SIM).

It has also been shown that the hop size estimate is dependent on not just the node density but also the distance between the intermediate estimating node and the final destination node. Taking both these factors into consideration, the Dynamic Hop count Computation (DHC) algorithm computes the distance covered per hop dynamically, further improving the accuracy of the distance estimation and consequently the localization.

Lastly, this chapter investigated critical issues in implementing hop count localization algorithms. Most, if not all, designs assume the radio signal radiation pattern to be circular which is rarely (if ever) true in the physical world. Furthermore, the radiation pattern changes dynamically with the environmental conditions. The hop count localization algorithms must also adapt to these changes and account for the irregular radiation patterns. Three modifications have been proposed, implemented and tested in experimental prototypes and shown to be able to mitigate the negative effects of the circular radiation pattern assumption. While there has been extensive research done in hop count based and other forms of range-free localization for WSNs, albeit with the similar unrealistic assumptions of circular signal radiation pattern and the like, the efforts on addressing implementation issues have not received the same amount of attention. To see WSNs eventually deployed, these implementation and engineering issues must be addressed and resolved. This will feature significantly in the ongoing and future work for localization in WSNs.

REFERENCES

[1]   D. Estrin, L. Girod, G. Pottie and M. Srivastava, "Instrumenting the World with Wireless Sensor Networks", in International Conference on Acoustics, Speech and Signal Processing (ICASSP), Utah, USA, pp. 2033-2036, May 2001.

[2]   B. Parkinson and J. Spilker, "Global Positioning System: Theory and Application", Washington, D.C., American Institute of Aeronautics and Astronautics, 1996.

[3]   C. Savarese, J.M. Rabaey and J. Beutel, "Locationing in Distributed Ad-Hoc Wireless Sensor Networks", in International Conference on Acoustics, Speech and Signal Processing (ICASSP), Utah, USA, pp. 2037-2040, May 2001.

[4]   J. Beutel, "Geolocation in a picoradio environment", M.S. thesis, ETH Zürich, Electronics Lab, 1999.

[5]   A. Savvides, C.C. Han and M. Srivastava, "Dynamic Fine-Grained Localization in Ad-Hoc Networks of Sensors", in MobiCom 2001, Rome, Italy, pp. 166-179, July 2001.

[6]   R. Peng and M.L. Sichitiu, "Angle of Arrival Localization for Wireless Sensor Networks", in IEEE SECON 2006, Reston, VA, USA, Sep 2006.

[7]   P. Bahl and V.N. Padmanabhan, "RADAR: An In-Building RF based User Location and Tracking System", in IEEE Infocom 2000, Tel-Aviv, Israel, Mar 2000.

[8]   D.Niculescu and Nath, "Ad Hoc Positioning System (APS)", in Globecom 2001, Texas, USA, pp. 2826-2931, Nov 2001.

[9]   D. Son, B. Krishnamachari and J. Heidemann, "Experimental study of concurrent transmission in wireless sensor networks", SenSys 2006, Boulder, CO, USA, Oct 31-Nov 03 2006.

[10]   G. Mao, B. Fidan and B.D.O. Anderson, "Wireless sensor network localization techniques", Computer Networks, vol. 51, pp. 2529-2553, 2007.

[11]   N. Bulusu, J. Heidemann and D. Estrin, "GPS-less Low Cost Outdoor Localization for Very Small Devices", IEEE Personal Communications Magazine, Vol. 7, No. 5, pp. 28-34, Oct 2000.

[12]   T. He, C. Huang, B.M. Blum, J.A. Stankovic and T. Abdelzaher, "Range-free localization schemes for large scale sensor networks", in ACM Mobicom, San Diego, CA, USA, Sep 14-19, 2003.

[13]   Y. Shang and W. Ruml, "Improved MDS-based localization", in IEEE INFOCOM, San Francisco, CA, USA, Mar 30-Apr 3, 2003.

[14]   L. Doherty, S.J. Pister and L. El-Ghaoui, "Convex position estimation in wireless sensor networks", IEEE Infocom, Anchorage, Alaska, USA, Apr 22-26, 2001.

[15]   D. Niculescu and B. Nath, "DV-based Positioning in Ad Hoc Networks", Kluwer Journal of Telecommunication Systems, Vol. 22, No. 1, pp. 267-280, Jan 2003.

[16]   R. Nagpal, H. Shrobe, and J. Bachrach, "Organizing a Global Coordinate System from Local Information on an Ad Hoc Sensor Network", in 2nd Int'l Workshop on Information Processing in Sensor Networks (IPSN), Palo Alto, CA, USA, Apr 2003.

[17]   K. Langendoen and N. Reijers, "Distributed Localization in Wireless Sensor Networks: A Quantitative Comparison", Elsevier Computer Networks, Vol. 43, No. 3, pp. 499-518, Nov 2003.

[18]   S.Y. Wong, J.G. Lim, S.V. Rao and Winston K.G. Seah, "Density-aware hop count localization (DHL) in wireless sensor networks with variable density", in IEEE Wireless Communications and Networking Conference (WCNC 2005), New Orleans, LA, USA, Mar 13-17, 2005.

[19]   S.Y. Wong, J.G. Lim, S.V. Rao and Winston K.G. Seah, "Multihop Localization with Density and Path Length Awareness in Non-Uniform Wireless Sensor Networks", in IEEE 61st Semiannual Vehicular Technology Conference (VTC2005-Spring), Stockholm, Sweden, May 30-Jun 1, 2005.

[20]   Jeffrey H.S. Tay, Vijay R. Chandrasekhar and Winston K.G. Seah, "Selective Iterative Multilateration for Hop Count-Based Localization in Wireless Sensor Networks", in Workshop on Mobile Location-Aware Sensor Networks (MLASN06), held in conjunction with the 7th International Conference on Mobile Data Management (MDM06), Nara, Japan, May 9-13, 2006.

[21]   Jeffrey H.S. Tay, Vijay R. Chandrasekhar and Winston K.G. Seah, "Range-free Localization Using Dynamic Hop Size Computation in Wireless Sensor Networks", in 4th IEEE Conference on Industrial Informatics (INDIN06), Singapore, Aug 16-18, 2006.

[22]   Eddie B.S. Tan, J.G. Lim, Winston K.G. Seah and S.V. Rao, "On the Practical Issues in Hop Count Localization of Sensors in a Multihop Network", in 63rd IEEE Vehicular Technology Conference (VTC2006-Spring), Melbourne, Victoria, Australia, 8-10 May, 2006.

[23]   M. Li and Y. Liu, "Rendered path: range-free localization in anisotropic sensor networks with holes", in MobiCom 2007, Montréal, Québec, Canada, Sep 09-14, 2007.

[24]   A. Savvides, C.C. Han and m. Srivastava, "Dynamic Fine-Grained Localization in Ad-Hoc Networks of Sensors", in Mobicom 2001, Rome, Italy, Jul 16-21, 2001.

[25]   A. Savvides, H. Park and M.B. Srivastava, "The N-Hop Multilateration Primitive for Node Localization Problems", in ACM/Kluwer Mobile Networks and Applications (MONET), Vol. 8, No. 4, Aug 2003.

[26]   J. Albowicz, A. Chen, and L. Zhang, "Recursive position estimation in sensor networks", in ICNP 2001, Riverside, CA, USA, Nov 11-14, 2001.J.

[27]   L. Kleinrock and J. Silvester, "Optimum transmission radii for packet radio networks or why six is a magic number", in Proceedings of National Telecomm Conference, Pages 4.3.1-4.3.5, 1978.

[28]   N. Reijers, G. Halkes and K. Langendoen, "Link Layer Measurements in Sensor Networks", in 1st IEEE International Conference on Mobile Ad-hoc and Sensor Systems (MASS), Forida, USA, Oct 24-27, 2004.

[29]   G. Zhou, T. He, S. Krishnamurthy and J. A. Stankovic, "Impact of Radio Irregularity on Wireless Sensor Networks", in 2nd International Conference on Mobile Systems, Applications, and Services (MobiSys) , Boston, MA, USA, Jun 6-9, 2004.

[30]   TinyOS – An Open-Source OS for the networked sensor regime, http://www.tinyos.net/.

CHAPTER 7

Data Gathering and Data Aggregation in Wireless Sensor Networks

Hongju Cheng*, Guolong Chen and Wenzhong Guo

College of Mathematics and Computer Science, Fuzhou University, P. R. China

Abstract: The wireless sensor network is emerging as a new hotspot by exploiting the cooperation of hundreds to thousands of cheap nodes. Data gathering and data aggregation are key issues in the network. This article has taken a deep view into the current solutions for the data gathering and data aggregation. First, it has introduced the basic concepts, *i.e.*, the data gathering system, data structure, data aggregation function and routing protocols. Secondly, it has explored the current data gathering protocols, and accordingly introduced three important tree-based / flat routing protocols, namely, SPIN, Directed Diffusion and ELECTION-based protocol, one cluster-based hierarchical protocol named as LEACH, as well as one location-based protocol named GAF. Finally, it has concerned with the real-time requirement in the applications, and introduced a novel solution by converting the real-time requirement into two constraints: node degree bounded and tree height bounded, and provided solutions for it.

INTRODUCTION

The Wireless Sensor Network [1] is emerging as a new hotspot in current science research and various application fields. It consists of hundreds to thousands or even more sensor nodes, which communicate through wireless channels, form a spatial-separate, reliable, robust and prize-low wireless network and can be placed in a large field. After deployment, nodes can sense, collect and encode data originated from the environment, and finally transmit the data to the sink nodes. The sink nodes are the specialized nodes in or close to the network that subscribe to an application-aware data streams from the sensor network by expressing interests or queries. The sink nodes also can serve as gateways between the sensor network and the outside wired or wireless backbone network. The collaboration of these sensor nodes gains significant improvement due to their improved model, capacity, calculation ability and ease of deployment.

By equipping the sensor nodes with different sensor model and various sensing objects, the wireless sensor networks can be applied in almost all fields of our life, For example, it can setup the battle field monitoring system for the military, environment monitoring system for the agriculture, traffic control and monitoring system for the city vehicles. With the further development of theory research and application technology, the wireless sensor networks are expected to change the state of all fields of our society significantly.

In fact, there appearing of wireless sensor networks are expected to have significant impact on the efficiency of the real-world applications. In these application scenarios, data gathering has played a key role in building the data monitoring system which is different from the traditional ones in many aspects.

One important character of wireless sensor network is its dense deployment in the application. A great number of nodes can be placed at the initial network setup phase and seldom be removed away after deployment because the cheapness of sensor makes it possible to get a large number of nodes with limited fund. There is redundancy among the data sensed by nodes that are in close in geographical location. By exploiting the spatial and temporal data redundancy, the data gathering process significantly increase the energy efficiency since that energy efficiency is crucial in the wireless sensor networks. Although a lot of works on the sensor networks have been done by many researchers during the recent years, it is still necessary and important to take a deep view into the current technology, and finally find and provide applicable data collecting solutions for the data gathering systems.

When one node transmits a packet to another in the wireless sensor network, the energy consumed by the communication is at least quadratic to the distance. One way to save energy is using radio with adjustable transmission power. The energy is saved just by reducing the power level to the minimum value while satisfying the communication requirement. Another way to save energy is the data aggregation technology. For example, in many applications it is common to collect data from all nodes in the network to one sink node. Note that the collected data is routed along a reversed broadcast tree with the sink as the root. Each non-leaf node can waits for data from its children, then summarizes the data with its own, and transmits the aggregated data to the parent. In this way, each node forwards the data for exactly one time in every query. The energy efficiency of the aggregation tree will finally increase the lifetime of the network.

The article is organized as following. The following section has introduced the basics mentioned in the article, including data gathering system, data structure, data aggregation function, and routing protocols. In the

Hai Liu / Xiaowen Chu / Yiu-Wing Leung (Eds.)

third section, the routing protocols are reviewed by deeply exploiting the current solutions in details. Three tree-based / flat protocols, one cluster-based hierarchical protocol and one location-based protocol, are introduced. In the fourth section, the article has focused on the real-time issue appearing as the quality-of-service requirement in many applications, and introduced a novel solution by transferring the real-time requirement to two constraints on the aggregation tree: degree-bounded and height-bounded. Heuristic algorithms for the real-time data aggregation are also introduced too. And finally are the conclusions.

BASICS OF DATA GATHERING AND DATA AGGREGATION

DATA GATHERING SYSTEM

The wireless sensor nodes are designed with limited computation ability, small communication power, raw memory, and constrained energy supply. The cheapness of the sensor nodes makes it possible to deploy a huge number of nodes in a geographically large range. Data is collected by each separate node and relayed to a special data center called as the sink. The data gathering process is a common and important operation in the sensor applications and its efficiency will significantly influence the operation and lifetime of the total network.

It shall be mentioned that the mechanism for the data gathering system relies heavily on the types of data collected in the network. Generally, there are two different collecting processes: event-driven collection or frequent collection. In the event driven system, the data gathering is carried out in case that some special events have appear, such as the detection of targets, the un-normal change of the sensed data, or just a new query originated from the sink. Data is collected only the special event has happened. In the frequent collecting system, nodes in the assigned area or position will sense and create data in a given interval, and the data is reported and relayed to the sink. In this situation data is gathered with a periodic operation, there is only one-way data flow (from the sources to the sink) in the network. Data gathering system is relatively simple and a careful design of the detailed process, such as path selection, the time selection for node to wake up, etc., will help to save the energy consumption in the global network.

Similar to the mechanism of the ad hoc networks, the data gathering system in the sensor networks also needs the cooperation of the in-network to deliver the detected information to the sink. Different sensor nodes may have collected the same types to data, which can be fused or aggregated before the consequent relay operation. Data aggregation is the combination of the raw data originated from different source nodes by a given function, which is named as aggregation function. The aggregation function can be as simple as the functions of maxima, minima and average, or as complicated as functions of fusing, duplicate suppression, etc. Data aggregation can achieve energy efficiency and reduce the number of data transmission. However, efficient data aggregation needs node cooperation, and synchronization and caching technologies might be necessary to achieve the aggregation operation. This also arises with extra cost and will increase the complexity and protocol reliability of the sensor nodes.

The data gathering and data aggregation needs supports from all layers of the network architecture. However, the basic ingredients that are necessary to the data gathering and data collecting are: proper data structure, efficient data aggregation function and robust routing protocol. It shall be mentioned that although the three ingredients are introduced separately here. The energy efficiency and prize constraint require the simplicity of the architecture. Note that senor nodes are generally application-aware. It can bee seen a good way to design the nodes with cross-layers protocols, including the data structure representation, data aggregation function and routing protocols.

DATA STRUCTURE

In generally, data is gathered from nodes in a correlated filed to the sink node in the sensor networks. Note that the number of sensor node will be hundreds to thousands or even more than that, a huge number of data will be observed in such large network. Then a proper data structure shall be designed to represent the raw data that the sink interests in. The data structure shall be considered and designed carefully so that different types of data can be expressed and outlined. Another consideration for the data structure is the data selection and processing. A sensor node will not store all generated or received information because of its limited storage capabilities. It needs to decide whether to store, discard, or transmit the relative data. It means that a good data structure is necessary to efficiently manage and store the data [3-4].

Another importance of data structure in the sensor networks is respectively concerned with the data aggregation process mentioned later. Notice that the raw data has inherited redundancy though it is in fact originated from difference source nodes. For instance, in case that the collected data is the temperature, the values at the sensor nodes are correlated and the data structure shall be designed with the spatial correlation or the physical position. A proper data structure will help the nodes to aggregate the incoming data together will the original data.

Distributed data structure for the information storage is researched recently [5, 6, 18-20]. The distributed data structure is trying to capture the spatial-temporal characteristic in data gathering system. Nevertheless, the energy-efficient storage of data structure is still an open area of research till now.

DATA AGGREGATION FUNCTION

In sensor networks, the energy cost by wireless communication is generally several times larger than that of the computation cost. The data aggregation is considered an effective technique to save the communication energy cost by reducing the number of transmission and fusing data from multiple source nodes. The collected raw data by the sensor nodes has inherent redundancy and relativity. This redundancy can often be eliminated by data aggregation. To conserve energy for a longer network lifetime, it is critical for the network to support high incidence of in-network data aggregation. The conclusion is drawn for some reasons. First, the individual raw data from one sensor node does not hold much value.   For a simple example, the observer in a traffic monitoring system needs only to know the total vehicles passing through a crossroad instead of a special car or taxi.   Secondly, the huge number of raw data will waste the limited memory and bandwidth in the sensor networks. It is more efficient to get an overview of the raw data in the global network with data aggregation. In the above traffic monitoring system, the aggregation function can be as simple as SUM. In addition to benefit of energy saving, data aggregation also helps to reduce the error of raw data by gathering and fusing a huge number of materials. The impact of data aggregation is well studied in [15, 16].

The granularity of the data aggregation function will influence the value of the collected data. For example, the SUM function will plus and merge information while the aggregation process is carried out and none raw data can be rediscovery after the process is finished. It means that we will lose the details and precision with respect to collecting all raw data. However, a lossless aggregation function will never suffer from it by compressing and preserving the raw information. It also means that all original data can be re-read and re-constructed from the aggregated information. This leads to extra cost, such as packet size, memory requirement, etc.

In fact, the data aggregation is a strongly proposed solution for the sensor networks and is always realized together with the routing protocols [16].

ROUTING PROTOCOL

Routing protocol is the most important ingredient in the data gathering and data aggregation system. It is very challenging because of the inherent characteristics of the wireless sensor networks as mentioned above. First, the relatively large number of sensor nodes makes it almost impossible to build a

global address-based protocol which is rather commonly used in other wireless networks, such as mobile ad hoc networks and cellular networks. Due to the loss of global identification, the routing protocols shall make path selections with limited local information. Secondly, the forwarding process in sensor networks is generally data-centric. That is, packets are forwarded if and only if the relay node is really interested in the data. This characteristic ensure that a new routing metric instead of the hop count, link bandwidth, etc., shall be designed to guide the path selection and path maintain in the wireless sensor networks. Thirdly, energy efficiency is one key object in the routing protocol design. It means a careful resource management among the nodes which have rather limited memory and link bandwidth. Although the sensor nodes are seldom moved after deployment, the topology might change because of the unreliability of the nodes and wireless links, the leave or coming of new nodes. The routing protocols shall be designed with strong robustness to meet with such different situations. Finally, the routing protocols shall take the advantage of data aggregation into realization. And as mentioned above, synchronization and caching are an important way to help the protocol to carry out the data aggregation process.

In spite of all these difficulties, a lot of works have been done in the routing problem in wireless sensor networks recently. The routing protocol is generally a summarization or the final solution for the data gathering and data aggregation problems. The following section will focus on the current works done in this field.

ROUTING PROTOCOLS FOR THE DATA GATHERING AND DATA AGGREGATION

A lot of works have been done on the routing problem in the sensor networks and protocols have been proposed for the data gathering and data aggregation. Generally, they can be classified as three types: tree-based / flat, hierarchical and location-based.

In this section we have first introduce several tree-based / flat protocols, namely, SPIN – Sensor Protocol for Information via Negotiation, Directed Diffusion, and en ELECTION protocol.   Then we have introduced the cluster-based protocol, LEACH –Low Energy Adaptive Clustering Hierarchy. Finally, we have discussed the real-time problem in data collecting system, and introduced some solutions for this problem.

TREE-BASED / FLAT PROTOCOLS

When data is collected from some sensor nodes to one special sink, a simple tree rooted at the sink can be build to gather data from these nodes, and the data aggregation happens at the non-leaf nodes, which waits for data from their children and use the aggregation function to aggregate the incoming data, and sends the final data to their parent node. Note the leaf node must gather data, but the non-leaf nodes might only aggregate the incoming data originated from different sources. A synchronization mechanism may be necessary in the tree-based protocols to make sure the parent node does not send data until it has received from all its children. Tree-based protocol is also named as flat protocol in the article. Tree-based protocol is also called as the flat protocol in some papers. Without loss of generality, it is named as tree-based /flat protocol in this article.

Shortest Path Tree (SPT), Greedy Increment Tree (GIT) [16], Minimum Steiner Tree (MST) can all be used to build the aggregation tree. The tree-based data gathering and data aggregation is well-studied. The advantages are discussed in many works [15, 16]. However, the tree-based protocols also have some drawbacks. First, in case that the sensor nodes or links on the tree fail to work for some out-of-control conditions, all information rooted at this node will lost. Secondly, dynamics of the topology such as node leaving and join may arouse the same problem. Thirdly, the building and maintaining of a tree in a distributed network is rather expensive which finally has reduced the network lifetime. Finally, if the tree is built without careful design, some nodes on the tree can be too far away from the root on the tree, the collected data may finally arrive at the sink with rather long delay, which is un-tolerated in many application because the sensed data is valid only for a given period of time.

Flooding and gossip is used in the routing while the sensor network appears. However, they consider neither the characteristics of the sensor network nor energy efficiency. The first flat protocol for the sensor network is SPIN, which had eliminated the data redundancy among nodes by negotiation. After that, a lot of protocols [9-12] have been proposed including Directed Diffusion, directed flooding, etc. In the following we will introduce several tree-based / flat protocols and highlight their advantages and shortcomings to fully understand the key ideas behind them.

SPIN – The SPIN (Sensor Protocol for Information via Negotiation) is a family of adaptive protocols based on data negotiation [9]. The idea behind the SPIN family of protocols is to name the sensed raw data with high level descriptor or meta-data. Only the data descriptor instead of the all data is exchanged between the node that the data is originally collected and the nodes that are expected or unwilling to obtain the data. After this negotiation process is finished, the real data is sent to nodes that really interest in it. Note that the data descriptor is generally shorter in length than that of the real data. The negotiation has

explored the property that the sensor nodes in close proximity have similar data, and hence there is a need to only distribute the data to other nodes that do not posses. It also helps to eliminate the implosion, overlap and energy-blindness problems that are very serious in traditional flooding and gossip protocols. In fact the negotiation process can significantly reduce the energy cost of the network, and finally help to increase the network lifetime.

There are three types of messages with the SPIN protocols.

∞ ADV, which is used to advertise the existing of new data. When a SPIN node has data to share with others, it can advertise this fact by an ADV message with the meta-data contained.

∞ REQ, which is used to request specific data. If one node wishes to receive the data packets from another node, an REQ message is sent.

∞ DATA, which is the packet for the requested data which is sent by the originator to the receiver.

The protocol starts when a node has received and is willing to share a new data. The node first advertises the meta-data of the real data by broadcasting an ADV message. All neighbors will receive this ADV message. If a neighbor is interested in this data, it just replies a REQ message back and finally the data is sent to this neighbor by a DATA message.

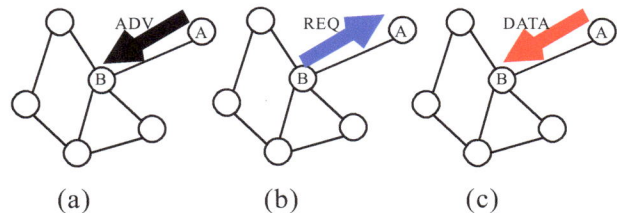

Fig. (1). An example of the SPIN protocol.

Fig. (1) shows an example to illustrate the mechanism of SPIN. Assume that node A has data to share with others, node A will broadcast an ADV message, as shown in (a). Upon receiving the ADV message from node A, node B checks whether it is interested in the data of node A, and sends back a REQ message back to node A if so, as shown in (b). When node A receives the REQ message, it sends the requested data to node B with a DATA message. Then node B can send the data out in the similar way until it reach the sink node.
In this example, data aggregation can happen at node B if has its own data while getting meta-data from node A. This makes the SPIN protocol very suitable for the data gathering and data aggregation process in wireless sensor networks.

It shall be mentioned that the node only needs to know its one-hop neighbors with the SPIN protocols. This advantage has ensured SPIN to be robust with topological changes. Furthermore, the three time handshakes (ADV-REQ-DATA) of SPIN can minimize the start-up cost of the network and is simple enough to be used by sensor nodes with memory limited. It shall be mentioned that nodes are not required to respond to every message in the network. If the meta-data has been obtained ever, the received ADV message can just be dropped. All these advantages ensure the SPIN protocol energy-efficient compared with the flooding and gossips protocols.

However, the data advertisement mechanisms in case nodes are not aware of the interests of the sinks, especially when nodes are far away from the sinks. And so nodes will not gather data when one neighbor sends an ADV. In means that SPIN is not suitable for applications which require a frequent data collection in the network.

Directed Diffusion – It is a reactive data-centric and application-aware routing protocol providing multipoint to multipoint communication [10]. Different from the SPIN, the Directed Diffusion is query-driven, that is, one / several sinks shall first indicate the interests and flood the interest into the network. An interest is defined as a list of attribute-value pairs such as the objects, event data rate, duration, geographical area of the interest, etc. Each node receiving the interest will rebroadcast the interest to the one-hop neighbors. The node also sets up interest gradients. A gradient is a vector specifying an attribute value and a direction (from the receiver to the neighbor who sends the interest), which can be characterized by the event data rate and data collection duration from the received interest. When the interest is flooded to all nodes in the network, the entries for the different interest and gradients are setup on each node, and finally paths are established between the sink and sensor sources. Note that the interest will be refreshed by the sink node periodically and two different interests can be aggregated into one simple interest if their tasks are similar to each other.

The Directed Diffusion is organized with three phases.
• Interest dissemination, which is used to deliver the interest from the sink to nodes in the network.

• Gradient setup, which is done by each node when receiving a different interest and path that satisfies the interest request is setup.

• Path reinforcement and forwarding, which is carried out when the interested data is forwarded to the sink. Fig. (2) has shown an example to illustrate the mechanism of Directed Diffusion. During the gradient setup process (b), several paths can be established with different gradient value on each link. However, only one single path with a special characteristic, such as lower delay or higher energy reserved, will be

reinforced and used to route the source data toward the sink. The further local flooding is reduced with this mechanism. And finally a good data gathering path is built from the sources nodes to the sinks. The sinks periodically refresh the interests, and the gradient on the selected path is reinforced periodically too. Note that no maintain and reservation is necessary in this paradigm. It ensures the protocol simplicity and easy realization in low-prize wireless sensor networks. Furthermore, path repairs are possible in Directed Diffusion protocol. The alternative path can be selected without any extra path searching process when the previously selected path is broken.

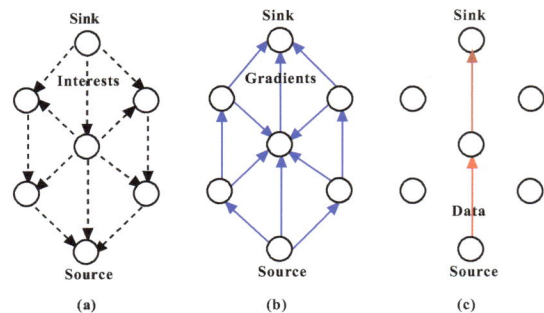

(a) Interests propagation.
(b) Initial gradient setup.
(c) Data delivery along the reinforced path.

Fig. (2). An example for the directed diffusion protocol.

Caching is important technologies in the Directed Diffusion protocol. Caching can increase the energy efficiency, network robustness and scalability in the data diffusion paradigm. First, the received interest by each node is cached before broadcasting to the neighbors. The new interest received can be aggregated into a simple interest with the cached interest if they have similar attribute-value. This combination will greatly reduce the data flow in the network. Secondly, the received data can also be aggregated with the cached data.

Directed Diffusion differs from the SPIN in two main aspects. First, the Directed Diffusion protocol is query-driven while the SPIN is data-driven. In Directed Diffusion the sink must send out an interest into the network to explicitly show what type of data it is interested in. In SPIN the node with new data will first notifies the existing to the neighbors by an ADV message, and only neighbors that are interested in the data will collect it by the REQ and DATA messages exchange. Secondly, it is unnecessary to maintain the global network topology, and nodes communicate with each other with only one-hop neighbor information with the Directed Diffusion.

However, directed diffusion is not suitable for applications that require continuous data collecting. It is because that the query requires extra overhead in the relatively static sensor network. In such a situation, static solutions such as directed flooding or ELECTION-based routing [11, 12] are more efficient.

ELECTION – The proposed ELECTION protocol in [12] is a tree-based protocol. Different from works mentioned above, the ELECTION builds a data gathering tree by a smart election process in order to improve the robustness and increase the lifetime of the total wireless sensor network while exploring the advantages of directed routing [11].

The ELECTION protocol is organized with two phases, namely, Initiation process and Election with Data Sending-out process. In the Initiation phase, rings are built centered at the sink to mark the distance of each node to the sink. The process can be done in the following. The sink first broadcasts a QUERY message with TTL (Time to Live) set to 0. Each node that has received this QUERY message will mark itself belonged to ring 1 (the set of nodes one-hop away from the sink), then plus the TTL value in the packet with 1. Note that each node maintains a *HOP* parameter to represent the distance to the sink which is initiated as infinity. If the modified TTL value is larger than *HOP*, the process is terminated. Otherwise, the node has found a neighbor (from which the QUERY message is received) closer to the sink. Then the node modifies the *HOP* as the TTL value, and broadcast the QUERY out. This process continues until the

QUERY message is received by all nodes in the network, and finally each node in the network knows its hops to each sink. It shall be emphasized that the Initiation phase is carried out periodically by the sink to maintain the robustness in dynamic topology.

The second phase is the Election and Data Sending-out process. An example is shown here to illustrate this process. Assume node *a* with distance to the sink as *HOP(a)* needs to send data to the sink. The candidate nodes that are suitable to forward this data are those neighbors with distance to the sink as *HOP(a)* - 1. Node *a* broadcasts an ELECTION message to notify neighbors. The neighbor nodes that have received the ELECTION message should check its *HOP* parameter. If the node finds itself to be a candidate, the potential service time is calculated with Equa. (1), which represents the time the candidate node is willing to be a leader.

$$time\_to\_work = current\_energy / Pt\_/2 \qquad (1)$$

In Equa. (1) *Pt_* means the power level that is necessary for data sending, and *current_energy* means the remaining energy on the node. Here we assume that a node is willing to act as a relay node till it consumes half of its remaining energy. The calculation result *time_to_work* is sent back by an ELECTION-REPLY message to the caller. After all candidate information is collected, the caller just elects the leader with maximum time to work.   Then the caller just sends data to the selected leader together the notification of the

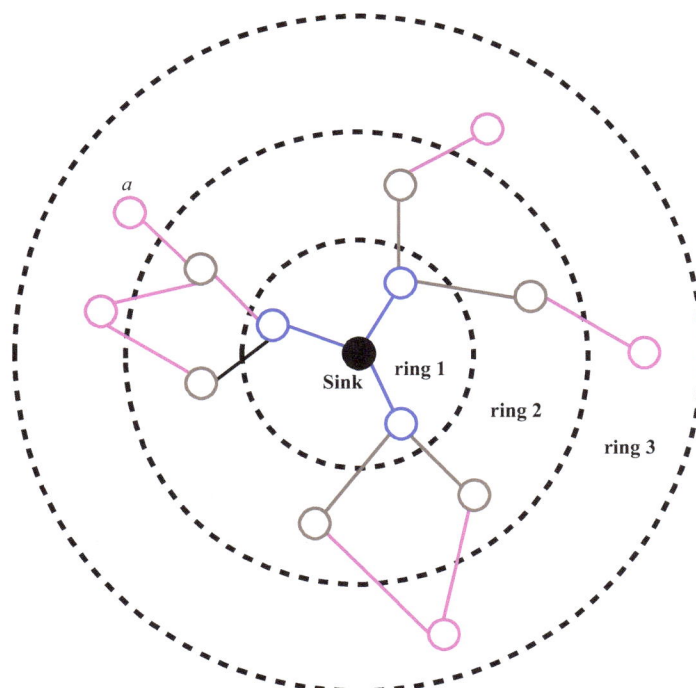

Fig. (3). The demonstration of rings in the network with the ELECTION protocol.

leader state.

It is common that several sensor nodes will collect and send data simultaneously in the wireless sensor networks. These source nodes can elect the leader separately. However, a common leader can aggregate the data from different sources. The elections rejoin process is also introduced in [12]. In case that a node intends to send data, it might find several leaders among its candidates. These leaders shall announce its LEADER state in the ELECTION-REPLY messages. The caller can just choose the node with maximum *time_to_work* as its forwarding relay node if such leader exists among the neighbors.

HIRARCHICAL PROTOCOLS

Another important technology to build the routing protocol is by the clustering method. In the cluster-based protocols nodes in the networks are divided into clusters, and each cluster has one cluster head that is responsible for the data gathering and data aggregation in the special cluster. The clustering protocols are rather energy-efficient in case that the source nodes are closing to each other in geography location. This situation is common in the data collecting system. The data in the same cluster can be aggregated and finally sent to the sink by the cluster. The clustering method has the similar problems as that in the tree-based protocols. For example, it may have high cost to maintain the cluster structure in dynamic network and lose robustness in case of node or link failure.

LEACH – Low Energy Adaptive Clustering Hierarchy (LEACH) is a famous self-organizing and adaptive clustering protocol for the sensor networks [13]. The basic idea of LEACH is to form clusters by dynamically and locally selecting some nodes as the cluster heads in the network. The clusters head will act as the backbone of the network. The sensed data on each sensor node will first be sent to the cluster head. And the cluster head will collect and aggregate all data from the respective cluster, and finally forward the result directly to the sink node. The cluster heads are randomly selected from all nodes, so that the high energy consumed to connect to the sink is spread to all nodes in the network. Optimal number of cluster heads is estimated to be about five percent of the total number of nodes in the networks. In case that the sensed data is locally, compared with the tree-based protocols, the cluster-based LEACH method will be rather efficient because data from different sources are aggregated first at the cluster head before further transmission, and the number of transmission will be reduced and energy be reserved significantly.

The operation of LEACH protocol is separated into two phases.

∞   Setup phase, which is used to elect the cluster head and build the cluster structure.
∞   Steady phase, which deals with the data gathering and data aggregation to the sink node.

In the setup phase the nodes are organized into clusters. Each node first chooses a random number between 0 and 1. And the node n becomes a cluster head if the random number is less than the following threshold $T(n)$ in round r:

$$T(n) = p/(1-p * (r \bmod 1/p)), \text{ if } n \in G \qquad (2)$$

where p is the desired percentage of cluster heads (for example, 0.05), r is the round number, and G is the set of nodes that have not been cluster heads during the last $1/p$ rounds.

In case that one node is elected as the cluster leader, it broadcasts a CLUSTER HEAD message to notify the rest nodes in the network that a new cluster head is selected. Nodes that are failed to be cluster heads in the current round will receive the notification and have to decide which cluster it belongs to. The decision is done by the signal strength of the CLUSTER HEAD message, that is, a node will select the node with highest signal strength as the leader. After that, the node sends a reply to the cluster head to notify its join. When all reply messages is received from the nodes in the respective cluster, the cluster head node assigns the time that the nodes can use to send data to it.

In the steady phase, the sensor node can begin sensing and transmitting data to the respective cluster head. Then the cluster heads, after receiving all data from the same cluster, will aggregate the data and finally forward the aggregation result directly to the sink node. Note that LEACH has assumed that all nodes can communicate with the sink directionally but it is not a fact in many applications.

After a certain period of time, the network goes back to the setup phase again, and enters another round of cluster head selecting process.

The LEACH has increased the lifetime of the network by selecting randomly nodes as the cluster heads to communicate with the sink. However, it might be impossible for all nodes to have enough power to communicate with the sink if the geographical range of the network very large. The deflect shows that LEACH is not applicable to network in large range. Furthermore, the idea of dynamic clustering brings extra overhead, which might eliminate the gain in energy consumption. In some special cases such as highly dynamic environments, the update information is necessary in order to keep the clusters consistent with the underlying topology. This requires rapid rebuilding of the cluster structure.

LOCATION-BASED PROTOCOL

Location-based protocols have utilized the node geographical information while building the routing paths in the data gathering process. In the sensor network, there is no global information such as internet address IP or identification. The key idea behind the location-based protocol is that the local location information can help to build the routing path by exploiting the characteristic of dense deployment in the wireless sensor network. Nodes relay the packets by forwarding to the neighbors who are close to the sinks. The location information of the neighbors can be obtained by strength of the incoming signals or the GPS equipments. A lot of works have been done in this field [24-26] and we will focus on the GAF (Geographical Adaptive Fidelity) protocol.

GAF – The Geographical Adaptive Fidelity (GAF) is primarily designed for the mobile ad hoc network but adaptive to the sensor network. The key idea behind the GAF is to divide nodes in the network into geographical grids. Nodes in the same grid are regarded as equivalent nodes and at any time it requires exactly one node maintain on work in any grid, while other members in the same grid just go asleep. The waken node is responsible for the packet relay originated from neighbor grids.

GAF assumed that each node is equipped with the GPS to locate the geographical position in the network. The covered network is divided into virtual grids. The grid size shall be calculated to ensure that nodes in the same grid can communicate with any node in the neighbor grid. Assume that sensor nodes have the same transmission range as R, and the grid size as r. It can be observed from Fig. (4) that the constraint shall be satisfied below:

$$r^2 + (2r)^2 \leq R^2 \tag{3}$$

There are three basic states in the GAF protocol.

- ∞ *sleeping*, which means that a node is shut down and can be waken up with the new cycle starts.
- ∞ *discovery*, which is used to find and collect the neighbors in the same grids.
- ∞ *active*, which is used to shown that the node is responsible for the data gathering in the current grid and data forwarding for packets from neighbor grids.

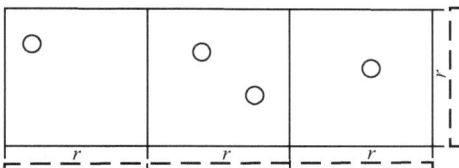

Fig. (4). A example of virtual grid in GAF.

Initially nodes start and set its state as *discovery*. Information about the node identification, grid identification, reserved energy, etc., is exchanged among neighbors in the same grid. The grid identification can be calculated with the node location. The node also set a timer while entering the *discovery* state. When the timer fires, the neighbor information of nodes in the same grid is collected and the node can choose to be an active node in the grid.

In case that a node enter *active*, a timer is also set to determine the time duration that this node is willing to keep on working. When this timer fires, the node returns to the *discovery* state and a new cycle starts.
Note that a node can turn to the *sleeping* state when it finds some other equivalent node in the same grid is handling routing.

REAL-TIME DATA GATHERING AND DATA AGGREGATION

With the development of wireless sensor technology, quality-of-service emerges as one important requirement. For example, some real-time applications needs to gather all the sensed data in the network, and the data shall arrive at the sink node in a given time interval. Real-time requirement might be satisfied with further modification on the above tree-based, hierarchical or location-based routing protocols. However, a theoretical study on this problem is still necessary. Here we have explored a novel solution for the real-time data gathering and data aggregation which is proposed in [14].

According to the relay mechanism, the delay for the data packet from one source to the sink is the total delay of all links on the path from the node to the sink, if we ignore the queuing delay on the nodes. However, notice that the link delay on a shared link is determined by the number of nodes contenting on the common channel. The work [21] shown that the cycle length for node to access a common channel in wireless network is upper-bounded by $K^2 + 1$, where K is the maximum node degree. It means that the maximum link delay in one hop is upper-bounded as $K^2 + 1$ with the maximum node degree as K by using the worst case analysis [21, 22]. In case that node degree bound is known, the bound on the height of the aggregation tree can also be concluded with the real-time constraint since that the total delay is the sum delay on each links, which is mentioned above. Then, there are two constraints when considering the real-time data aggregation: 1) node degree bounded, where the maximum node degree on the tree shall not exceed a bound; and 2) tree height bounded, where the tree height shall not exceed a bound.

When data is gathered from all nodes in the networks, an energy-efficient data gathering scheme shall be designed while satisfying the real-time requirement. In the sensor network, as mentioned, the energy consumed by the communication is at least quadratic to the distance. One way to save energy is using radio with adjustable transmission power. The energy is saved just by reducing the power level to the minimum value while satisfying the communication requirement.

The real-time data gathering and data collecting problem is described as following. A weighted graph $G = (V, E)$ can be used to represent the sensor network, with V be the set of sensor nodes, and E the set of links between these nodes. There is a link between two nodes if their distance is no more than the maximum transmission range, while the link weight is the minimum energy cost needed to connect the two nodes incident to this link. Here we assume that the nodes are symmetric and the maximum transmission range is distinct to all nodes. The real-time data aggregation problem is formulated as: given a weighted graph $G = (V, E)$, find a spanning tree rooted at the sink $s \in V$ with the total energy cost on the tree minimized, in which each node's degree is no more than the degree constraint D, and the number of hops of each node to the sink is no more than the hop constraint H.

It is already concluded that the Minimum Spanning Tree (MST) of any Euclidean graph in the plane is a 6-degree MST (a tree is denoted as a K-degree tree is the node degree on the tree is no more than K), and it can be transformed into a 5-degree MST in [17]. This transformation is as follows which are shown in Fig. (5). Assume that the node degree of u is 6 on the MST and let $v_0, v_1,..., v_5$ be the neighbors of u on the MST. It can be proved that nodes $v_0, v_1,..., v_5$ must locate at the vertexes of a regular-hexagon with node u as the center. The degree of node u is reduced to 5 if we swap the edge (u, v_0) with (v_0, v_1). Note that the new spanning tree has the same total weight because these nodes form a regular hexagon. It means the new spanning tree is a minimum spanning tree too. The transformation process continues until all nodes with degree as 6 are reshaped in the similar way above. Finally a 5-degree minimum spanning tree is built. Motivated by above analysis, the following conclusion can be drawn accordingly [14].

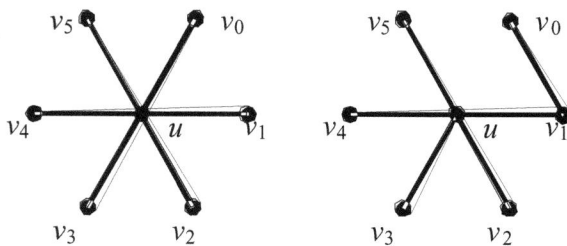

Fig. (5). A 6-degree MST is transformed into a 5-degree MST.

Lemma 1: *Given a weighted graph $G = (V, E)$ in the plane with the link weight $w(u, v)$ as a function of the distance d between the two nodes (u, v), i.e. $w(u, v) = f(d)$, for any given d, $f'(d) > 0$. The minimum spanning tree for this graph is a 6-degree MST which can be converted into a 5-degree MST.*

The energy consumption in the sensor network is generally calculated with the FIRST ORDER RADIO MODEL [23]. Assume that one node transmits a k-bit packet to another node with distance as d, the total energy cost is:

$$E(k, d) = 2 \cdot E_{elec} \cdot k + \varepsilon_{amp} \, k \cdot d^2. \tag{4}$$

where E_{elec} and ε_{amp} are two constants independent to the packet size k and node distance d.

It can be observed that $E'(d) > 0$ which means that the lemma 1 stands in the sensor networks. In the following sections we will introduce the heuristic algorithms in [14] to build a degree-bounded and hop-bounded MST.

Node-First Heuristic (NFH)

The Node-First Heuristic (NFH) is to build a 5-degree and H-hop spanning tree, where H is a parameter determined by the real-time requirement in applications. The key idea of the NFH is originated from the Prim algorithm, i.e., adding nodes onto the spanning tree in sequence and checking the node degree and tree height simultaneously. The initial spanning tree T contains only the sink s. Then select one node, namely u to T who is not on T but has the minimal edge weight connected to T. Simultaneously, check the degree of the node, namely v, who is the parent of u. If $deg(v)$ is equivalent to 6, just transfer the current spanning tree to a 5-degree tree. By the way, we check the hop to sink of node u, namely, $hop(u)$. If $hop(u) = (H + 1)$, node u must select a new parent on T. If no such candidate can be found, v shall change its parent in order to decrease its own hop to the root. This can be done in the similar way as u does. However, if v fails too, this back-track process iteratively runs until one node on T is found and its parent is changed. Otherwise, the algorithms just terminated and no solution is found. This process continues until all nodes are added to the T.

Tree-First Heuristic (TFH)

The aim of the Tree-First Heuristic (TFH) is also to build a 5-degree and H-hop spanning tree which is similar with NFH. The building of the spanning tree is carried out in two phases, namely, initialization phase and re and reshape phase. In the initialization phase, a minimum spanning tree is built with the Prim's algorithm. However, the selected node, namely, u, just joins T if it does not violate the hop constraint. Otherwise, the node u is refused, and its state is marked as FROZEN and is not allowed to join the tree during the rest of first phase. This process continues until all nodes that do not conflict with the hop-constraint are added to the tree. In the second phase, the nodes with state as FROZEN are to select a new parent on the current spanning tree with the hop constraint satisfied. This is feasible because there are a lot of nodes on the spanning tree when the first phase ends, and there might exist more than one candidate among the node's neighbors that is already on the tree. The sink broadcasts a message to unfreeze these FROZEND nodes. This process continues until all nodes in FROZEN state have selected a new parent.

Note that in the TFH and NFH, the joining time of a node that conflicts with the constraints is different. In the NFH, the node is always asked to join the tree if it is selected by select a new parent or the re-selection of its parent, and so on. However, in the THH, the un-suitable nodes are frozen until the first phase ends.

Hop-Bounded Heuristic (HBH)

The Hop-Bounded Heuristic (HBH) is to build a D-degree and H-hop spanning tree. The key idea is that we first build a tree satisfying the hop constraint, and then the tree is re-shaped according to the degree constraint.

The spanning tree with the hop constraint can be obtained with the modified Bellman-Ford's algorithm. The key difference from the traditional Bellman-Ford's algorithm is the running time of the loop cycle. During the ith loop, nodes built their shortest path to the sink with the path length no more i. And Finally an H-hop tree is built after the first phase ends. Then node degree is checked. A function TRIM_AND_DRAFT is used to cut and draft to proper nodes. Details of this process can be seen in [14].

CONCLUSIONS

There wireless sensor network consists of a huge number of cheap nodes with limited resources. It can be used in various fields of our economy and society. Among all these application scenarios, the data gathering has played a key role in building the monitoring system. Energy efficiency is crucial in the wireless sensor networks. Exploring the dense deployment and data redundancy of the sensor network will help to reduce the energy cost which leads to the data aggregation solutions.

The data structure, data aggregation and routing protocols are three main ingredients in building data gathering system. Data structure illustrates how data is organized in the memory constrained sensor node. A proper data structure will help nodes to observe,

collect, cache and aggregate information. Distributed data structure is studied recently but is still an open area of research. The data aggregation is considered an effective technique to save the communication energy cost by reducing the number of transmission and fusing data from multiple source nodes. In fact, data aggregation is a strongly proposed technology for the sensor networks and is always realized together with the routing protocols.

The article has explored the current data gathering protocols, and has introduced three tree-based / flat data aggregation and routing protocols, namely, the SPIN, Directed Diffusion and Election-based Aggregation protocol. When data is collected from some sensor nodes to one special sink, a simple tree rooted at the sink can be build to gather data from these nodes, and the data aggregation happens at the non-leaf nodes. The tree-based data gathering and aggregation is well-studied. However, tree-based protocols have some drawbacks, such as loss of robust to the link / node failure, the heavy cost to build and maintain the tree structure and no guarantee on the real-time requirement. Cluster-based hierarchical protocols are reasonable in case that the source nodes are close. The data in the same cluster can be aggregated at the cluster head, and finally sent directly to the sink by the cluster head. A cluster-based protocol names as LEACH is also introduced in this article which is proved to be energy efficient compared with other protocols. However, it may have high cost of maintaining the cluster structure in dynamic network and lose robustness in case of node and link failure.

Location-based protocols have utilized the node geographical information while building the routing paths in the data gathering process. The key idea behind the location-based protocol is that the local location information can help to build the routing path by exploiting the characteristic of dense deployment in the wireless sensor network.

Quality-of-service is emerging as one important requirement in the wireless sensor networks. The article has aimed at the intention and has introduced a novel idea to build the aggregation tree by transferring the real-time requirement into two constraints: node degree and tree height. Three heuristics algorithms, namely, Node-First-Heuristic, Tree-First-Heuristic, and Height-First-Heuristic, are proposed to solve this real-time requirement.

REFERENCES

[1]   Akyildiz IF, Su WL, Sankarasubramaniat Y, *et al*. A survey on sensor networks. IEEE Communcations Magazine, 2002: 102-114.

[2]   Fasolo E, Rossi M, Widmer J, *et al*. In-nework aggregation techniques for wireless sensor networks: a survey. IEEE Wireless Communications, 2007: 70-87.

[3]   Nath S, et al. Synopsis diffusion for robust aggregation in sensor networks. In Proc. ACM/IEEE SenSys'04, Baltimore, MD, Nov. 2004.

[4]   Cohen E, Kaplan H. Spatially-decaying aggregation over a network: model and algorithms. In Proc. ACM SIGMOD'04, Paris, France, June 2004.

[5]   Shrivastava N, Buragohain C, Agrawal D, et al. Median and beyond: new aggregation techniques for sensor networks. In Proc. IEEE SenSys'04, November 3-5, Baltimore, Maryland, USA, 2004.

[6]   Yick J, Mukherjee B, Ghosal D. Wireless sensor network survey. Compter Networks, vol 52, 2008: 2292-2330.

[7]   Akkaya K,Younis M. A survey on routing protocols for wireless sensor networks. Ad Hoc Networks, vol 5, 2005: 325-349.

[8]   Lindsey S, Raghavendra C, Sivalingam KM. Data gathering algorithms in sensor networks using energy metrics. IEEE Transaction on Parallel Distribution Sysystem, vol. 13, no. 9, 2002: 924–35.

[9]   Kulik J, Heinzelman WR, Balakrishnan H. Negotiation-based protocols for disseminating information in wireless sensor networks. ACM Wireless Networks, vol 8, 2002: 169-185

[10]   Intanagonwiwat C, Govindan R, Estrin D. Directed diffusion: a scalable and robust communication paradigm for sensor networks. In Proc. IEEE/ACM MobiCom'00, Boston, MA, August 2000.

[11]   Ko YB, Choi JM, Kim JH. A new directional flooding protocol for wireless sensor networks. In Proc. ICOIN'04, LNCS 3090, 2004: 93-102.

[12]   Cheng HJ, Jia XH. An energy efficient routing algorithms for wireless sensor networks. In Proc. IEEE WCNC'05, Wuhan, China, September 2005.

[13]   Heinzelman WR, Chandrakasan A, Balakrishnan H. Energy-efficient communication protocol for wireless sensor networks. In Proc. of the Hawaii International Conference System Sciences, Hawaii, January 2000.

[14]   Cheng HJ, Liu Q, Jia XH. Heuristic algorithms for real-time data aggregation in wireless sensor networks. In Proc. ACM IWCCC'06, Vancouver, BC, Canada, July 2006.

[15]   Leang D, Kalis A. Smart SensorDB: sensor network development boards with smart radios. In Proc. IEEE ICCCAS'04, vol 2, 2004: 1476-1480.

[16]   Krishnamachari B, Estrin D, Wicker S. The impact of data aggregation in wireless sensor networks. In Proc. 22nd Distributed Computing Systems Workshops, July 2002: 575-578.

[17]   Monma C, Suri S. Transitions in geometric minimum spanning trees. In Proc. 7th annual symposium on Computational geometry, 1991: 239-249.

[18]   Newsome J, Song D. GEM: Graph EMbedding for routing and data centric storage in sensor networks without geographic information. In Proc. ACM/IEEE Sensys'03, San Diego, CA, 2003.

[19]   Desnoyers P, Ganesan D, Shenoy P. TSAR: a two tier sensor storage architecture using interval skip graphs. In Proc. ACM/IEEE Sensys'05, San Diego, CA, 2005.

[20]   Ganesan D, Greenstein B, Perelyubskiy D, et al. An evaluation of multi-resolution storage for sensor networks. In Proc. ACM/IEEE Sensys'03, Los Angeles, CA, 2003.

[21]   Chlamtac I, Pinter S. Distributed nodes organization algorithm for channel access in a multihop dynamic radio network. IEEE Transactions on Computers, vol. C-36, no. 6, 1987: 729-737.

[22]   Cheng HJ, Xiong NX, Yang LT, et al. Distributed scheduling algorithms for channel access in TMDA wireless mesh networks. Journal of Supercomputing, vol. 45, 2008: 105-128.

[23]   Heinzelman, WR, Chandrakasan A, Balakrishnan H. Energy-efficient communication protocols for wireless microsensor networks. In Proc. 33rd Annual Hawaii International Conference on Jan 2000.

[24]   Xu Y, Heidemaann J Estrin D. Geography-informed energy conservation for ad hoc routing. In Proc. ACM/IEEE Conf. Mobile Computing and Networking, 2001: 70-84.

[25]   Yu Y, Estrin D, Govindan R. Geographical and energy-aware routing: a recursive data dissemination protocol for wireless sensor network. UCLA Technical Report, UCLA-CSD TR-01-0023, 2001.

[26]   Stojmenovic I, Lin X. GEDIR: loop-free location based routing in wireless netoworks. In Proc. Paraallel and Distributed Computing and Systems, Boston, MA, USA, Nov. 3-6, 1999.

CHAPTER 8

Area Coverage in Wireless Sensor Networks

Antoine Gallais

University of Strasbourg, France
Image Sciences, Computer Sciences and Remote Sensing Lab (CNRS UMR 7005)

Abstract: Wireless sensor networks are deployed to observe remote or sensitive environments. To avoid difficult or dangerous manipulations after the deployment, power-saving strategies are used to prolong the network lifetime. Selecting active sensors, that perform the monitoring task while passive ones save energy, is one of them. The ensuing sensor area coverage issue is thus formulated as follows: every part of the deployment area, initially sensed by n deployed sensors, must be sensed by at least k active ones (k varying between 1 and n). This chapter investigates proposed techniques to designate those sensors along with existing assumptions and tools that they use.

1 Introduction

1.1 Activity scheduling in wireless sensor networks

Wireless sensor networks are often considered as dense and redundant sets. Depending on the application, the number of deployed sensors may vary in order to ensure an adapted lifetime of the so-formed network. Indeed, the redundancy is viewed as a way of disposing spare sensors that could be activated once others start running out of power or simply fail. This redundancy conveniently allows nodes that are not required for the local application task to turn into sleep mode, in order to increase their own lifespan, and the lifetime of the created network. Activity scheduling especially consists in designing the set of active sensors that participate in the application while, on the opposite, passive ones are saving energy for further duty. Scheduling sensors' activities can be made through various schemes, either in a static way or dynamically. In a static scheduling, each sensor is programmed with an embedded timetable that imposes the activity periods. This timetable can be computed before the deployment or regularly updated during the deployment. If no static timetable is available, then it should be defined dynamically, depending on several factors such as network state or sensors' environment for instance.

Regarding the reduced size of the objects we are dealing with, constraints linked with energy limitations must be carefully considered. As one of the wireless sensor networks ambitions is to be deployed over distant and sensitive areas, there is no point considering battery charging strategies. Even for small scale deployments where sensors would be accessible, the fact is that charging hundreds or thousands of sensors could be painful. Then, as energy sources are drying up during the deployment, this constraint is the determining factor that limits the network lifetime.

There are several reasons why wireless sensors consume energy. Their ability to sense and to communicate are the two principal ones. Considering power consumption induced by sensing, it must be said that it mainly depends on the material and the target of the sensing. Considering wireless communication, scheduling activities allows large energy savings that lowly vary with the radio chipset embedded on the sensors. When activity is scheduled, a passive node does not communicate. During multi-hop communications, only active devices may act as forwarders. By this way, passive sensors do not compete to access the medium either. In infrastructure-less networks, there is no entity responsible for assigning communicating slots to nodes willing to communicate. This is why many efforts are made to develop Medium Access Control (MAC) protocols in wireless networks that allow every node of the network to access the medium in order to communicate with others. These protocols aim at minimizing costly collisions during wireless communications. As long as some occur, nodes have to transmit their data several times to deliver their data. In wireless sensor networks, several MAC protocols have been proposed so far. They have ensured that the competition for the medium would not be too costly for the sensors.

Actually, very few of them have been subjected to tests in highly dense networks composed of thousands of nodes. Reducing this density therefore remains a prime goal in energy saving strategies.

Nevertheless, energy is not the only reason why activity must be scheduled in a wireless sensor network. Reducing the network density has also an impact on the data collect process and on the medium access policy for instance. For instance, in time-driven applications, it could be useless to regularly gather excessive and redundant information about the same portion of area. For that reason, leaving as few active sensors as possible is an interesting goal. Moreover, when event-driven approaches are implemented, sensors do not transmit data until an event occurs (e.g. sudden temperature raise, humidity exceeding a given threshold). If every object able to sense the event initiates a report, then the routing and MAC protocols must be scalable enough to ensure proper working with a large set of nodes.

It is therefore crucial to investigate activity scheduling strategies as it can ensure both energy savings and less problems related to MAC and routing layers once large wirelessly communicating populations must be managed.

Some nodes are passive while active ones participate in the application. These roles can be switched regularly in order not to always exhaust the same nodes. In this chapter, we will review the solutions related to the designation of active and passive sensors. The hardware techniques to wake up a wireless node are out of the scope of this contribution. Note that sensed events could be used to wake up the sensors (e.g. [1]).

The activity scheduling cannot compromise the running application. Among existing criteria, we focus on the permanent monitoring of the deployment area. We thus address the issue of scheduling sensors' activities from the *area coverage* point of view.

1.2 Area coverage problem

Once assumed that a large and redundant set of sensors is deployed over a target area, the goal of the so-formed wireless sensor network is to monitor this zone. Sensor area coverage problem is to determine a small number of active and connected sensors that still cover the same area as the fully deployed set. This enables active sensors to detect any event in covered area and report it to a monitoring center. Today's sensors can acquire various information from their environment (e.g. temperature, humidity, pressure, light) and applications are numerous. On one hand, applications that aim at continuously monitoring a phenomenon (e.g. habitat [2], glacier monitoring [3]) are said to be time-driven, due to the data collection scheme they use

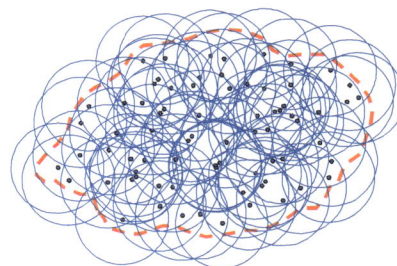

(a) A deployed wireless sensor network.

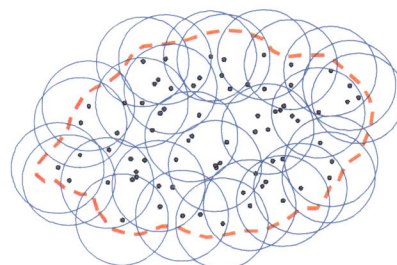

(b) Only a subset of nodes is sufficient to ensure full coverage of the area

Fig. (1): Scheduling activity while preserving area coverage.

(i.e. periodic monitoring reports sent from sensors to the sink stations). On the other hand, applications referred to as event-driven ones, are intended for measurement of a response to stimuli (e.g. volcano monitoring [4], structural health monitoring [5]). In both cases, any portion of the deployment area must be sensed by at least one active node. Scheduling activity in a wireless sensor network with the area coverage criterion means that the set of active sensors must be able to sense as large an area as the whole set of sensors. Fig. (1)(a) illustrates a wireless sensor network deployed over a target area delimited by a doted line. The sensing ability of every node is symbolized by a disk centered on the node itself. As we can observe, the monitoring task does not require every sensor to be active at the same time since only a small subset is able to cover the whole area (see Fig. (1)(b)). Along with the monitoring task, sensing reports (emitted by each node in time-driven applications), alert messages (that may occur in event-driven deployments), or simple control information impose a communication path to exist between every sensor and at least one of the sink stations.

1.3 A review of commonly used assumptions

We are now presenting some assumptions that are commonly used in solutions that address the area coverage problem.

1.3.1 Deployment of the sensors

Before starting the monitoring task, the sensor network must first be deployed. Several methods are envisioned. Their use depends on both the application requirements and on the constraints related to the target area on the other hand.

- **Deterministic deployment**

  Depending on the conditions over the target area (e.g. accessibility, prior knowledge), a deterministic deployment can be conducted. In such cases, it is assumed that the nodes can be placed precisely, thus allowing the elaboration of a preliminary deployment map. Then, considering the area coverage problem, sensors' activities could be scheduled ahead of the deployment. Each sensor would therefore be implemented to ensure regular activity and energy saving periods throughout its lifetime. This kind of deployment is often considered for applications such as structural health monitoring [5] or maintenance of equipments [6].

- **Random deployment**

  Using sensors in unreachable or sensitive areas prevents any deterministic deployment that would assign a precise position to every sensor. Then, nodes must be deployed in a different manner. This has been compared for long with throwing seeds over a field. Indeed, sensors can be disposed randomly over the area, after having been dropped by a plane for instance. Considering the costs of sensors, this method has not been widely developed yet. Still, considering sensors deployed over an unstable environment, a random deployment would also be obtained.

1.3.2 Localization of the sensors

It is often assumed that sensors are aware of their location. This position can be exact or relative to some reference points. Indeed, this assumption is essential once the coverage evaluation must be dealt with, as we will further detail in section 2. Many solutions have been proposed to enable location-aware sensors. Some are inherited from classical ad hoc networks while others are especially dedicated to the field of wireless sensor networks [7].

Relying on the Global Positioning System (GPS) is quite never considered, unless nodes benefit from miniaturized GPS receivers and are powered correctly to compute this position using the satellites' signals. However, this is getting more and more credible and we have recently observed many changes in objects that are supposed to compose ad hoc networks for instance. Yet, as we study infrastructure-less networks, it would be ironic to rely on a GPS solution that is based on a satellite infrastructure.

Apart from the GPS solution, several contributions have been proposed for ad hoc networks. They are either centralized [8] or distributed [9]. Most of the existing works that do not rely on the GPS solution are using reference nodes. Each of those nodes may know their self position, which is then spread all over the network. Non-reference nodes can compute their positions by using triangulation. To do so, some distances must also be known. Several methods exist to evaluate the distance between two communicating nodes. The Received Signal Strength Intensity (RSSI) can be used for instance. Yet, the accuracy of this measure highly depends on the features of the radio chipset, which remain low-cost in the field of sensor networks. One could also use the time spent during a transmission, which implies nodes to be precisely time-synchronized. Once the area where the node probably is has been determined, the exact position can be determined by various means (e.g. [10]).

We can also talk about the number of reference points that is required to ensure correct computation. The reference nodes must be numerous enough and should be smartly spread inside the network in order to limit the impact of potential errors. Identifying the reference points can be achieved thanks to specific nodes that are aware of their exact position. These are said to be anchor nodes. They may use a GPS receiver or any other positioning system since they can rely on enough power supply and great computation capabilities. In a wireless sensor networks, those nodes could be the sink stations themselves for instance. Once agin, determining the dimension of the system is a matter of prime importance since it could otherwise lead to very bad results (e.g. [11]).

The results can be improved by finely spreading the anchors so that every node of the network would stand at a rational distance form at least one of them. These solutions have been tested with networks of variable communication density. It has been shown that the computation task required to ensure accurate positioning was inducing already significant latency with small-scale networks (e.g. 10 minutes in a network composed of 10 nodes [12]). This latency can even be more important once the network is unstable during the computation effort [13].

As the time required to ensure proper location might not be bounded (e.g. simple nodes can become reference points only once their self positions have been computed) , some solutions adopt a hierarchical approach. In such methods, nodes can initiate their position computation only once a superior node has finished to do so [14, 15]. Some works have also investigated non structured approaches in which nodes regularly observe their neighborhoods to evaluate their positions. For instance, a node can not initiate the computation process until enough reference nodes appear in its communication area [12].

Recently, new solutions have proposed precise position evaluations thanks to a low number of anchor nodes and a fully decentralized algorithm [16]. Some others do not rely on those anchors anymore and are rather based on some features of the network deployment (e.g. the beacon scheme [17]). Most of these solutions do not use any GPS receivers nor anchor nodes and instead use a virtual coordinate system [18]. If the so computed positions might be insufficiently accurate to be used in applications such as precise object localization, they can perfectly be of prime interest once the area coverage evaluation is considered in wireless sensor networks as we will further elaborate on in section 2.

1.3.3 Time-synchronization among sensors

In wireless sensor networks, time-synchronization is also a matter of prime importance. For instance, it is essential to allow accurate dating of the data in order to ensure proper data fusion since it will be used to characterize the sensed event. As the embedded hardware may not allow fine synchronization (clock drifts can be of some seconds per day between two sensors), some other solutions must be used to guarantee this.

Many techniques have already been proposed to synchronize wireless communicating devices. In wireless sensor networks, the time-synchronization can be required during the whole lifetime to overcome time drifts. As we will see, activity is mainly

organized in a rounded fashion, each round having its set of active sensors. Considering activity scheduling processes that occur at the beginning of each round, a simple point synchronization could be sufficient. Then, such time synchronization can be achieved through various ways (e.g. using a helicopter signal [19]). However, these strategies imply heavy infrastructures or at least external operations. In [20], the clocks of the nodes can converge thanks to the wireless communications. Some nodes emit messages that transit over multi-hop paths before reaching back the emitting node. This node can then evaluate the minimal and the maximal bounds for the accumulated delays (the timestamp is updated depending on the local time at the receiver and the creation date of the message). This approach is robust since it can work among networks whose connectivity is intermittent. In [14] and [15], computing the average of the delays increases the accuracy and allows time to be computed at a given point of the network.

Time synchronization can be achieved through different ways, depending on whether an infrastructure is present or not. We can also mention, that the IEEE 802.15.4 standard [21] allows time-synchronization to be maintained thanks to specific frames and a hierarchical mode (e.g. the star topology).

1.4 Classifying approaches to designate monitoring sensors

Activity scheduling can be achieved through different methods. We classify existing solutions in three categories as it can be observed on Fig. (2). Centralized approaches assume the presence of a central entity able to communicate with every sensor and to be aware of the current topology, thus allowing easier computations and role assignments. Hierarchical strategies are inherited from centralized ones as the central entity is transformed into several distributed authorities, each being responsible for a given part of the network. Finally, localized solutions rely on decisions made by nodes solely based on local information. Their goal is then to provide a global coherent behavior regarding the application requirements without relying on any central entity.

1.4.1 Centralized approaches

In centralized activity scheduling solutions, there is a need for a central entity being aware of the whole network. This entity (figured as a square on Fig. (2)(a)) can then designate active and passive

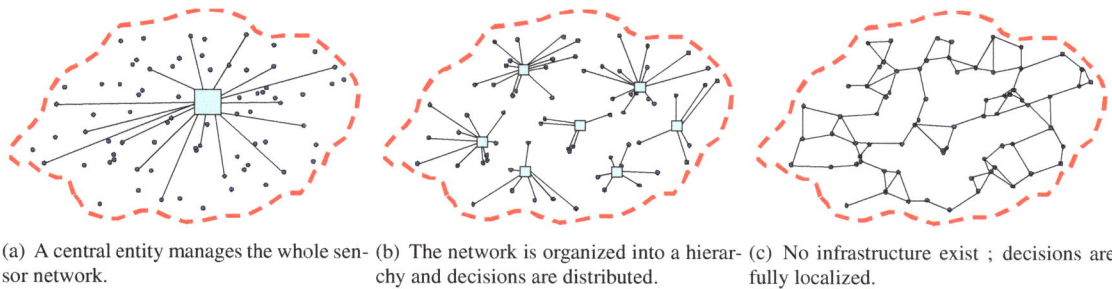

(a) A central entity manages the whole sensor network.

(b) The network is organized into a hierarchy and decisions are distributed.

(c) No infrastructure exist ; decisions are fully localized.

Fig. (2): Three algorithmic strategies to address the activity scheduling issue.

sensors regarding the coverage goals of the application. Topology changes due to mobility or failures must be accurately monitored in order to maintain a correct view of the network at any time. In dynamic networks, the information about these changes must be propagated throughout the network, to maintain the information needed for each node to make decision. These solutions therefore imply regular status messages from the sensor nodes to the central entity. They also suppose that the central entity can either directly communicate with the sensors or can rely on multi-hop communication paths to reach every node of the network.

1.4.2 Hierarchical approaches

In hierarchical approaches, the network is organized into subsets, each having to be self-managed. Then, it allows to relax the full information propagation required by centralized solutions. Still, hierarchical approaches use instead a wave type of computation and communication that can induce some problems depending on the network characteristics (e.g. memorization at nodes, unbounded delays). To solve these issues and to correctly achieve the management of these sets, designating a managing entity is one solution (squares on Fig. (2)(b)). This entity can be designated during the initialization process or elected by the sensors. If this entity were one of the sensors, then it could be regularly changed in order to balance the induced charge. In a hierarchical organization, the topological information are propagated within the subset only. This is why they are considered as a good tradeoff between centralized and fully localized approaches. However, the way sensors must be assigned to one of the subset depends on many parameters and the criteria and methods used to build those subsets in a decentralized fashion lies in the field of network clustering [22].

1.4.3 Localized approaches

Localized approaches do not rely on any network infrastructure and do not aim at building a hierarchy among sensor nodes. By this way, they have significantly lower communication overhead, as no global view of the network is required. The prime goal is to obtain a global coherent behavior, regarding the application requirements, solely based on local decisions. A decision is said to be local as long as it is based on local information (e.g. decisions made by its communication neighbors). Moreover, in a fully localized protocol, decisions are not impacted by distant nodes (e.g. in clustering type protocol, where nodes wait until some decisions arrive and unblock the decision making criterion). This approach is illustrated by Fig. (2)(c). The topological changes (due to role switching, failures or mobility) should have local consequences only as they stand for simple neighborhood modifications. In wireless sensor networks, and especially in area coverage protocols, localized approaches allow the impact of these changes to be restricted to only nodes whose sensing regions overlap. These solutions are suitable for networks of any size and density. They are needed for dynamic networks, such as sensor networks, because of changes in activity status, or changes due to failures or adding more nodes. This is the reason why this chapter especially focuses on localized area coverage solutions.

1.5 Modeling wireless sensor networks

1.5.1 Communication model

A wireless network can be modeled by a graph $G = (V, E)$, V being the set of vertices and $E \subseteq V^2$ the set of edges. An edge between two vertices u and v exists if u is physically able to send a message to v.

The neighborhood set of u, noted as $N(u)$, is defined as:

$$N(u) = \{v \in V \mid v \neq u \wedge (u,v) \in E\}$$

Each sensor has a communication range CR meaning that the communication area of a node u is modeled as a disk of radius CR, centered on the node itself :

$$(u,v) \in E \equiv d(u,v) \leq CR$$

with $d(u,v)$ being the euclidean distance between nodes u and v.

1.5.2 Area modeling

Nodes monitor an area using their various embedded sensing modules. The sensing radius of a node is denoted by SR. Monitored area of a sensor node u is denoted as $S(u)$. It is modeled as a disk of radius SR, centered on the node itself. We so have:

$$S(u) = \{p \mid d(u,p) \leq SR\}$$

with $d(u,p)$ being the euclidean distance between a node u and a physical point p. The area covered by a set of nodes $A = \{a_1, a_2, \ldots, a_n\}$ is denoted by $S(A)$:

$$S(A) = \bigcup_{i=1}^{i=|A|} S(a_i)$$

2 Existing methods to evaluate coverage provided by a set of sensors

In this chapter, we survey solutions that exist to schedule activity among sensors, based on the area coverage criterion. Nodes have to be organized so that those deciding to be active remain able to cover as large an area as the original whole set of deployed sensor nodes. Area coverage protocols require some nodes to be able to evaluate the coverage of a given target zone (either their own or the one covered by other nodes).

In this section, we review the various techniques that have been proposed in the literature to enable proper coverage evaluation by sensor nodes. Most of the time, it is assumed that a sensor evaluating the coverage of an area is aware of its position and of the sensing radii of the nodes it considers during the process.

2.1 Discrete area coverage evaluation

We first describe three discrete methods that allow sensors to evaluate the coverage of a target area. For the sake of clarity, the sensing region of the node will be considered as this target area.

2.1.1 Using reference points

A sensor node can discretize its sensing area in order to model it as a set of points. Then, the coverage of its area is approximated by the number of points that are covered:

$$S(u)_{eval} = \frac{|\{p \in Ref(u) \mid p \in S(N(u))\}|}{|Ref(u)|} \times 100$$

$Ref(u)$ being the set of reference points and $S(u)_{eval}$ the evaluated percentage of the area covered by node u and which can be sensed by its neighborhood $N(u)$. Choosing the reference points can be achieved according to various schemes. Some solutions use a grid to represent the sensing region while some others randomly fix a set of points within the target area. In both strategies, the accuracy of the evaluation straightly depends on the number of reference points.

2.1.2 Discretizing sensing area perimeter

Another method consists in discretizing the perimeter of the sensing region into portions. Fig. (3) shows two neighboring nodes, u et v, with u trying to evaluate the coverage provided by v. Therefore, the coverage of a perimeter portion means that the corresponding part of the sensing disk is also covered, as it can be observed on Fig. (3). The $[A,B]$ segment is fully covered by v since its extremities A and B are within the sensing range of v. Node u can so assume that the corresponding portion of $S(u)$ is covered by v. As soon as the extremities of a given segment are not within the sensing range of a neighbor, u considers the region as non covered. This is the case for the $[C,D]$ segment.

The accuracy of this method depends on the size of every segment. Longer segments lead to fewer points thus inducing a lighter computation task. Yet, it increases the probability of unsolvable cases. Indeed, when a segment is considered, if only one of its extremities is covered, then no information regarding the coverage of the portion can be extracted. Moreover, once sensing and communicating radii differ, this method cannot be used. For instance, a

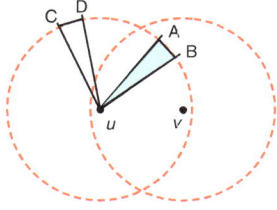

Fig. (3): Once sensing and communicating radii are equal, the coverage of two points of the perimeter (e.g. points A and B) is an information about the coverage of the corresponding portion of $S(u)$.

communicating neighbor may have a sensing range shorter than its communicating radius. Therefore, the coverage of a segment could not be interpreted as the coverage of the whole sensed portion. Generally speaking, this perimeter based scheme can not be applied as soon as $CR > SR$. Some other methods must then be used (e.g. [23]), making the coverage evaluation a more complex and greedy computation task.

2.2 Exact area coverage evaluation

Several mechanisms have already been studied in area coverage protocols to reach an exact computation of the coverage. Some of them rely on a well known geometric theorem, which is generally applicable. Moreover, it is applicable to any shape of monitored region by a sensor. This covering criterion has been already applied in [23, 24, 25]. It efficiently confirms whether or not a sensing region is fully covered by other sensing regions. It is applied on the borders of the sensing areas of each sensor. As mentioned in our modeling assumptions (see section 1.5.2), these borders are normally circles, and we will express the theorem first in circle terminology. This criterion, expressed in the following theorem, is fast to compute and works whatever the ratio between the sensing and the communicating radii is.

Theorem 2.1 *If there are at least two covering circles and any intersection point of two covering circles inside the sensing area is covered by a third covering circle, then the sensing area is fully covered.*

In other words, a disk d is fully covered by other disks if and only if every intersection point of two disks $d1$ and $d2$ inside d is covered by another disk $d3$. In addition, intersection points of any other disk

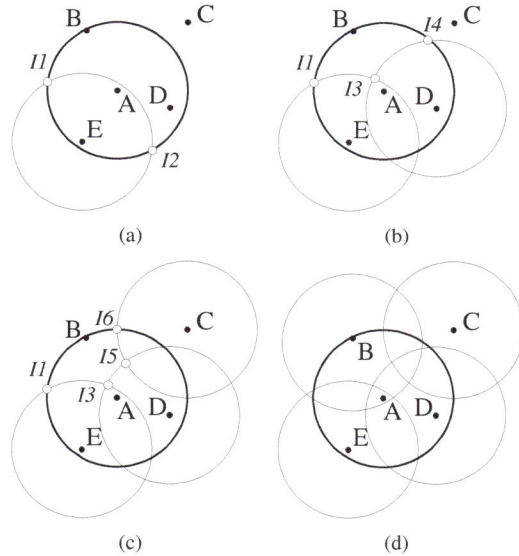

Fig. (4): Deterministic coverage evaluation thanks to the intersections of the sensing circles.

$d1$ with d must also be within a third circle $d2$. Note that circles are not required to have the same radii. Here is a short example to illustrate this coverage criterion. As observed on Fig. (4), a node A evaluates the coverage of its sensing region, and is aware of some of its neighbors, noted as B, C, D et E. On this figure, only the sensing disk of each node is drawn. We consider that the communicating range is larger as A and C are neighbors without C being in the sensing region of A (i.e. $SR < CR$).

Fig. (4)(a) shows both intersection points ($I1$ and $I2$) of the sensing circles of nodes A and E. $I2$ is within the sensing disk of node D (Fig. (4)(b)) but two new intersection points must then be considered. These non covered intersection points are noted as $I1$, $I3$ and $I4$. On Fig. (4)(c), we can observe that $I4$ has been covered by node C. Yet, once again, two new intersection points must be considered, noted as $I5$ and $I6$. Finally, node B covers the four intersection points $I1$, $I3$, $I5$ and $I6$ and every intersection point that has been induced is covered by at least one node among C, D and E. We therefore observe that A is fully covered (Fig. (4)(d)). For the sake of clarity, this example is illustrated with equal sensing radii but the coverage criterion could be used with sensing disks of various dimension.

This simple method allows area coverage evaluation in networks whose sensor nodes have heterogeneous sensing radii without increasing the complexity of the computation task. This also means that a deterministic coverage evaluation is feasible through the use of reference points (the intersection points of the sensing circles).

2.3 Various existing extensions

2.3.1 Ignoring border regions

The coverage criterion that uses intersection points of the sensing circles can be modified to avoid the problem of border nodes effect. Indeed, the original sensing coverage and the monitored area must be distinguished. The original sensing coverage is the coverage provided by the whole set of sensors while the monitored area is a geometrical figure, such as a rectangle for instance, inside which sensors are deployed. It represents the physical environment over which sensors will be spread. During the coverage evaluation, depending on whether the application requires the original sensing coverage to be preserved or solely aims at ensuring the coverage of the monitored area, the nodes located near the borders of this monitored area may have different behaviors. Indeed, if the original sensing coverage must be guaranteed, then those sensors have no other choice but to be always active as they are the only ones able to monitor the furthest pieces of their own sensing areas. If only the monitored area is to be covered, then some portions of the sensing regions covered by the border nodes (i.e. those outside the monitored area) do not require any coverage.

In such a case, the coverage criterion can be extended to take into account the intersections of sensing areas with the monitored area. Nodes simply find the intersection of their sensing area with the monitoring area, and consider it as their revised sensing area. For example, in Fig. (5)(b), node A considers shaded area (the mentioned intersection) as its new sensing area. If node A applied the same reduction to its neighbors, special cases, with regions intersecting along line segment rather than in a singe point, would occur. To keep algorithm simple for implementation, node A preserves covering regions of neighbors as circles. This does not impact the accuracy of this criterion. The modified covering region prevents border nodes from being active at every round. For instance, Fig. (5)(a) shows four nodes, A, B, C and D within a square area. In order to preserve the coverage of the whole region that it is able to sense, A should be active in each round. However, if only the rectangle is to be monitored, then A could get into sleep mode. As observed in Fig. (5)(b), circle centered at C covers all intersec-

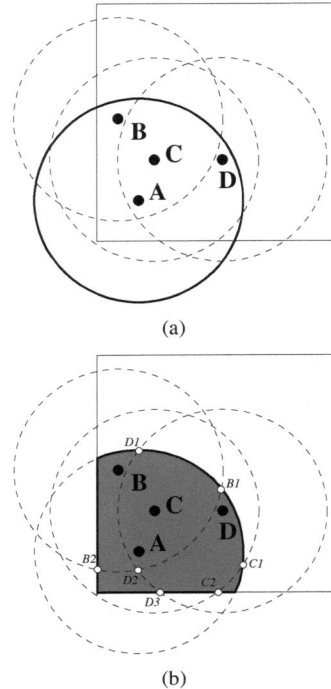

(a)

(b)

Fig. (5): Considering the borders of the deployment area during coverage evaluation.

tion points created by other circles and revised monitoring region of A, while $C1$ and $C2$ are covered by circle centered at D.

This method is computationally very efficient. It allows dynamic evaluation of the criterion, by keeping the list of nodes to be covered by new active neighbors. As soon as the criterion is satisfied, the verification of this condition can be terminated. In this way, the criterion does not require excessive computation time in case of highly dense networks. Yet, it must be assumed that nodes are aware of the field they have to monitor, and can adjust the covering criterion in order to consider portions of sensing regions located inside the monitored area only (see also [24]).

2.3.2 Evaluating multiple coverage

Once sensor nodes are deployed over a target area, the monitoring application may impose various degrees of coverage. In other words, regarding the redundancy induced by the deployment, multiple area coverage can be achieved (see 3.3 for details). Then, the coverage evaluation methods must allow sensors to determine whether an area is multiply covered or not.

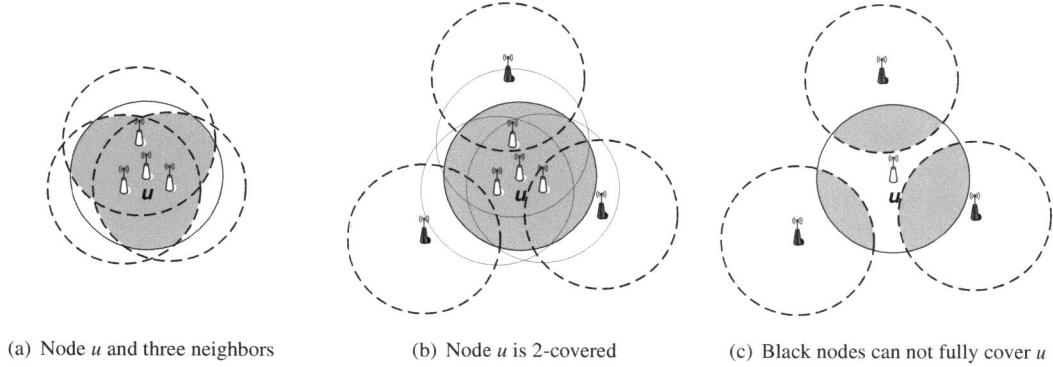

(a) Node u and three neighbors   (b) Node u is 2-covered   (c) Black nodes can not fully cover u

Fig. (6): A k-covered area may not be covered by k distinct sets

Let us formally describe the multiple area coverage. Given a set of nodes, noted as V, deployed over an area A, V is able to cover k times A if every physical point $p \in A$ is covered by at least k distinct sensor nodes:

Definition 1 (*Flat k-area-coverage*) *An area is k-covered if every physical point p is covered by at least k active sensors.*

We will designate this issue as the flat k-area-coverage problem. The k-coverage of an area A is so formulated as follow:

$$A_{k-covered} \Leftrightarrow \forall p \in A, \|\{v \in V \mid p \in S(v)\}\| \geq k$$

A more restrictive definition is that k-area-coverage consists in k distinct subsets of active nodes, called activity layers and denoted C_i, each covering the area once:

$$A_{k-covered}$$

$$\Leftrightarrow$$

$$(\|\{C_i \mid A \subseteq S(C_i)\}\| \geq k) \wedge (\forall i \neq j, C_i \bigcap C_j = \emptyset)$$

Definition 2 (*Layered k-area-coverage*) *An area is k-covered if there exist k distinct sets of sensors so that each one fully covers the area.*

We will further refer to this second definition of the k-area-coverage issue as the layered k-area-coverage problem. For the sake of clarity, a k-covered node u will stand for a node whose monitored area $S(u)$ is k-covered.

$$u_{k-covered} \Leftrightarrow S(u)_{k-covered}$$

Note that solving the layered k-area-coverage problem necessarily implies the flat k-area-coverage issue to be solved also; each of the k nodes monitoring any physical point belongs to a distinct activity layer. Meanwhile, ensuring any physical point of the area to be covered by at least k sensors (flat approach) does not imply k-area-coverage by k distinct layers of nodes (layering approach). In other words, the area can be k-covered by a set of nodes from which no k disjoint subsets can be extracted.

For instance, on Fig. (6)(a), u is fully covered by a set of three nodes. The gray part of its sensing region is covered twice while white subregions are covered by only one sensor each. Fig. (6)(b) shows that new neighbors can appear (black nodes) to ensure 2-coverage of these three subregions. Therefore, u is 2-covered. Meanwhile, finding two distinct subsets of neighbors of u that fully cover its sensing region is impossible as Fig. (6)(c) shows that the subset composed of the black nodes does not fully cover u.

Still, these two formulations of the k-area-coverage problem can each fit to various classes of applications. Both can be easily handled by a node which must evaluate its coverage. In order to evaluate multiple area coverage, a node must have a required coverage degree, noted as k. It can therefore compare the provided coverage level to k, thus deciding to be fully k-covered or not. Note that such a parameter could be heterogeneous over the set of nodes.

We now show how any node of the network could locally evaluate the k-coverage of a target area. Given a node u and according to the flat k-area-coverage definition, the basic idea is that u can use methods such as those described earlier (e.g. perimeter and intersection schemes) while simply modifying the coverage criterion. Then, in order to evaluate the k-coverage of a target area, u must check that each computed point (e.g. extremities of perimeter segments or intersection points) is sensed by at least k nodes

If k-coverage is envisioned from the *activity layer* point of view (according to the layered k-area-coverage problem definition), then a node u must check that the set of nodes able to sense the zone can be separated into independent subsets, each covering the area once. Several methods can be used to compute such sets. Further details are given in section 3.3.

3 Existing sensor area coverage protocols

3.1 Covering and connectivity

As we already mentioned, the monitoring set of active nodes should be connected in order to ensure communication paths along which reporting or alert messages could transit between sensor nodes and sink stations. Connectivity and coverage have been considered as two separated matters for a long time. First because connectivity of a given set had been deeply studied, especially regarding the field of dominating sets, and second because area coverage was not a subject of prime importance yet, being a problem specific to wireless sensor networks.

Let us give some details about the dominating sets. Given a graph, a Dominating Set (DS) involves vertices so that any vertex of the graph is either in the dominating set or is a neighbor of a dominant node. A DS is not necessarily connected as shown on Fig. (7)(a) where the disks represent the communication areas and the lines stand for the communication links (nodes B, C and G cannot communicate). Then, a Connected Dominating Set (CDS) is a dominating set whose all nodes are connected (see Fig. (7)(b)).

Many solutions have been proposed to build CDS. Wu and Li [26] have first allowed the computation of DS that was later improved by Stojmenović et al. [27], ensuring low communication overhead for the construction provided that 2-hop knowledge was available at each node. Indeed, a node must become dominant as soon as some of its neighbors can not communicate with each other. Several contributions have followed as Dai and Wu proposed a generic rule for a node to decide whether to be dominant or not [28]. This rule was used in many contributions (e.g. [29], [30]). Decisions rely on

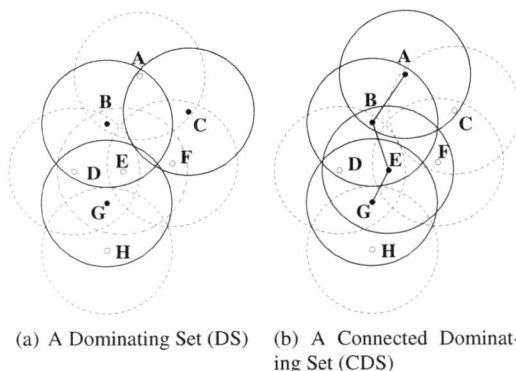

(a) A Dominating Set (DS)   (b) A Connected Dominating Set (CDS)

Fig. (7): Dominating sets used for node coverage.

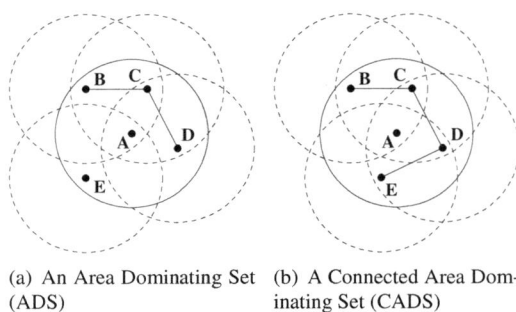

(a) An Area Dominating Set (ADS)   (b) A Connected Area Dominating Set (CADS)

Fig. (8): Area dominating sets ($CR = SR$).

unique identifiers, whose computation is also an important concern as the size of the dominant set varies according to the distribution of the identifiers. Some works have thus proposed different computation schemes [31, 32].

Some of these definitions have been extended to consider area coverage [30]. An Area Dominating Set (ADS) implies every pieces of the surface formed by the union of the monitoring areas to be covered by at least one node in the dominating set. Fig. (8)(a) shows that the initially covered area is fully covered by the set formed by A, B, C, D, F and H. Nevertheless, the fact that G is not required implies that H cannot communicate with the other dominating nodes.

At last, a Connected Area Dominating Set (CADS) is an ADS in which no partition exists. For instance, Fig. (8)(a) can be modified to obtain a Connected Area Dominating Set. If G is dominant, as shown on Fig. (8)(b), then the set of dominating nodes is connected and fully covers the area.

The protocols detailed hereinafter aim at building CADS. As we will see, the existing contributions try to maintain the whole set of sensors connected while ensuring the connectivity with the sink stations only would be sufficient regarding the context of wireless sensor networks.

3.2 Solutions for simple coverage

Here we essentially describe algorithms that assume randomly deployed sensor networks. Some works have assumed a given topology to start the study (e.g. a grid [33]) or have study given deployment patterns that would ensure both coverage and connectivity once wireless sensors are deployed over a sensing field [34]. Moreover, several centralized and distributed approaches have emerged from literature [35, 36] but this chapter focuses on localized algorithms as argued in 1.4.3.

3.2.1 Asynchronous area coverage protocols

Concerning localized algorithms, several asynchronous solutions have already been proposed. The first one is a simple localized PEAS algorithm which was proposed by Ye et all in [37]. Asynchronous networks are considered. Initially, all nodes are in sleep mode. Periodically, each sensor wakes up and sends a probing message. All active nodes within a given transmission radius R (which is identical for all nodes) receive this message. They then evaluate if their distance from the probing sensor is less than a range P, which is also equal for all nodes. This can be done due to signal strength or time delay measurements. If so, they advise the probing sensor accordingly, to allow it to continue sleeping for another period. Otherwise, no message is sent and the probing node decides to be active. Once it activates, it remains active until the end of its lifetime. This protocol is highly fault tolerant. However it does not ensure full area coverage.

Cai, Li and Wu [38] described a sensor area coverage protocol for asynchronous sensor networks. Their algorithm corrects and completes PECAS protocol [39] (which is an extension of PEAS [37]) which leaves holes in coverage. Each node maintains the portion of its area which is not covered by other sensors (net area). In protocol [38], each sensor is in sleep or one of four active states (pre-wake, awake, overdue, pre-sleep). Sensor activates at its own decision and sends message to neighbors. Awake neighbors respond (attaching their location and the remaining activity times), and sensor can decide to go back to sleep state or to move to Awake state (and informs neighbors). After working for time TW, the sensor remains in the active mode until its sleep neighbors wake up and replace it. Sensors in Awake or Overdue state may move to pre-sleep state when they notice that their net area is below threshold. Sensor in pre-sleep state announce their intention to sleep, in order to avoid multiple sleeps and creation of void areas. Neighbors in Awake or Overdue states respond. If sleep intention message is heard from another neighbor within a timeout, sensor decides to sleep only if its net area remains below threshold when these neighbors are ignored, or is below net areas of all these neighbors. Note that, when net areas are 0 for several such neighbors, but above threshold when any of such neighbors is removed, all of them remain active, although node in fact could move to sleep mode (provided other such neighbors remain active). Thus the case of multiple sleeps could be improved in its performance.

3.2.2 Hexagonal and square grid coverage

Zhang and Hou [24] described an efficient algorithm for selecting covering sensors in time synchronized network. Sensors periodically make new decisions about their active or sleeping status. In each round, a single sensor starts the decision process, which then propagates to the whole network. New sensors are selected so that the priority is given to sensors located near optimal hexagonal area coverage, obtained when the area is ideally divided into equal regular hexagons. The coverage is indeed quite good, given the distributed nature of the decisions. However, the need for a single sensor to start the process may cause problems in applying it, including increased latency. If several sensors start the process then the decisions at *meeting* points would be suboptimal. Another problem is that the original sensing area coverage may not be preserved (as shown by experimental results).

The algorithm presented in [40] divides the area into small grids, and then covers each grid with a sensor. Each sensor that can cover a grid maintains a list of other sensors that can also cover it, in a priority order. All sensors covering the same grid can communicate with each other. When sensor density is significant, sensors need a lot of memory and processing time to maintain priority lists, plus the communication overhead for making covering decisions in cooperative manner is nontrivial.

3.2.3 Coordinated area coverage

Hsin and Liu [41] investigated random and coordinated area-coverage algorithms. Each sensor covers a circle of radius R. In their coordinated-coverage scheme, a sensor may decide to sleep after receiving *permission* from sponsoring neighbors, for the time such permission is given. A node that sponsors any other node must be active. The decisions are not synchronized, since each sensor can *negotiate* with its sponsors independently, and the scheme allows for several variants with (sophisticated) protocol details. The authors suggest that nodes collect information about residual energy from neighboring sensors. Sensors with low residual energy are more likely to enter the sleep state than sensors with high residual energy. Each sensor maintains its own delay counter, which is used for role alteration. Coordinated schemes performed better in their experiments. Although the coordinated scheme by Hsin and Liu [41] has some desirable properties, such as localized behavior, it may select too many sponsor nodes to be active, since there is no coordination between nodes for the selection of as many as possible common sponsor nodes.

Carle et al. [42] proposed a localized scheme based on a relay selection phase. Every node selects a set of relays among its 1-hop neighbors. The relays cover an area as large as the area covered by whole neighborhood. Then, an activity decision is made based on a unique key. Any node which has the smallest priority in its neighborhood or which has been selected as relay by its neighbor with the smallest priority will decide to remain active. This decision allows connectivity to be preserved along with full area coverage. However, the algorithm involves sending *hello* messages to learn 1-hop neighbors, and sending messages informing neighbors about relays (the later messages are even of extended size), which may induce a high communication overhead.

Sheu, Yu and Tu [43] propose the following protocol. First, each sensor A sends or routes its priority to all sensing neighbors. Then it considers the perimeter of its sensing circle, and portions of perimeters of sensing neighbors with higher priority which are inside its own sensing circle. If all these perimeters are fully covered by other sensing neighbors with higher priorities then A may sleep. To decide about some neighboring active sensors, each of the considered perimeters is subdivided into segments, based on intersections with other considered circles. For each such segment, the sensor with the highest priority, among nodes covering this segment, is active. Note that some neighboring active sensors may not be discovered. However, those discovered suffice to construct connected query tree, for reporting from A to the sink. This elegant localized protocol requires one message per node for $CR > 2SR$ but for other ratios CR/SR the routing overhead and complexity (e.g. if greedy routing fails) may become excessive.

3.2.4 Low communication overhead schemes

Tian and Georganas [44] proposed a solution for sensor area coverage in synchronous homogeneous networks where sensing range is equal to the transmission range. It requires that every node knows the positions of all its neighbors before making its monitoring decision. At the beginning of each round, each node selects a time-out interval. At the end of the interval, if a node sees that neighbors (that have not yet sent *retreat* message) together cover its monitoring area, the node transmits a *retreat* message to all its neighbors and moves into the sleep mode. Otherwise, the node remains active, but does not transmit any message. The process repeats periodically to allow for changes in monitoring status. While this scheme ensures full area coverage, it can not be guaranteed that covering sensors are connected; thus, reporting to a monitoring station may not succeed. Then to ensure connectivity of the set of active nodes, an assumption can be made regarding the ratio between sensing and communication radii ($SR \leq CR$). Such an assumption had already been used and proved as preserving network connectivity as long as area coverage was provided [24, 25]. Tian and Georganas therefore extended their scheme in [45] by considering this assumption and thus allowing their covering sets to be connected.

Yet, another concern is about neighboring active sensors that may fail without notice. Neighboring sensors may not activate, believing that the sensor is *alive* and monitoring. This problem can be resolved if neighboring information is exchanged before the decision making process.

In [23], Jiang and Dou describe several improvements to the algorithm in [44]. They assume that $CR \geq 2SR$, and apply the intersection based criterion to evaluate area coverage. Nodes apply a random backoff before making decisions. In the algorithm presented in [23], at the beginning of each round, each node sends a hello message to inform about its position. The algorithm from [44], which relies on node retreat messages, is then applied. Experimental data in [23] show that this algorithm outperforms PEAS [37] with respect to the number of nodes needed in the coverage, while completely preserving sensing coverage of the original network.

Some solutions have also been proposed for arbitrary ratios CR/SR. In [46], authors add a connectivity criterion when $CR < 2SR$. The coverage is evaluated thanks to the intersection based method and several variants are proposed so that nodes can make decisions without inducing much communication overhead. several localized sensor area coverage protocols are proposed for heterogeneous sensors, each with arbitrary sensing and transmission radii. Sensors are assumed to be time synchronized, and active sensors are determined at the beginning of regular periods, named activity rounds. Prior knowledge about neighbor existence is not required thus avoiding regular neighbor discovery phases. Indeed, each node selects a random timeout and listens to messages sent by other nodes before the timeout expires. Sensor nodes whose sensing areas are not fully covered (or fully covered but with a disconnected set of active sensors) when the deadline expires decide to remain active for the considered round, and transmit an *activity* message announcing it. There are four variants in this approach, depending on whether or not *withdrawal* and *retreat* messages are transmitted. Covered nodes decide to sleep, with or without transmitting withdrawal message to inform neighbors about the status. Still, after hearing from more neighbors, some active sensors may observe that they became covered. Such cases can occur especially with nodes having the shortest timeouts. In order to reduce the number of active nodes, authors propose that these nodes can decide to alter their original decision and transmit a *retreat* message. Simulations show largely reduced message overhead while preserving coverage quality, compared to existing methods based on hello messages followed by retreat ones. Moreover, where excessive message loss contribute to excessive coverage holes in these methods, the approach proposed in [46] has shown robustness by still building connected sets of active nodes that fully cover the area. Authors finally investigate the impact of the timeout functions, showing that activity-aware timeout functions could help extend the network lifetime.

3.3 Solutions for multiple coverage

We now review some of the papers that exist in literature concerning k-area-coverage.

In [47], authors consider networks in which nodes are in sleep mode most of their lifetime. This paper firmly formulates the lower bounds for the number of nodes that should be deployed to ensure k-area-coverage.

Abrams, Goel and Plotkin [48] study the problem of partitioning the sensors into covers so that the number of covers that include an area, summed over all k areas, is maximized. They so address the layered k-area-coverage problem (see def. 2 in section 2.3.2). Three approximation algorithms, assuming k is fixed, are described. Randomized algorithm assigns to each sensor one of k covers at random. In distributed greedy algorithm, each sensor sets a timeout and listens to decisions made by neighbors, increasing the counter in the appropriate set for each message announcing decision by a neighbor. When timeout expires, each node selects a set for which the corresponding counter is minimal. Centralized greedy algorithm adds some weights but otherwise runs a similar procedure. In this article, no discussion is made concerning connectivity preservation with different ratios of communication and sensing radii.

Actually, network connectivity is rarely treated in existing works. Meanwhile, if $CR \geq 2SR$, k-connectivity is proved to be achieved once the network is k-covered [49]. Therefore, most of reviewed solutions rely on this theorem to focus on area coverage only without addressing the problem of the connectivity preservation.

In [50], Yang et al. have studied to what extent point coverage could approximate area coverage. Two non-centralized solutions are given to build k-covering sets. Only the second proposal can be said to be localized and ensures full point coverage and network connectivity. Then, dominating sets described in [51] are used to ensure k-coverage, thus requiring a 2-hop neighborhood knowledge.

In [35], Gupta, Das and Gu show that the connected coverage problem is NP-hard. In [52], this statement is generalized for connected k-coverage problem. Zhou, Das and Gupta [52] propose three algorithms to solve this issue. The first one is a centralized greedy protocol while the two others are distributed versions of it. The distributed greedy algorithm is very close to the distributed approximation algorithm that is provided in [35]. Let M be the set of nodes that should k-cover the query region. Initially, a random sensor is in M. Then, it must select the best candidate sensor and path to complete both the coverage and the connectivity. This is done by broadcasting a search message to all sensors within $2r$-hops where r is said to be the *link radius* of the network, that is the maximum number of hops that separate two nodes of the network whose sensing areas intersect (then $2r$ might be very large and the broadcast will be much energy-consuming). After a treatment on received response messages, a candidate sensor is added to M. This is repeated until the query region is k-covered. The communication overhead induced by this phase can be very high and authors propose a distributed priority algorithm to reduce it. Meanwhile, in this solution, every node must gather $max(t, r)$-hop (t is a constant and r is the *link radius*) neighborhood information (that include the unique priorities of nodes). Once again, the amount of information that needs to be collected might lead to high energy consumption. Indeed, t is fixed at 2 in the simulation results and so at least 2-hop information is required. Although no discussion is provided on how t can be fixed (t is set to 2 for the provided simulation results), authors propose a simple computation of r depending on the network density. For instance, r equals to $2SR/t + 1$ in dense networks, that is 5-hop information could be required ($SR = 4$, $t = 2$). The communication cost induced is not deeply studied while a 5-hop information could be hard to achieve and to maintain within highly dense networks.

Actually, most of contributions that address the k-area-coverage issue do not consider either fully localized approaches nor unreliable wireless communications. Still, it would be very hard to enable acknowledgments for control traffic in wireless sensor networks. Due to the very high communication densities, it would lead to both huge communication overhead and power consumption.

To lower the communication overhead, the protocols presented in [46] have been extended by considering k-coverage rather than simple sensing coverage for the deployment area. In [53], authors propose to enable k-area-coverage with connected active nodes sets by either modifying the coverage evaluation scheme or the protocol itself. They base these extensions on ideas presented in [46], in order to maintain low communication overhead. Their first extension uses the same area coverage protocol and focuses on the coverage evaluation scheme. Following the flat k-area-coverage definition (see def. 1), a node u decides to be passive and turns into sleep mode if it is completely k-covered. Otherwise, u remains active and sends a positive acknowledgment, containing the values of its communicating and sensing radii along with its position. Any node with a longer timeout that receives this message will therefore add u to its neighbor table. Authors show that this approach ensures k-area-coverage. They also point the fact that protocols originally designed to preserve 1-coverage, can be similarly extended to handle k-area-coverage.

Their second extension is a modification of the activity scheduling protocol. As multiple coverage is also achieved if there exists k disjoint subsets of active nodes, each covering the area once, they propose an adaptive localized protocol based on the layered k-area-coverage definition. Therefore, they try to build k activity layers, whose members cover the area fully and are connected. The difference with protocols detailed in [46] is that nodes, after listening for messages during the timeout period, make their activity decision and also choose an activity layer whose number is included in the control messages (used to notify the activity of a neighbor or its decision to get passive). Upon reception of these messages, a node u must evaluate the coverage that is provided by each activity layer. As soon as a layer is either not fully covering $S(u)$ or is not connected, u decides to be active and sends an activity message to announce its status. In this solution, u chooses the uncovered activity layer which has the lowest number. Depending on the local density, the number of reached layers might reach k or not. If it does not, then the adaptive aspect of this solution ensures that at least i layers will be constituted, with $i \leq k$. The four variants that have already been described for 1-coverage in [46] have also been modified, with some adjustments for those using negative messages. Indeed, any node v receiving a negative message from a node u can deduce that $S(u)$ is k-covered by k distinct activity layers. Then, when evaluating the coverage provided by any layer, v must consider that every physical point $p \in S(u) \cap S(v)$ is already k-covered. It is shown that all variants are able to build k distinct layers consisting of low percentages of active sensor devices in a fully decentralized manner.

4 Conclusions

In this chapter, we reviewed some important localized solutions in the field of area coverage protocols for wireless sensor networks. We have exposed the various assumptions on which most of these works still rely (e.g. communication and sensing models, nodes with static positions) and we focused our analysis on energy-effciency aspects and communication paradigms used in area coverage protocols.

Because of their flexibility, localized and distributed approaches are often viewed as interesting strategies to schedule activities among wireless sensors. While fully centralized or localized solutions have their own drawbacks depending on the network characteristics (e.g. size, density), some mixed solutions could be envisioned in order to allow more configurability in energy-saving strategies. For instance, the one detailed in [52] allows users to tune the protocol in order to control its induced communication costs. Indeed, authors proposed a simple computation for the number of hops at which information is gathered by a node to locally compute its decision. In [54], the proposed methods allow to tune the coverage degree as well as the sensing probabilities of a wireless sensor network thus tending toward configurability of activity scheduling protocols. In this chapter, we did not discuss about what parameters should be taken into account to tune or configure such protocols. Indeed, depending on the deployed application, some of the classical communication protocols (e.g. Medium Access Control, routing) could impose or require various degrees of activity. For instance, while a sufficient number of nodes would be activated to accurately monitor the target area, the so-induced communication redundancy might still be too high for routing schemes. These schemes could therefore tune activity scheduling protocols so that only a subset of the active sensors would be needed for routing, thus allowing longer sleep periods for the radio modules. We will further investigate these potential interactions within the communication stack that could lead to higher flexibility, configurability and versatility.

5 Perspectives regarding the area coverage problem

We are now giving some perspectives regarding some of the commonly used assumptions. Indeed, as many contributions have focused on activity scheduling and area coverage issues, more and more people, trying to develop wireless sensor networks in the real world (e.g. MoteLab testbed[1], SensorScope deployments[2], SensLab project[3]), are looking for energy-saving solutions able to pass the theory-to-practice transition. Yet, considering the feedbacks from these deployments, existing theoretical solutions are not satisfying. Most of them rely on assumptions that may not hold in the real world anymore (e.g. disk models for communications and sensing, time-synchronization) thus leading to wireless sensor networks built from scratch [55]. Moreover, it is always difficult to estimate the scalability

of these algorithms along with their efficiency once real deployment scenarios are considered (e.g. mobility of the sensors).

5.1 Characterizing the sensing abilities

We firstly presented the sensing area of a node as a disk. Some solutions have used this model to propose some variants. For instance, adjusting the sensing range can be used to optimize the number of nodes participating in the application and thus reducing the total amount of spent energy [56, 57]. Considering the area as a portion of the disk only (i.e. directionnal sensors) has also been investigated. Those sensors are able to sense events in some given directions, rather than in an omnidirectional fashion as often assumed so far. The problems induced by such kind of sensors have been sum up in [58]. Recently, a deployment solution was proposed in order to take advantage of this new feature, ensuring both full coverage of the target area and connectivity of the active nodes subset [59].
Still, those solutions keep considering that the sensing area is a disk, or a portion of a disk. Very few works indeed investigate area modeling as it lies in the field of electronics essentially. Depending on the sensing (e.g. temperature, humidity), the model should be adjusted. Some generic ones have been proposed in order to observe both the sensing ability of some existing sensors [60] and the adaptations that should be made in area coverage protocols (e.g. coverage evaluation scheme [54]).

5.2 Mobility in wireless sensor networks

Once deployed, sensor nodes are most of the time assumed to be static. Mobility is hardly envisioned and the area coverage protocols detailed in this chapter make the same assumption. Recently, this requirement has been relaxed with the emergence of mobile sinks and actor nodes. Mobility has already been considered in the field of localization or time-synchronization, meaning that previous assumptions might still make sense for mobile sensors. In [12], authors show that maintaining accurate location is hard and takes time because of the latency induced by the computation task. It has been proposed to tune the frequency of the control messages, depending on the mobility of each node, in order to reach the target accuracy [15, 11]. Considering the area coverage problem itself, mobility

---

[1]http://motelab.eecs.harvard.edu
[2]http://sensorscope.epfl.ch
[3]http://www.senslab.info

might improve coverage as pointed in [61]. So far, most of contributions talk about the mobility of the sink stations. Indeed, as communications inside the sensor network are from the sensors to the sinks and reverse, having mobile sinks would delete the connectivity constraint [62]. The sink would have to move across the network in order to collect the sensing reports. The mobility of the sensors themselves is hardly addressed even if some solutions already exist to ensure coverage with mobile sensors [63, 64].

Acknowledgments

Author is grateful to Jean Carle, François Ingelrest, David Simplot-Ryl and Ivan Stojmenović for the fruitful joint work they have participated in.

References

[1] L. Gu and J. A. Stankovic, "Radio-triggered wake-up capability for sensor networks," in *Proceedings of 10th IEEE Real-Time and Embedded Technology and Applications Symposium (RTAS)*, Toronto, Canada, 2004, pp. 27–37.

[2] R. Szewczyk, A. Mainwaring, J. Polastre, J. Anderson, and D. Culler, "An analysis of a large scale habitat monitoring application," in *Proceedings of ACM Conference on Embedded Networked Sensor Systems (SenSys)*, Baltimore, MD, USA, 2004, pp. 214–226.

[3] G. Barrenetxea, F. Ingelrest, G. Schaefer, M. Vetterli, O. Couach, and M. Parlange, "Sensorscope: Out-of-the-box environmental monitoring," in *Proceedings of IEEE/ACM International Symposium on Information Processing in Sensor Networks (IPSN)*, St. Louis, Missouri, USA, 2008, pp. 332–343.

[4] G. Werner-Allen, K. Lorincz, M. Welsh, O. Marcillo, J. Johnson, M. Ruiz, and J. Lees, "Deploying a wireless sensor network on an active volcano," *IEEE Internet Computing*, vol. 10, no. 2, pp. 18–25, March/April 2006.

[5] N. Xu, S. Rangwala, K. K. Chintalapudi, D. Ganesan, A. Broad, R. Govindan, and D. Estrin, "A wireless sensor network for structural monitoring," in *Proceedings of ACM Conference on Embedded Networked Sensor Systems (SenSys)*, Baltimore, MD, USA, 2004, pp. 13–24.

[6] L. Krishnamurthy, R. Adler, P. Buonadonna, J. Chhabra, M. Flanigan, N. Kushalnagar, L. Nachman, and M. Yarvis, "Design and deployment of industrial sensor networks: Experiences from a semiconductor plant and the north sea," in *Proceedings of ACM Conference on Embedded Networked Sensor Systems (SenSys)*, San Diego, CA, USA, 2005, pp. 64–75.

[7] K. Römer, "Time synchronization and localization in sensor networks," Ph.D. dissertation, Swiss Federal Institute of Technology Zurich (ETH Zurich), 2005.

[8] L. Doherty, K. Pister, and L. E. Ghaoui, "Convex position estimation in wireless sensor networks," in *Proceedings of IEEE International Conference on Computer Communications (INFOCOM)*, vol. 3, Anchorage, AK, USA, 2001, pp. 1655–1663.

[9] D. Niculescu and B. Nath, "Ad hoc positioning system (aps) using aoa," in *Proceedings of IEEE International Conference on Computer Communications (INFOCOM)*, vol. 22, San Francisco, CA, USA, 2003, pp. 1734–1743.

[10] N. Bulusu, J. Heidemann, and D. Estrin, "Gps-less low cost outdoor localization for very small devices," *IEEE Personal Communications Magazine*, vol. 7, no. 5, pp. 28–34, October 2000.

[11] C. Savarese, J. M. Rabaey, and K. Langendoen, "Robust positioning algorithms for distributed ad-hoc wireless sensor networks," in *Proceedings of the General Track: 2002 USENIX Annual Technical Conference*, Monterey, CA, USA, 2002, pp. 317–327.

[12] M. Maroti, B. Kusy, G. Simon, and A. Ledeczi, "The flooding time synchronization protocol," in *Proceedings of ACM Conference on Embedded Networked Sensor Systems (SenSys)*, Baltimore, MD, USA, 2004, pp. 39–49.

[13] W. Su and I. F. Akyildiz, "Time-diffusion synchronization protocol for wireless sensor networks," *IEEE/ACM Transactions on Networking*, vol. 13, no. 2, pp. 384–397, 2005.

[14] S. Ganeriwal, R. Kumar, and M. Srivastava, "Timing-sync protocol for sensor networks,"

in *Proceedings of ACM Conference on Embedded Networked Sensor Systems (SenSys)*, Los Angeles, CA, USA, 2003, pp. 138–149.

[15] J. V. Greunen and J. Rabaey, "Lightweight time synchronization for sensor networks," in *Proceedings of ACM international conference on Wireless Sensor Networks and Applications (WSNA)*, San Diego, CA, USA, 2003, pp. 11–19.

[16] J. Liu, Y. Zhang, and F. Zhao, "Robust distributed node localization with error management," in *Proceedings of ACM Mobile Ad Hoc networking and Computing (MobiHoc)*, Florence, Italy, 2006, pp. 250–261.

[17] L. Fang, W. Du, and P. Ning, "A beacon-less location discovery scheme for wireless sensor networks," in *Proceedings of IEEE International Conference on Computer Communications (INFOCOM)*, Miami, FL, USA, 2005, pp. 161–171.

[18] S. Capkun, M. Hamdi, and J.-P. Hubaux, "GPS-free positioning in mobile ad hoc networks," *Cluster Computing*, vol. 5, no. 2, pp. 157–167, April 2002.

[19] I. Stojmenović and S. Olariu, "Data centric protocols for wireless sensor networks," *Handbook of Sensor Networks: Algorithms and Architectures (I. Stojmenović, ed.), Wiley*, pp. 417–456, 2005.

[20] K. Römer, "Time synchronization in ad hoc networks," in *Proceedings of ACM Mobile Ad Hoc networking and Computing (MobiHoc)*, Long Beach, CA, USA, 2001, pp. 173–182.

[21] "IEEE standard for information technology - telecommunications and information exchange between systems - local and metropolitan area networks specific requirements part 15.4: wireless medium access control (MAC) and physical layer (PHY) specifications for low-rate wireless personal area networks (LR-WPANs)," 2003.

[22] A. A. Abbasi and M. Younis, "A survey on clustering algorithms for wireless sensor networks," *Computer Communications Journal (Elsevier), special issue on Network Coverage and Routing Schemes for Wireless Sensor Networks*, vol. 30, no. 14-15, pp. 2826–2841, 2007.

[23] J. Jiang and W. Dou, "A coverage preserving density control algorithm for wireless sensor networks," in *Proceedings of 3rd International Conference on AD-HOC Networks and Wireless (ADHOC-NOW)*, Vancouver, BC, Canada, 2004, pp. 42–45.

[24] H. Zhang and J. C. Hou, "Maintaining sensing coverage and connectivity in large sensor networks," *Ad Hoc and Sensor Wireless Networks journal (AHSWN)*, vol. 1, pp. 89–123, 2005.

[25] G. Xing, X. Wang, Y. Zhang, C. Lu, R. Pless, and C. Gill, "Integrated coverage and connectivity configuration for energy conservation in sensor networks," *ACM Transactions on Sensor Networks (TOSN)*, vol. 1, no. 1, pp. 36–72, August 2005.

[26] J. Wu and H. Li, "On calculating connected dominating set for efficient routing in ad hoc wireless networks," in *Proceedings of the 3rd International Workshop on Discrete Algorithms and Methods for Mobile Computing and Communications (Dial M)*, Seattle, WA, USA, 1999, pp. 7–14.

[27] I. Stojmenović, M. Seddigh, and J. Zunic, "Dominating sets and neighbor elimination-based broadcasting algorithms in wireless networks," *IEEE Transactions on Parallel and Distributed Systems (TPDS)*, vol. 13, no. 1, pp. 14–25, 2001.

[28] F. Dai and J. Wu, "Distributed dominant pruning in ad hoc networks," in *Proceedings of IEEE International Conference on Communications (ICC)*, Anchorage, AK, USA, 2003.

[29] I. Stojmenović and J. Wu, "chapter broadcasting and activity scheduling in ad hoc networks," *Mobile Ad Hoc Networking (S. Basagni and M. Conti and S. Giordano and I. Stojmenović, eds.), IEEE Press*, pp. 205–229, 2004.

[30] J. Carle and D. Simplot, "Energy efficient area monitoring by sensor networks," *IEEE Computer Magazine*, vol. 37, pp. 40–46, 2004.

[31] J. Wu, B. Wu, and I. Stojmenović, "Power-aware broadcasting and activity scheduling in ad hoc wireless networks using connected dominating sets," *Wireless Communications and Mobile Computing*, vol. 4, no. 1, pp. 425–438, 2003.

[32] J. Shaikh, I. Stojmenović, and J. Wu, "New metrics for dominating set based energy efficient activity scheduling," in *Proceedings of the International Workshop on Wireless Local Networks (WLN)*, Bonn, Germany, 2003, pp. 425–438.

[33] S. Shakkottai, R. Srikant, and N. Shroff, "Unreliable sensor grids: Coverage, connectivity and diameter," in *Proceedings of IEEE International Conference on Computer Communications (INFOCOM)*, San Francisco, CA, USA, 2003.

[34] C. Liu and Y. Xiao, "Random coverage with guaranteed connectivity: Joint scheduling for wireless sensor networks," *IEEE Transactions on Parallel and Distributed Systems (TPDS)*, vol. 17, no. 6, June 2006.

[35] H. Gupta, S. Das, and Q. Gu, "Connected sensor cover: Self-organization of sensor networks for efficient query execution," in *Proceedings of ACM Mobile Ad Hoc networking and Computing (MobiHoc)*, Annapolis, MD, USA, 2003, pp. 189–200.

[36] J. V. B. Carbunar, A. Grama and O. Carbunar, "Coverage preserving redundancy elimination in sensor networks," in *Proceedings of IEEE Conference on Sensor and Ad Hoc Communications and Networks (SECON)*, 2004, pp. 377–386.

[37] F. Ye, G. Zhong, J. Cheng, S. Lu, and L. Zhang, "Peas: A robust energy conserving protocol for long-lived sensor networks," in *Proceedings of International Conference on Distributed Computing Systems (ICDCS)*, Rhode Island, RI, USA, 2003, pp. 28–37.

[38] Y. Cai, M. Li, W. Shu, and M.-Y. Wu, "Acos: A precise energy-aware coverage control protocol for wireless sensor networks." *Ad Hoc & Sensor Wireless Networks, An International Journal*, vol. 3, no. 1, pp. 77–98, 2007.

[39] C. Gui and P. Mohapatra, "Power conservation and quality of surveillance in target tracking sensor networks," in *Proceedings of ACM Mobile Computing and networking (Mobicom)*, Philadelphia, PA, USA, 2004, pp. 129–143.

[40] T. Yan, T. He, and J. A. Stankovic, "Differentiated surveillance service for sensor networks," in *Proceedings of ACM Conference on Embedded Networked Sensor Systems (SenSys)*, Los Angeles, CA, USA, 2003, pp. 51–62.

[41] C.-F. Hsin and M. Liu, "Network coverage using low duty-cycled sensors: random & coordinated sleep algorithms," in *Proceedings of the third international symposium on Information Processing in Sensor Networks (IPSN)*, Berkeley, CA, USA, 2004, pp. 433–442.

[42] J. Carle, A. Gallais, and D. Simplot-Ryl, "Preserving area coverage in wireless sensor networks by using surface coverage relay dominating sets," in *Proceedings of IEEE Symposium on Computers and Communications (ISCC)*, Cartagena, Spain, 2005, pp. 347–352.

[43] J. Sheu, C. Yu, and S. Tu, "A distributed protocol for query execution in sensor networks," in *IEEE Wireless Communications and Networking Conference (WCNC)*, vol. 3, New Orleans, LA, USA, 2005, pp. 1824–1829.

[44] D. Tian and N. Georganas, "A coverage-preserving node scheduling scheme for large wireless sensor networks," in *Proceedings of ACM international conference on Wireless Sensor Networks and Applications (WSNA)*, Atlanta, GA, USA, 2002, pp. 32–41.

[45] D. Tian and N. D. Georganas, "Connectivity maintenance and coverage preservation in wireless sensor networks," *Ad Hoc Networks Journal (Elsevier Science)*, vol. 3, pp. 744–761, November 2005.

[46] A. Gallais, J. Carle, D. Simplot-Ryl, and I. Stojmenović, "Localized sensor area coverage with low communication overhead," *IEEE Transactions on Mobile Computing*, vol. 7, no. 5, pp. 661–672, May 2008.

[47] S. Kumar, T. H. Lai, and J. Balogh, "On k-coverage in a mostly sleeping sensor network," in *Proceedings of ACM Mobile Computing and networking (Mobicom)*, Philadelphia, PA, USA, 2004, pp. 144–158.

[48] Z. Abrams, A. Goel, and S. Plotkin, "Set k-cover algorithms for energy efficient monitoring in wireless sensor networks," in *Proceedings of IEEE/ACM International Symposium on Information Processing in Sensor Networks (IPSN)*, Berkeley, CA, USA, 2004, pp. 424–432.

[49] X. Wang, G. Xing, Y. Zhang, C. Lu, R. Pless, and C. Gill, "Integrated coverage and connectivity configuration in wireless sensor networks," in *Proceedings of ACM Conference on Embedded Networked Sensor Systems (SenSys)*, Los Angeles, CA, USA, 2003, pp. 28–39.

[50] S. Yang, F. Dai, M. Cardei, and J. Wu, "On multiple point coverage in wireless sensor networks," in *Proceedings of IEEE Mobile Ad hoc and Sensor Systems (MASS)*, Washington, DC, USA, 2005, pp. –764.

[51] F. Dai and J. Wu, "An extended localized algorithm for connected dominating set formation in ad hoc wireless networks," *IEEE Transactions on Parallel and Distributed Systems (TPDS)*, vol. 15, no. 10, pp. 908–920, October 2004.

[52] Z. Zhou, S. Das, and H. Gupta, "Connected k-coverage problem in sensor networks," in *Proceedings of 13th International Conference on Computer Communications and Networks (IC-CCN)*, Chicago, IL, USA, 2004, pp. 373–378.

[53] A. Gallais and J. Carle, "An adaptive localized algorithm for multiple sensor area coverage," *Ad Hoc and Sensor Wireless Networks journal (AHSWN)*, vol. 4, no. 7, pp. 271–288, 2007.

[54] A. Gallais, J. Carle, D. Simplot-Ryl, and I. Stojmenović, "Ensuring k-coverage in wireless sensor networks under realistic physical layer assumptions," in *Proceedings of 5th IEEE Conference on Sensors (Sensors)*, Daegu, Korea, 2006.

[55] G. S. G. Barrenetxea, F. Ingelrest and M. Vetterli, "The hitchhiker's guide to successful wireless sensor network deployments," in *Proceedings of ACM Conference on Embedded Networked Sensor Systems (SenSys)*, Raleigh, NC, USA, November 2008, pp. 43–56.

[56] J. Wu and S. Yang, "Energy-efficient node scheduling models in sensor networks with adjustable ranges," *International Journal of Foundations of Computer Science*, vol. 16, no. 1, pp. 3–17, 2005.

[57] M. Cardei, J. Wu, and M. Lu, "Improving network lifetime using sensors with adjustable sensing ranges," *International Journal of Sensor Networks (IJSNet)*, vol. 1, no. 1/2, pp. 41–49, January 2006.

[58] H. Ma and Y. Liu, "Some problems of directional sensor networks," *International Journal of Sensor Networks*, vol. 2, no. 1/2, pp. 44–52, 2007.

[59] X. Han, X. Cao, E. Lloyd, and C.-C. Shen, "Deploying directional sensor networks with guaranteed connectivity and coverage," in *Proceedings of IEEE Conference on Sensor and Ad Hoc Communications and Networks (SECON)*, San Francisco, CA, USA, 2008, pp. 153–160.

[60] J. Hwang, Y. Gu, T. He, and Y. Kim, "Realistic sensing area modeling," in *Proceedings of IEEE International Conference on Computer Communications (INFOCOM)*, Anchorage, AK, USA, May 2007, pp. 2421–2425.

[61] B. Liu, P. Brass, O. Dousse, P. Nain, and D. Towsley, "Mobility improves coverage of sensor networks," in *Proceedings of ACM Mobile Ad Hoc networking and Computing (MobiHoc)*, Urbana-Champaign, IL, USA, 2005, pp. 300–308.

[62] G. Yang, B. Tong, D. Qiao, and W. Zhang, "Sensor-aided overlay deployment and relocation for vast-scale sensor networks," in *Proceedings of IEEE International Conference on Computer Communications (INFOCOM)*, 2008, pp. 2216–2224.

[63] A. Sekhar, B. S. Manoj, and C. S. R. Murthy, "Dynamic coverage maintenance algorithms for sensor networks with limited mobility," in *Proceedings of 3rd Annual IEEE International Conference on Pervasive Computing and Communications (PerCom)*, Kauai island, HI, USA, 2005, pp. 51–60.

[64] W. W. V. Srinivasan and K.-C. Chua, "Tradeoffs between mobility and density for coverage in wireless sensor networks," in *Proceedings of ACM Mobile Computing and networking (Mobicom)*, Montréal, Québec, Canada, 2007, pp. 39–50.

Index